WE SHOULD
HAVE SEEN
IT COMING

WE SHOULD HAVE SEEN IT COMING

From Reagan to Trump— A Front-Row Seat to a Political Revolution

★ ★ ★

GERALD F. SEIB

RANDOM HOUSE

NEW YORK

Published in the United States by Random House, an imprint and
division of Penguin Random House LLC, New York.

RANDOM HOUSE and the HOUSE colophon are registered trademarks
of Penguin Random House LLC.

Library of Congress Cataloging-in-Publication Data

Hardback ISBN 9780593135150
Ebook ISBN 9780593135167

Printed in the United States of America on acid-free paper

randomhousebooks.com

2 4 6 8 9 7 5 3 1

First Edition

Book design by Victoria Wong

To Barb, Joseph, Jake, and Luke,
who made this journey with me, and whose love
and companionship were the most cherished gifts
received along the way

Preface

We all should have seen it coming.

For almost four decades, the Republican Party had been defined by a man, Ronald Reagan, and his movement, the Reagan Revolution. Reagan was the most unlikely of revolutionary figures, a modestly successful actor with a self-effacing style and no intellectual pretensions. Yet he personally had made the Republican Party into a conservative party, and his legacy continued to inspire the movement's leaders, animate its policy debates, and stir its voters' emotions long after he left the scene.

Over time, however, emerging signs—chief among them grassroots anger at the political and financial establishments and frustration over the impact of conservative policies on the party's new working-class base—suggested that the foundation Reagan had built was starting to crack, though those signs were largely ignored or dismissed. Finally, the foundation collapsed. In fact, it's possible to pinpoint the moment when Republicans closed the door on the Reagan Revolution and opened the door to a new era, the populist and nationalist era of Donald Trump. It came on the evening of July 20, 2016, when Senator Ted Cruz strode to the podium at the Republican National Convention at Quicken Loans Arena, in Cleveland.

Cruz, a tall and striking figure with a shock of jet-black hair, a perpetually intense air, and the kind of self-assured oratorical style born of years as a college debater, was there to deliver a concession speech, acknowledging that he had lost a bitter nomination fight to Trump. The arena floor was crowded and buzzing in anticipation. Like boxing fans bored by the preliminary fights and eager to see the main card, delegates were milling around restlessly, waiting for the Cruz speech to begin. As he waited behind stage, text of his speech tucked into his pocket, Cruz wasn't sure exactly what he was heading into, though he sensed it might be dramatic.

Cruz had arrived in Cleveland after running for president explicitly as the heir to Ronald Reagan. Indeed, Ted Cruz loved Reagan, and had been preparing to follow in his footsteps his entire life.

One of Cruz's most vivid early memories was, as a nine-year-old, cheering on from afar as Reagan debated President Jimmy Carter in the 1980 presidential campaign. As the son of a Cuban émigré, Cruz admired Reagan's staunch anti-Communism, his embrace of free markets, his vision of America as a shining city on a hill that attracted people from around the globe.

The senator's father, Rafael, had been a young pro-Castro revolutionary in Cuba. After being jailed and beaten by soldiers of Cuba's old Batista regime, he fled to the United States in 1957 with nothing but a hundred dollars his mother had sewn into his underwear.

Two years later, after Castro had taken over, Rafael returned to Cuba for a visit and was horrified at what he saw as the tyranny of the country's new Communist government. Rafael Cruz became an ardent anti-Communist. In his new home in America, he naturally became a champion of the most anti-Communist party he saw on the scene, the Republican Party. "I've joked that in a Cuban household, there were two parties, the Republicans and the Communists," Ted Cruz says now. "That is only somewhat tongue in cheek."

Cruz remembers growing up in a home that was passionately political. "There was an urgency about politics," Ted Cruz recalls. "You didn't just read the newspaper or watch the news and go, 'Oh, that's interesting.'" Cruz's aunt Sonia had fought in the counter-revolution against the Castro regime and was thrown in prison and tortured for doing so, and that pain burned bright within the family. "What I heard growing up," Cruz says, "is that having principled men and women in office is how we protect ourselves from tyranny. And so, as a little boy, if you'd asked me, 'What do you want to do in life?' I would have said, 'I want to defend freedom.'"

When Reagan won that 1980 presidential election, launching a conservative wave that would become the most powerful force in American politics, Cruz knew he wanted to be part of it. "I think there is an entire generation of conservatives for whom Ronald Wilson Reagan will always be our president, in much the same way the World War II generation referred to FDR as our president," he says.

He was ardent in his beliefs and the way he expressed them; indeed, some considered him obnoxious in his certitude and self-confidence. He entered Princeton University, and one of his roommates there would later recall Cruz saying his life's goal was "to become like Ronald Reagan—a principled conservative and great communicator." He became a star debater at Princeton and then a top law student at Harvard. His outsider status as an outspoken conservative in largely liberal institutions didn't bother him. He reveled in it.

After law school at Harvard, he entered private practice, but he also worked on the presidential campaign of George W. Bush in 2000. He then became Texas's solicitor general, effectively the state's top lawyer. His entry into elective politics was typically audacious: In his first run for public office, in 2012, he defeated a far more entrenched Texas Republican to win a seat in the United States Senate.

After that victory, he was approached by Stephan Penley, an artist who does patriotic art, who offered to create a painting of Reagan for Cruz's Senate office. Cruz accepted, and commissioned a painting of the iconic moment when Ronald Reagan stood at the Berlin Wall and beseeched the leader of the Soviet Union to "tear down this wall." The resulting piece, a ten-foot-long monster, hangs in a place of honor in Cruz's Senate office.

So, heading into the 2016 presidential campaign, if there was anybody who thought himself entitled to claim the Reagan mantle, it was Ted Cruz. In his announcement speech, he specifically harked back to Reagan's successful 1980 presidential campaign. He invoked Reagan regularly.

Others in a crowded Republican field, who thought they themselves had pretty good records as lovers of Ronald Reagan, chafed at Cruz's claiming of the Reagan legacy for himself. Yet Cruz seemed to fit into Reagan's footsteps pretty well. Many in the old Reagan coalition and the conservative old guard did, in fact, line up behind him: David Keene, who worked for Reagan as long ago as 1976 and later ran the American Conservative Union, backed Cruz, as did longtime conservative fundraising wizard Richard Viguerie, who thought Cruz would march to the nomination.

But it was not to be. As Ted Cruz and the rest of the world learned in 2016, the Republican Party had changed. It had become more blue-collar, more rooted in rural and small-town America, more disillusioned with the existing party establishment, more skeptical of free-market economics and global trade, more anti-immigration, and simply more angry. Its voters were ready to consider something different—radically different, in fact. They were ready for Donald J. Trump.

Trump was a populist and a nationalist, but certainly not a traditional conservative. Former House Speaker Newt Gingrich, who would become a Trump fan, says simply: "He's not a conservative. He didn't sit around reading *National Review*," the traditional bible for conservative thinkers. Instead, Gingrich defines Trump as an "anti-liberal . . . a commonsense, practical person who understands how much of modern political correctness is just total baloney and how much our bureaucracies are decrepit and failing."

Corey Lewandowski, Trump's campaign manager in 2016, when asked whether Trump is a conservative, replies: "He's a pragmatist."

In fact, most conservatives were scornful of Trump. He certainly didn't share a Reaganesque belief in the virtues of immigration. When Reagan launched his general-election campaign in 1980, he did so with a speech in front of the Statue of Liberty in which he praised generations of immigrants for the work they did in building the United States: "They brought with them courage, ambition, and the values of family, neighborhood, work, peace, and freedom. We all came from different lands, but we share the same values, the same dream." When Trump launched his campaign, he did it a few miles away, in his eponymous Fifth Avenue skyscraper, with a speech in which he called Mexican immigrants rapists and drug dealers.

Nor did Trump share conservatives' devotion to free trade. In fact, he was utterly disdainful of the North American Free Trade Agreement, a trade pact with Canada and Mexico that was the culmination of a dream Reagan laid out when he called for a North American Accord in that same 1980 campaign. Trump openly praised tariffs as a tool in trade wars—even calling himself "Tariff Man" at one point—while conservatives disdained tariffs as a form of taxation paid by regular citizens. Conservatives believed in the magic of a free market unconstrained by government interference, while Trump openly tried to pressure and coerce private companies to act as he thought they should.

Conservatives believe in limited executive power; Trump envisioned himself as a president with wide latitude to use executive orders to do as he pleased. Conservatives seek to reduce government spending; Trump proudly proclaimed he had no desire to cut the fastest-growing government programs, Medicare and Social Security. He scorned the seemingly endless war in Iraq that was championed by the Republicans' neoconservative wing. Trump had been married three times, with a history of bragging about his extramarital sexual exploits, which would seem to have been a surefire turnoff for the party's substantial evangelical religious wing.

Yet none of that background disqualified Donald Trump in 2016. Much of it, it turned out, made him attractive. He was a disrupter at a time when many in a significantly changed Republican Party wanted precisely that: disruption.

Cruz and Trump fought hard, even bitterly, to the end of that 2016 primary season. Trump called Cruz "Lyin' Ted," mocked the appearance of his wife, and, bizarrely, seemed to advance a theory that Cruz's father had something to do with the assassination of President John F. Kennedy. Cruz, in turn, called Trump "a sniveling coward" and a "pathological liar." Cruz won eight million Republican votes and even harbored some hopes right up until the party's nominating convention that delegates would have second thoughts and bolt from Trump—something, as it happened, Trump's campaign managers also worried was possible. But Trump's strength was simply too much to overcome. He had won primaries and caucuses in thirty-six states and commanded news coverage throughout the primary season. By the time convention week opened in Cleveland, it was over.

It was a bitter pill to swallow, not just for Cruz but for many other conservatives. It was as if an alien virus had invaded and taken over the body that conservatives had controlled for decades.

As the candidate who had come closest to winning the nomination before it fell to Trump, Cruz was entitled to a nationally televised prime-time speech at the convention. Anticipation was high as the speech approached. How would Cruz handle the moment? What would he say about Trump, who had been formally nominated the night before?

Against that backdrop, Cruz strode to the podium and began to speak. It began normally enough. The Texan was warmly welcomed by the crowd, and it seemed the moment might be one of unity. He talked about freedom and liberty and America's promise to the world.

But as the speech rolled forward, people noticed something: He mentioned Trump's name only once, early in his remarks. When it became clear that Cruz didn't intend to endorse Trump, the noise from Trump supporters began to swell. As it happens, I was on the floor of the convention at that moment, standing between the New

York delegation, a hotbed of loud Trump supporters, and Cruz, high above on the podium. It was like straddling two worlds. "Say his name!" the Trump delegates shouted. Others yelled, "We want Trump!" and "Goldman Sachs!"—a reference to the investment bank where Cruz's wife works, a favorite target for scorn from the populist troops in Trump's army.

Then, in a remarkable moment, Cruz seemed to implicitly suggest that conservatives *not* vote for the nominee of his Republican Party: "If you love our country, and love your children as much as I know that you do, stand and speak and vote your conscience, vote for candidates up and down the ticket who you trust to defend our freedom and to be faithful to the Constitution."

Boos rained down from Trump supporters in the crowd. The noise was so loud that at one point Cruz had to stop speaking for almost a full minute. At that point, there was more raw emotion—tension, anger, anxiety—than I'd ever experienced at any of the dozen or so conventions I've attended.

As it turned out, the reaction was neither spontaneous nor accidental. Cruz had given a copy of his speech to Trump team members several hours ahead of time. They were pretty sure they knew what he would say—and what he wouldn't say. Trump aides had pressured Cruz until the moment he walked onstage to add a line endorsing Trump, but he wouldn't commit to do so. So the Trump team had their lieutenants in the state delegations—whips, in the political vernacular—organize an effort to shout down Cruz as he spoke. "What I did not anticipate is that the Trump campaign had whips on the floor of the convention," Cruz recalls. "And they made a political decision to whip the delegates into booing. For a candidate who was looking to unify the party and win a general election a few months later, that was a surprising decision for their campaign to make."

Trump was watching this from out of sight, in a back room at the convention hall. Lewandowski, a brusque New Hampshire political operative with crew-cut hair and piercing eyes, had recently been deposed as Trump's campaign manager, but that night he was sitting with the Trump family. The nominee-to-be, he recalls, "grew more and more agitated as Cruz went on and on." There was still some hope that Cruz might ad-lib an endorsement. But when it became clear that wasn't happening, Trump chose to upstage Cruz by walking out into the arena. "It was not planned," Lewandowski says. "But as Ted continued to speak, it became more and more apparent that he was going to come out and make an appearance."

As the noise on the floor grew, Trump emerged into the seating area directly across the auditorium from Cruz and, before walking to his seat, flashed a thumbs-up at his supporters, which served to egg them on. Word of Trump's arrival flashed through the crowd. Heads that had been watching Cruz swiveled to see Trump.

At that moment, the conservative movement and the Republican Party, which together had been the most powerful force in American politics for the preceding forty years, essentially parted company. The party of Reagan had become the party of Trump.

The story of how this happened is the most important political story of the new millennium. The primary lesson that emerges from a look back over the four decades of this evolution is as simple as it is profound: None of us should have been surprised by the rise of Donald Trump. The signs were there for years. The populist presidential campaigns of Pat Buchanan and Ross Perot; the anti-establishment, anti-intellectual vice presidential campaign of Sarah Palin; the Tea Party revolt; and, above all, the rancorous debates over immigration reform were just the most obvious of indicators. Most of us either didn't take them seriously enough or had other explanations. The arc of this change also happens to track with my own journalism career. I arrived in Washington in early 1980, just as Reagan was seeking the presidency, and, save for a stint in the Middle East, have been chronicling this narrative ever since. As a result, I was lucky enough to see much of the history chronicled here firsthand, and to record it in the pages and on the website of *The Wall Street Journal*. In short, I had a pretty good seat for a very good show, and have woven in my own reporting and observations along the way in the telling.

It is a tale filled with fascinating characters, many of whom I have come to know, as well as strange twists and more than its fair share of drama. Still to be answered, though, is the core underlying question: Is this turn toward nationalism and populism permanent, or a passing fad?

Contents

WE SHOULD
HAVE SEEN
IT COMING

CHAPTER 1

The Rise of the Reagan Revolution

Sunday, July 15, 1979, was a typically muggy summer day in Washington. The oppressive humidity merely added to the feeling that a hostile world was pressing in on the beleaguered capital, and the beleaguered Democratic president, Jimmy Carter.

Newspaper headlines of the weekend spoke of gas shortages, soaring inflation, global chaos spreading across the land. *The Wall Street Journal*'s front page summarized the feeling on the Friday heading into that weekend with a long, gloomy story headlined "Public Turns Moody, Cuts Buying in Wake of Inflation, Gas Woes."

There was little doubt who was on the spot because of all this bleak news: Carter. Halfway through his third year as president, his job approval in the Gallup poll had dropped from 75 percent early in his first year to 28 percent—the lowest of his presidency, and just four points above the approval rating Richard Nixon scored before he resigned amid the Watergate scandal.

The president himself was, if anything, adding to that sense of doom and gloom. Carter was an unusual political figure in almost every way—a kind of natural outsider who made the dramatic leap from peanut farmer to president in a relatively short time, and without making a lot of close friends along the way. He was a devout man who taught Sunday school, and whose moralistic style some saw as a sign of his inherent decency. Others viewed it as the mark of a sanctimonious attitude. Over the previous week and a half, Carter had done something nobody in Washington had ever seen before: He canceled a widely anticipated televised speech, fled the capital, and retreated to the presidential Camp David getaway to mull over the state of affairs.

He asked dozens of prominent Americans to join him there to ponder how the country should proceed. Members of Congress were summoned, as were governors and religious and labor leaders. Walter Cronkite was there, as was Bill Clinton, the young governor of Arkansas. It went on for ten days. Carter soaked in advice and opinions and took notes with a blue felt-tip pen. The original, ostensible point of the retreat was to figure out how to deal with an international energy crisis. But soon the quest became something much bigger: how to get the country out of its funk.

When the visitors had left, Carter sat down with his vice president, Walter Mondale, and a few staff members and speechwriters and began hashing out a different kind of nationally televised address to the nation.

Finally, on the night of July 15, Carter sat at his desk in the White House and delivered one of the most remarkable speeches ever presented by an American president. It became known, universally, as the "Malaise Speech." In fact, Carter never uttered the word "malaise," but that term aptly captured how both the country and its president seemed to view their predicament in mid-1979.

"I want to talk to you right now about a fundamental threat to American democracy," Carter told the nation. "The threat is nearly invisible in ordinary ways. It is a crisis of confidence. It is a crisis that strikes at the very heart and spirit of our national will."

This loss of confidence, he declared, "is threatening to destroy the social and the political fabric of America." Then, in a striking reversal from normal presidential rhetoric, Carter seemed to point the finger of blame not at his domestic opponents, or at bad luck, or at himself. Instead he pointed the finger of blame directly at American citizens—his countrymen—who were listening:

"In a nation that was proud of hard work, strong families, close-knit communities, and our faith in God, too many of us now tend to worship self-indulgence and consumption. Human identity is no longer defined by what one does, but by what one owns." The nation, he said, had never fully recovered from the assassinations of Martin Luther King Jr. and John and Robert Kennedy, or from the Vietnam War, or from Watergate, much less from the more recent shocks of hyperinflation and fuel shortages. "We are at a turning point in our history," he told the nation.

Nobody had ever heard a presidential address like it. In the end, Carter seemed to confirm for citizens that they were in a year that was shaking their world—and their confidence—to the core.

More than that, the troubled summer of 1979 marked the end of a long period of liberal dominance, as embodied by the modern Democratic Party. The story of public life in America is, in many ways, the story of the ebb and flow of great ideological movements. At the end of the nineteenth century, the Second Industrial Revolution spawned the era of progressivism, personified by Teddy Roosevelt. That phase was brought to an end by Herbert Hoover and the Great Depression. The Depression, followed by World War II, gave rise, in turn, to Franklin Roosevelt's New Deal liberalism and the era of big government.

For half a century, Roosevelt's brand of liberalism was the dominant force in American politics. Liberals believe in the power of government to do good; starting with Roosevelt, they had put that belief into action. Just one small example: Virtually every town in America still carries monuments to the New Deal's belief in public works—parks, libraries, bandstands, museums. Go online to a site called livingnewdeal.org and you can see a map of America covered coast to coast with measles-like dots. Each dot represents a Roosevelt-era project still in use today.

Liberals were responsible for the two most important and beloved government programs in history, Social Security and Medicare. Under President Lyndon Johnson and his Great Society programs, liberals expanded the social safety net. They desegregated the military and championed the greatest civil rights advances since the end of slavery. They enacted minimum-wage laws, made workplaces safer, and allowed unions to grow in power.

But by the late 1970s, liberalism had become creaky. Inflation was running wild, and unemployment was soaring. High tax rates appeared to be sapping the American economy of its vitality. The American auto industry, the very symbol of American manufacturing prowess, had lost its international edge, saddled as it was by high labor costs and even higher bills for generous retirement benefits promised to two generations of workers.

The welfare programs that had saved so many Americans became the object of caricature on the right. Big cities, the epicenter of liberal politics, were a mess. Over-regulation had hobbled the American oil industry and left the nation dependent on foreign energy. As if to prove liberalism's identity crisis, Democrats, the party that believed in the virtues of government regulation, had, in Carter, a president who tried to pivot to a new strategy of deregulation.

Abroad, to show that they weren't soft on Communism, liberals bent over backward to show they were tough, an impulse that led Lyndon Johnson to lock the country into a bloody conflict in Vietnam. The failure there appeared to diminish international fear of American might. The gas lines that snaked around American towns and cities by the late 1970s seemed a metaphor: To many Americans, it felt as though liberalism had, like the cars in everyone's driveways, run out of gas.

Certainly, the events that followed Carter's speech drove home that impression of an America adrift in a world it no longer controlled. Three days later, the Sandinistas swept into power in Nicaragua. That fall, Islamic radicals launched a siege at Mecca, in Saudi Arabia. On November 4, students seized the American embassy in Tehran. And on December 24, the Soviet army invaded Afghanistan, setting off a chain of events that ultimately would lead to the demise of the entire Soviet system.

At home, meanwhile, the economy headed into dangerous, uncharted waters that signaled, among other things, the decline of the post–World War II American dominance of global economic affairs. Inflation ran at an astonishing 10.4 percent for the year. Home mortgage rates soared well above 10 percent. Global oil producers had discovered that they truly had the United States over a barrel, and the result was soaring gasoline prices and shortages.

The year's events marked the transition of the American economy from one driven by cheap oil and heavy manufacturing into one that would come to be dominated by technology and services. U.S. manufacturing employment hit its historic peak in 1979, then began a long decline. Union membership did the same. Real hourly wages of Americans hit a peak and began a slide that continued for three decades.

In sum, powerful forces of change that had been bubbling just below the surface for years, gathering heat and power, burst to the surface in the latter half of 1979. It's hard to overstate now just how disconcerting all this was. America was supposed to control the world; now it was being pushed around. America was supposed to make the best cars, but the cars Detroit was producing were ugly and unreliable and were now being surpassed in quality by, of all things, Japanese cars. The indignities came in forms large and small. At a little restaurant in my hometown of Hays, Kansas, inflation was pushing up costs so fast that the owner decided to order menus with no prices printed on them; instead he would simply write the prices in erasable ink, to make it easier to raise them in the weeks and months ahead.

Events this psychologically disorienting are bound to have profound political consequences. In this case, there were two big impacts. The first affected Jimmy Carter personally. Many Americans concluded he was a good man but simply in over his head. His problems were so abundant that people actually speculated whether the presidency had become too big for any one person and should be split into two, with one president for foreign affairs and another for domestic affairs.

The other, broader impact had to do with how Americans

viewed the entire political system. They began to seriously question the continued viability of the liberal compact that had prevailed since the Great Depression. In retrospect, it took Jimmy Carter's failures to set the stage for Ronald Reagan's success.

On the day Carter delivered his Malaise Speech, Reagan was living in California, four years removed from his last official political position as governor of California and busying himself doing regular radio commentaries and writing a newspaper column. He remained a household name in America—and was at least the titular leader of the conservative movement.

Reagan's journey to this point in life was, as he well understood, the stuff of American myth. Before World War II, he had made the unlikely journey from mediocre student to Iowa sportscaster to Hollywood film star. In perhaps his most famous role, he played Notre Dame football star George Gipp, picking up along the way a dip-of-the-head mannerism when speaking that he later said was a boon to him as a political speaker. That role also earned him the nickname that would follow him through his political career, "the Gipper," sometimes used fondly, sometimes mockingly.

As his film career began to fade, he moved on to television and then to corporate hucksterism, serving as a kind of national spokesman for General Electric Co. The GE role came as Reagan's political views were evolving, and his corporate job pushed that evolution along. Though he once was a fan of Franklin Roosevelt's Democrats, he traveled the country preaching the virtues of free enterprise and minimal government interference in economic affairs. That was the GE gospel, but it also reflected the way Reagan's encounters with Communist sympathizers in Hollywood had soured him on the politics of the left. He committed his best thoughts, lines, and stories to a growing stack of index cards that provided the material for his speeches; an assortment of those cards, all covered in Reagan's tight handwriting, is on display at the Reagan Presidential Library, in California. They fleshed out his worldview, one skeptical of government intervention in the private economy.

Reagan was, as one would expect, given his Hollywood background, a handsome man with an easy and approachable style. He brought to the political stage, as he had to the silver screen, a shock of dark brown hair, perpetually ruddy cheeks, an easy grin, and a kind of glint in his eye. He usually seemed easygoing, though he also could set his chin and harden his gaze when seeking to add some gravity to a point. All those characteristics helped him develop a bit of a national following on the right in the early 1960s. That following exploded in size when, in 1964, on the eve of the presidential election, he delivered a rousing nationally televised speech on behalf of Senator Barry Goldwater, the Republican presidential nominee and an outspoken conservative. The Reagan speech was entitled "A Time for Choosing." But it came to be known as simply "The Speech." In it, Reagan explained why he had switched from Democrat to Republican and, beyond that, delivered the purest distillation of the emerging conservative creed.

He decried the nation's tax burden, Washington's deficit spending, the mounting federal debt, and the size of the government. Though the budget deficit was minuscule by today's standards, and economic growth was humming along at more than 5 percent annually, it was true that federal spending was creeping upward. Government growth, Reagan declared, would sap away individual freedom in service of a ballooning central government run by elitists in Washington: "This is the issue of this election: whether we believe in our capacity for self-government or whether we abandon the American Revolution and confess that a little intellectual elite in a far-distant capital can plan our lives for us better than we can plan them ourselves." He closed with a rousing passage extolling America as both land of the free and beacon for the world, in words with which he would forever be identified: "You and I have a rendezvous with destiny. We'll preserve for our children this, the last best hope of man on earth, or we'll sentence them to take the last step into a thousand years of darkness."

The speech was an instant success, though not nearly enough to save Goldwater, who lost to President Lyndon Johnson in a landslide of historic proportions.

In retrospect, it's clear that Goldwater was both ahead of his time and the wrong man to turn the country to the right. The successes of liberal governance were too abundant and widely appreciated in 1964. The American economy still dominated the globe; the American middle class was growing. Unions had helped blue-collar workers make spectacular gains; they could send their kids to college, enjoy luxuries in life that eluded their parents, and look forward to a secure retirement, thanks to Social Security and, soon, Medicare. The assassination of President John Kennedy just a year earlier had helped make the Democratic president a revered figure and served to rally many American voters to the side of his successor, Johnson.

The threat to liberty from creeping government intrusion, about which Goldwater was so alarmed, seemed too distant and esoteric to too many Americans. Besides, Goldwater himself was a bit scary. He talked as if he was prepared to consider nuclear war with the Soviet Union if that was what it would take to rid the planet of the Communist threat. His words could sound extreme, an assessment Goldwater seemed to confirm when he declared that "extremism in the defense of liberty is no vice."

It was decidedly not yet time for a conservative revolution.

Still, the fame Reagan himself earned in 1964 convinced him to run for governor of California two years later. He won, and did so again in 1970. From there, Reagan ran for president, and hard, in 1976, daring to challenge the incumbent president from his own party, Gerald Ford. Ford, mild-mannered and a great believer in the virtues of bipartisan compromise, was the very embodiment of his party's moderate faction. Reagan was the conservative rabble-rouser. But, it should never be forgotten, he was also an entertainer. He knew how to strike the chords that would move an audience, and he listened carefully for for the opportunity to hit those chords. David Keene, then a young political operative who ran the Reagan operation in the South in that campaign, recalls that Reagan was still in the habit of talking off note cards, which he would shuffle around between stops, testing which lines worked best with which audience.

Almost by accident, he found an issue that excited the conservative Republican base. At a speech in Sun City, Florida, Reagan threw in a line he'd used before, without great effect, objecting to the Ford administration's efforts to negotiate a treaty turning control of the Panama Canal over to the country of Panama. He declared, "We bought it, we paid for it, it's ours, and we're going to keep it." At that, Keene says, "the roof blew off the place." So Reagan used the line again at the next stop, and the next stop, to the same reaction, and he kept hammering the issue for the remainder of the campaign.

Reagan made it a close race—close enough that the outcome of the nomination fight wasn't clear until delegates cast their ballots at the party's convention in Kansas City, nominating President Ford as the Republican standard-bearer. As the Reagan challenge wound down, Ford called Reagan to the convention's podium and invited him to speak.

Reagan seemed to address the crowd extemporaneously, though in fact he gave a truncated version of the acceptance speech he had prepared, just in case. He called on Republicans and disillusioned Democrats alike to band together to end "the erosion of freedom that has taken place under Democrat rule in this country, the invasion of private rights, the controls and restrictions on the vitality of the great free economy that we enjoy. These are our challenges that we must meet." It was a virtuoso performance; the crowd roared in response to Reagan's defense of conservative principles. Ford, the nominee, seemed stiff and boring by comparison.

By 1979 Reagan was preparing to run again, against Jimmy Carter, who had narrowly beaten Ford in the general election. But his path to the nomination was hardly assured. He had come close in 1976, but he also had been portrayed as a conservative extremist by moderates in his own party. "It was easy to paint him into a right-wing corner, which was the whole point of the Ford '76 campaign," recalls Charlie Black, then a top Reagan political aide. "In that campaign we did some pretty conservative things, [speaking] against the Panama Canal treaties and attacking Henry Kissinger and all those kinds of things." So, Black says, after the 1976 campaign Reagan ended up being seen in many quarters as an extremist: "He didn't have support or a lot of friends in the Northeast, in the Midwest, [but he] had a lot of grassroots conservative support."

While Reagan should have been the natural Republican frontrunner at the outset of the 1980 campaign, he had problems. Tom Roeser, a former Nixon aide who subsequently worked for Quaker Oats in Chicago, got a call early in the campaign season from John Sears, Reagan's campaign guru, saying Reagan was going to be visiting Chicago and asking Roeser to put together a group of business figures to have lunch with the prospective candidate. Years later, in a conversation with Chicago Democratic political operative David Axelrod, Roeser recalled that he called some of his business acquaintances and then reported back to Sears that he was embarrassed to say that nobody would agree to have lunch with Reagan. *Okay,* Sears replied, nonplussed. *Will you have lunch with him?*

Initially, Reagan's fundraising went just as poorly as that luncheon. A series of formidable fellow Republicans, all more mainstream than Reagan, had gotten into the race: Senator Howard Baker, former Central Intelligence Agency chief and China envoy George H. W. Bush, former Texas governor John Connally, and Illinois representative John Anderson. There even was a direct challenge from a fellow conservative, Illinois representative Phil Crane.

By the spring of 1979, many of them appeared to be gaining ground, as the Reagan campaign machine malfunctioned. In fact, in the spring of that year, *U.S. News & World Report* ran an item about the Carter team's view of Reagan in its Washington Whispers column: "White House political strategists have concluded— regretfully—that Ronald Reagan is fading and will have little chance of winning the Republican presidential nomination in 1980. Why the regrets? Because Carter's aides are convinced that the conservative, 68-year-old former California governor is an easy target." It was almost a Reagan political obituary.

What the Carter camp failed to grasp was how Carter's struggles were leaving voters increasingly open to a conservative message that had previously seemed unthinkable. Ronald Reagan understood, though. Several months later, in November 1979, he formally announced his presidential bid with a speech that could be read as almost a point-by-point response to Carter's Malaise Speech.

"In recent months leaders in our government have told us that we, the people, have lost confidence in ourselves; that we must regain our spirit and our will to achieve our national goals," Reagan said. "Well, it is true there is a lack of confidence, an unease with things the way they are. But the confidence we have lost is confidence in our government's policies."

Then Reagan began to reel off the classic conservative solutions he would advance to address these problems. The federal government "has overspent, overestimated, and over-regulated" and must be reined in. "The key to restoring the health of the economy lies in cutting taxes. At the same time, we need to get the waste out of federal spending. . . . We must put an end to the arrogance of a federal establishment which accepts no blame for our condition, cannot be relied upon to give us a fair estimate of our situation, and utterly refuses to live within its means." He called for closer ties with Canada and Mexico. He said he'd ask those countries to send representatives to sit in on American government meetings and declared, "It is time we stopped thinking of our nearest neighbors as foreigners."

It was all familiar terrain for Reagan, and it worked. He regained his campaign footing and was seen as the front-runner—until the first actual votes were cast, in the Iowa caucuses. Reagan had campaigned a total of forty-one hours in the state. Bush, by contrast, spent thirty-one days grinding his way through the midwestern winter. And he was rewarded for his efforts, narrowly beating Reagan in the caucuses.

The Reagan campaign, in a panic, threw out the old, aloof strategy and put the candidate on the road full-time for the first-in-the-nation primary in New Hampshire. There, aided by a dramatic debate in Nashua in which he publicly stared down Bush in a tussle over allowing other candidates to join in, Reagan won the primary.

From there, his front-runner's status was secure, and he cruised to the nomination. Meantime, yet another disaster befell Carter. In April 1980, desperate to end the Iranian hostage crisis, he approved the dispatch of eight helicopters bearing Special Forces soldiers into Iran on a daring operation designed to spring the American diplomats being held in the embassy in Tehran. But when only five of the helicopters reached their staging point inside Iran in working condition, Carter, on the advice of military leaders, aborted the mission. One of the helicopters crashed into an American transport plane as they tried to withdraw; both went up in smoke, and eight servicemen were killed. As it happens, I arrived in Washington to begin my service there for *The Wall Street Journal* the morning the news of the failed hostage mission broke. I heard about it as soon as I woke up in the Key Bridge Marriott, just across the Potomac River from Georgetown. By the time I got in to the *Journal* bureau, it was a frenzy of reporters and editors rushing about trying to make sense of what had happened, and what it meant for the seemingly cursed Carter administration. *This,* I thought, *is going to be an interesting place*.

What's important about that 1980 campaign, though, isn't simply that Reagan won his party's nomination. Along the way, he took a series of steps that expanded the conservative movement into a fully formed political force—and pulled the entire Republican Party into this new conservative tent.

First, Reagan won over a group of high-profile hawkish Democrats in the national security establishment—the so-called neoconservatives. These intellectuals and activists were disciples of the late Senator Henry "Scoop" Jackson of Washington State, a Democrat who sought to weld together Democrats' traditional left-of-center economic policies with a fierce anti-Soviet, pro-defense philosophy. Jackson ran against Carter in 1976 and lost. His followers stayed in the Democratic Party, but they increasingly found Carter's policies too soft for their liking, and his emphasis on other countries' human rights records rather than their anti-Communist policies the wrong way to set priorities in international affairs.

Their misgivings came to a head when the Soviet Union invaded Afghanistan in December 1979 to install a pro-Moscow government there, a move the neoconservatives surmised the Soviets undertook because they saw Carter as too weak to respond forcefully. Knowing of their grumbling, Carter called the hawks in his party to a meeting in the White House the following month to hash things out. It was a disaster. Carter was offended by their criticisms of him, and they were appalled at his defensiveness.

The Reagan campaign moved in to pick off the neocons. At his request, he joined a group of them for dinner at the house of columnist George Will, on a quiet street in Maryland just beyond the District of Columbia line. Reagan specifically asked that the group include a sometimes acerbic professor and writer named Jeane Kirkpatrick. The candidate had read and admired an essay she wrote for the conservative magazine *Commentary* entitled "Dictatorships and Double Standards," which argued that the United States was perpetuating a double standard by tolerating Communist totalitarian regimes of the left while spurning military regimes of the right in Latin America and elsewhere. On the night of that meeting, Kirkpatrick and others walked into Will's lovely colonial brick home carrying their doubts about Reagan and his level of experience and intellectual heft. Kirkpatrick warned Reagan that she was, and always had been, a Democrat. Reagan disarmed her by replying, "So was I once."

In the end, his staunch anti-Communism was enough to win them over. By the spring of 1980, the Reagan campaign announced a team of foreign policy advisers populated with neoconservative thinkers, including Kirkpatrick, who later would become Reagan's ambassador to the United Nations. Reagan had successfully pulled the hawkish wing of the Democratic Party directly into his orbit.

The second step seemed innocuous enough: a lunch in Los Angeles. Reagan's campaign team arranged for him to dine with a garrulous young congressman from New York, Jack Kemp, and his wife, Joanne. Kemp had become an evangelist for a kind of sunny, upbeat conservative economics built entirely around the idea of a giant tax cut. At the urging of his two top aides, Arthur Laffer and Jude Wanniski, Kemp was pushing what became known as the theory of supply-side economics, which held that a big tax cut would produce such a surge in economic growth that even a lower tax rate on those surging incomes would keep government revenues more or less stable—in other words, from the federal government's point of view, a big tax cut could pay for itself. People would pay a lower tax rate, the economy would boom, incomes would go up, and the government wouldn't have to run a big deficit or severely cut into the services it offered to save money. Everybody would win.

To Kemp, the idea was the answer to what he always considered conservatives' Achilles' heel: a grim economic message that stressed balanced budgets and low-tax austerity, implying that pain was a necessary side effect of fiscal responsibility. Worse, conservatives had a tendency to lash out in anger at liberals who disagreed with them. That approach, Kemp thought, was a guaranteed turnoff to poor, working-class, and minority voters, ensuring Republicans would never expand their appeal.

"Root-canal conservative politics of the 1970s was far from where my father was," recalls Jimmy Kemp, the late congressman's son. "You don't whip up anger; you explain what you are for. And he was for economic growth, with a bleeding heart that wanted to leave nobody behind. He was always for equality of opportunity, though never for equality of outcome unless that was earned."

Kemp's brain trust wanted him to take this message, and his supply-side tax cut, into the presidential race himself. Maybe young Jack Kemp, not old Ronald Reagan, could be the conservatives' darling of 1980. At a minimum, by running on his signature message, he would position himself to become Reagan's running mate.

But the Kemp bandwagon stalled out before it even got started, largely because of the would-be candidate himself. Team Kemp expected that Reagan would be cool toward Kemp's economic theories. Instead, when the congressman described his ideas over lunch, Reagan embraced them so completely that Kemp threw his support behind the Gipper.

Kemp eventually joined the campaign as an adviser. Reagan, in return, got full ownership of an economic plan that, while controversial, was the kind of dramatic and specific gesture his campaign had been looking for. It set him apart not just from other Republicans—Bush would famously call it "voodoo economics"—but from previous conservative figures as well. Moreover, its cheery promise that economic growth could reduce or eliminate troublesome concerns that tax cuts would explode the deficit fit nicely with Reagan's naturally optimistic view of the world. The growing conservative revolution had its economic battle plan.

The third crucial step came in Detroit, at the Republican National Convention, where Reagan would be officially nominated. He came to Detroit without having chosen a running mate. As the convention approached, the Reagan team saw that the party establishment—East Coast in orientation, and considerably less conservative than their presumptive nominee—remained unconvinced that the party had picked a winner. And they had an idea: Reagan should take the radical step of picking a former president, Gerald Ford, as his running mate to reassure the party's old mainstream.

"The establishment—to them Ronald Reagan was an interloper from the West," recalls Edwin Meese, the aide who was perhaps closest to Reagan at the time. "A lot of the establishment money people were not sure Ronald Reagan was really up to the job. And so that's where you had this boomlet of Ford as the vice president."

The Reagan team decided there was enough support for the idea that it had to be taken seriously. So two small teams of Reagan and Ford advisers were put together to meet privately and discuss it. It was a powerful group. On the Ford side were former secretary of state Henry Kissinger and future Federal Reserve chairman Alan Greenspan. The Reagan side included a future head of the Central Intelligence Agency, William Casey, and Meese, a future attorney general. Together, these men began discussing whether it was possible for a new president and a former president to somehow divide the duties of the most powerful office in the land.

The subtext of the conversations was the idea that Reagan needed a centrist running mate at his side to reassure establishment Republicans, to say nothing of the country more broadly, that he wasn't too far to the right for the job. And for a couple of days it appeared it might happen.

As a young, impressionable reporter, I found myself in Detroit that week, covering the first political convention I had ever attended. The question of whether the "dream ticket" of Reagan and Ford would come together consumed the gathering through its first two days, and then the speculation hit its peak as the convention opened its Wednesday night session, where a running mate selection would have to be announced. Most delegates and reporters assumed it was on the way to completion. I didn't have enough experience, that steamy Detroit week, to be sure how unusual all this really was, but I could tell the air was electric with excitement at the idea that something unprecedented—putting a former president at the number-two spot on a national ticket—might actually be taking shape in full public view.

Behind the scenes, though, the arrangement was falling apart. The Reagan team was growing increasingly uncomfortable with the idea of seeming to divide the powers of the presidency in two. The idea died when Ford appeared in a live interview on CBS's evening news program, talking as if the ticket were a done deal and describing what sounded an awful lot like a co-presidency. The Reagan team gathered and decided to pull the plug—though they hadn't yet told anyone outside the inner circle.

Late that night, as delegates milled around the floor and completed the roll call that formally nominated Reagan, William Brock, the chairman of the Republican National Committee, caught the eye of my *Wall Street Journal* colleague Al Hunt, who was in the press stand just above the convention floor. Amid the din, Brock used an elaborate set of hand signals to tell Al the dream ticket was dead: He folded his hands and put his head on them as if on a pillow (that was the signal for "dream") and then ran his finger across his throat (the signal for "dead"). Al rushed back to the *Journal*'s work space, and he and his sidekick in political coverage, Jim Perry, frantically rewrote the story they had prepared to herald the Reagan-Ford ticket, turning it in a matter of minutes into one that told of its demise.

While that drama played out on the convention floor, the Reagan team gathered in its headquarters to decide where to turn next. Whatever was going to happen now had to happen quickly. In their back pockets, Meese recalls, the brain trust had been carrying around a secret internal campaign poll, so closely guarded that only Meese, Casey, Reagan pollster Richard Wirthlin, and Reagan himself knew of its existence. It showed that the two people who could clearly help Reagan win the election were Ford and George Bush. Bush, tall and slender, with patrician good looks and a reassuring lopsided grin that he deployed regularly, was well known, well regarded, and offensive to almost no one. With time running out, Reagan called Bush, the man who had so belittled supply-side economics, and asked him whether he could support all the Reagan positions and, if so, whether he would accept a place on the ticket. Bush agreed immediately to both propositions.

As that suggests, the marriage between the conservative leader and the man who had been the consummate establishment moderate was an act of pure political expediency. But its implications for the Republican Party—and for the conservative revolution—were momentous and long-lasting. By forging a partnership with Bush, Reagan instantly brought the party's moderate wing into the fold. That included not just Bush himself but Bush's closest friend, James Baker, who went on to become Reagan's White House chief of staff and Treasury secretary, and a passel of Bush-supporting moderates in Congress. The Republican Party united—and united under conservative leadership.

The fourth and final big step came when Reagan married the conservative movement with the evangelical movement—then known as the new religious right. This marriage was consummated just days after that Republican convention, when Reagan flew to Dallas to attend a rally of the newly minted Religious Roundtable in Reunion Arena in August 1980.

More than ten thousand loud, cheering evangelicals were there, as was the full roster of leaders: Jerry Falwell, Pat Robertson, James Robison. A young conservative Christian activist named Mike Huckabee, later to be governor of Arkansas and a presidential candidate, helped organize the meeting.

Ironically, Carter had in some ways opened the door for evangelicals to move more deeply into the political sphere by proclaiming himself a born-again Christian and talking openly about how his faith influenced his political life. Evangelical leaders were happy about that at first, but soon soured on Carter and his leadership. So, in 1980, the evangelicals decided to cast aside fully their traditional aversion to political activism and jump into the political arena with both feet. They were activated, in part, by the Supreme Court's decision legalizing abortion seven years earlier in the *Roe v. Wade* case, which conservative Christians thought had taken America over a kind of cultural Rubicon and into a new era of disrespect for sacred life. If such decisions were going to be made in the world of politics and policy, and by judges appointed and confirmed by politicians, religious conservatives wanted to be part of that world.

In Reagan they had found the man with whom they wanted to lock arms. He wasn't overtly religious, but he talked frequently of God and old-time values in words that resonated with evangelical Christians. And he shared their view on abortion. For his part, Reagan was ready to link arms as well, unconcerned as past candidates had been about the dangers of mixing religion and politics. His mere decision to show up in Dallas said that loud and clear.

He was introduced by Robison, who, with his shock of thick dark hair, brooding good looks, and booming southern voice, resembled a real-life version of actor Gregory Peck, planted behind a dark brown podium. Waving a Bible and thrusting his arms forward toward the crowd, Robison implored the Reunion Arena crowd: "If the righteous, the pro-family, the moral, the biblical, the godly, the hardworking, and the decent individuals in this country stay out of politics, who on this earth does that leave to make the policies under which you and I live and struggle to survive. . . . It's time for God's people to come out of the closet and the churches and change America."

Reagan then rose to speak and, using the precise words the religious leaders there had suggested, he declared: "I know this is a nonpartisan gathering, and so I know that you can't endorse me. But I only brought that up because I want you to know I endorse you and what you're doing."

I was in Reunion Arena for that moment. After the nominating convention, the *Journal*'s political reporters had gone off on a brief vacation, leaving me to fill their spot on the Reagan campaign plane. I've been to many a big sporting event, but I'm not sure I've heard any arena louder than that one as Reagan finished his remarks. The speeches before his had been fiery, and were marked with some angry jabs at the assembled national press corps for its alleged hostility to the religious right. Reagan only turned up the temperature higher. As the crowd roared upon his conclusion and turned some of its fire on us, Howell Raines, of *The New York Times*, who later became the paper's top editor, turned to me and joked, "We better get out of here before somebody gets lynched." The passion was not just noteworthy; it represented an entirely new force in American politics, suddenly unleashed on Reagan's behalf.

With those four developments, Reagan had constructed in 1980 the complete conservative package. By combining economic conservatives, national security conservatives, and religious conservatives, he formed what would be referred to for years afterward as the movement's three-legged stool. It is no exaggeration to say that American politics would never be the same.

The Republican moderate wing took one last shot at stemming the conservative tide, and it came courtesy of John Anderson. The Illinois congressman had a moderate voting record, a professorial look, a chippy style, and a disdain for what Reagan had done to his Republican Party. Having failed to win the GOP nomination for himself, he set off on an extreme long-shot quest to win the presidency as an independent candidate. He backed a big gas tax to reduce oil consumption, favored gun control, and argued that Reagan's tax-cut ideas would be disastrous. In a tumultuous year, he wagered, there just might be enough moderate Democrats disillusioned with President Carter and enough moderate Republicans scared by Ronald Reagan to put together a winning coalition.

And for a while, it seemed that might be possible. In mid-June, Anderson was winning the support of as many as 25 percent of voters in national polls. He formed something called the National Unity Party, then fundraised and spent heavily to gather the signatures needed to qualify for the ballot in all fifty states. Reagan agreed to debate Anderson, but Carter didn't, and the two-man debate ended up helping Reagan.

I spent most of that fall traveling with John Anderson for the *Journal* as he played Don Quixote, tilting at windmills in his independent run. The journey was great fun, particularly as the campaign became ever looser as Anderson's chances of making a difference started to fade, with the candidate's young staff and the traveling journalists sharing inside jokes and after-hours drinks. Anderson picked a man few in the nation knew, Patrick Lucey, the former Democratic governor of Wisconsin, as his running mate, in an effort to show he really did stand between the two main parties. (I have found that a sure way to stump the crowd in a parlor-game discussion of politics is to ask people to name Anderson's running mate.) The campaign entourage made what seemed to be countless stops at the supposed hotbeds of moderate politics, such as Madison, Wisconsin. Anderson tried, tirelessly, to defend the political middle and champion a third party in a country where loyalties to the two parties and their ideological leanings almost inevitably overpower dissenters.

He campaigned hard to the end. But Republicans united behind Reagan. Carter, meanwhile, tried to portray Reagan as a conservative extremist, in part by wheeling out recordings Reagan had once made suggesting the Medicare program was "socialized medicine."

It didn't work. Reagan won in a landslide, carrying forty-four states and winning 489 Electoral College votes, to Carter's 49. Even liberal bastions such as New York, Wisconsin, and Vermont went for Reagan. Blue-collar voters became "Reagan Democrats" that day, abandoning their traditional party. Anderson won just 6.6 percent of the vote.

The size of the Reagan juggernaut became clear on Election Night. I was dispatched to ABC News headquarters in New York to sit in as the network's analysts analyzed the results of their national exit poll. The effort seemed anticlimactic when the polling team appeared at about 6 P.M. and said, essentially, *It's over. Reagan will win in a walk.* Then, perhaps an hour later, the drama was revived when the analysts returned with shocked looks on their faces to say, essentially, *Hold on, Republicans might actually take back the Senate, too.* I was utterly unprepared for that. Sometimes, in the course of a journalistic career, you realize only afterward that you've watched something big and historic. This was one of those rarer occasions in which it was clear *at the moment* that something big and historic was unfolding before your eyes.

In the end, Republicans picked up twelve seats in the Senate that night to take control away from the Democrats. The new senators who swept in on Reagan's coattails included several notable conservatives: Steve Symms of Idaho, Chuck Grassley of Iowa, Mack Mattingly of Georgia, Paula Hawkins of Florida. Nobody saw it coming.

Conservatives suddenly had a measure of power beyond anything they had dared hope for. The crisis atmosphere, in turn, made it all the easier for President-elect Reagan to begin putting conservative ideas into motion. The Reagan Revolution was under way.

CHAPTER 2

★ ★ ★

Storming the Gates

In the closing scene of the film *The Candidate,* Robert Redford, whose character has just won election to the U.S. Senate, looks at his top adviser and asks, "What do we do now?"

It's a question Ronald Reagan might well have asked after winning the presidency in 1980. He and other conservatives had long wandered in the American political wilderness. They were well practiced in proclaiming what they were against—liberals and Communism and socialism and big government and high taxes—but a lot less adept at detailing a real, conservative governing agenda.

Reagan himself was hardly a policy wonk. No intellectual, he had limited interest in the details of public policy. In fact, he seemed under-equipped to lead an ideological movement.

Yet he did bring to the presidency two crucial attributes. First, he believed deeply in basic conservative principles. And second, in an era in which political salesmanship was becoming key to success, he knew how to frame those beliefs in an unthreatening, optimistic manner for a public ready for change. Put more succinctly, he knew what he thought and he knew how to explain it to a mass audience.

Lou Cannon, a reporter who long covered Reagan and became his most authoritative biographer, described Reagan's views this way: "He preached love of country, distrust of government, the glories of economic opportunity, the dangers of regulating business, and the wonders of free markets and free trade. He believed in the manifest destiny of the United States of America. . . . As president, he was at once the most malleable and least movable of men."

To the surprise of some who considered him a lightweight, Reagan actually was well read. As he moved from Democrat to Republican, from the political left to the right, for example, he read *The Conscience of a Conservative,* the book by Barry Goldwater that was the bible of modern conservatives. The book created a philosophical framework for modern conservatism, one built around devotion to the American Constitution. Goldwater described the Constitution as "a system of restraints against the natural tendency of government to expand in the direction of absolutism." And it carried these words of warning, which some conservatives would revive decades later in the era of Donald Trump: "The framers were well aware of the danger posed by self-seeking demagogues—that they might persuade a majority of the people to confer on government vast powers in return for deceptive promises of economic gain."

In his campaign, Reagan had put some meat on those bare conservative bones. He embraced big tax cuts, a big increase in defense spending, and a North American Accord that would grow into the North American Free Trade Agreement. By their own acknowledgment, though, most conservatives hadn't really developed a detailed plan for running a federal government they disliked. Happily for Reagan, Ed Feulner was ready, with a solution to that problem in hand.

Feulner, a large, bespectacled man with a hearty laugh, was a founder of the Heritage Foundation, one of the few outposts for conservatives in a Washington that was far more populated with liberal institutions. Heritage was born in the early 1970s, a time when Feulner was working in Congress for conservative representative Phil Crane. A friend of his, Paul Weyrich, was working on the other side of the Capitol, for conservative senator Gordon Allott. (As it happens, another young staffer in the Allott office at the time was George Will, who would go on to be a leading voice of conservatives in his widely read newspaper columns and TV appearances.)

Feulner and Weyrich were frustrated at the absence of a strong voice for conservative policy positions in Washington debates. They considered the dominant Republican-oriented think tank at the time, the American Enterprise Institute, to be too stuffy and aloof, often speaking up too late in the game to really make a difference. The Brookings Institution, the leading Democratic-leaning think tank, did a much better job of weighing in from the left in ways that actually moved the outcome, they felt.

They wanted a think tank—really more of an "action tank"—on the right that would both generate policy arguments from a conservative perspective and then inject them straight into the Washington bloodstream. They got their chance, serendipitously enough, when a letter arrived in the office of Senator Allott in 1972.

Allott represented the state of Colorado, which also happened to be home to beer magnate Joseph Coors and his brewery, which made much of its Rocky Mountain locale in its marketing. Coors was deeply conservative, and in his letter to Allott he said he would be coming to Washington seeking ways to push policy in a more conservative direction. The letter normally would have gone to Will, but he had just left Allott's office. So it landed on the desk of Weyrich—who knew what to do with it.

Weyrich arranged to meet with Coors and to bring Feulner along. Together, they pitched him on the idea of a new conservative think tank that would participate more actively in policy fights. Perhaps more important, they had conspired ahead of time with a staff member then serving in Richard Nixon's White House, Lyn Nofziger, to bring Coors to Nofziger's office in the stately Old Executive Office Building, next to the presidential mansion. Nofziger was a like-minded conservative who had worked for Reagan in California (and would do so again when Reagan ran for president). Weyrich thought gathering in his office within the White House compound would lend some gravitas to the conversation with Coors.

As the group sat down together in Nofziger's office, Coors pointed to Weyrich and Feulner and said that they wanted to start a new conservative organization and were seeking his money. But, Coors noted, AEI already was operating as a think tank on the right. What did Nofziger think? At that point, Nofziger got up, walked to the bookshelf in his office, and pulled out an AEI policy report, on which he had strategically sprinkled some dust ahead of time. He blew off the dust in dramatic fashion, Feulner recalls, and declared, "That's what your AEI study is worth. They fill up your bookcases, but they don't matter. They're either too late or they're too ponderous. People don't pay attention to them."

As a result of that meeting, Coors gave Weyrich and Feulner a quarter of a million dollars to help launch what would become the Heritage Foundation. (The name of the foundation came to Weyrich when he was walking in his Northern Virginia neighborhood one night, passed a development called Heritage Homes, and decided that Heritage would be a good name.)

Heritage started small, in a couple of townhouses on Capitol Hill, and soon became a scrappier, edgier place for framing conservative arguments on important policy issues. At the time, Feulner also was a casual friend of Ed Meese, Reagan's longtime aide and attorney general. So when Reagan was in the early stages of preparing to run for president in 1980, Meese had dinner with Feulner and asked him whether Heritage would put together some policy guidance to implement a conservative agenda in case Reagan won. "There was no real handbook in terms of how you do it," Feulner says.

Feulner took the idea to Heritage's board of directors, who decided not only to say yes but to jump in with both feet. Soon Heritage's leaders were creating an entire conservative governing plan. They started reaching out to conservative academics and policy wonks, lobbyists and like-minded congressional staffers, and eventually formed twenty-three teams of experts, each charged with coming up with recommendations for how to steer policy in every conceivable corner of the government and its bureaucracy.

So while the Reagan campaign went about the day-to-day busi-ness of winning an election, the Heritage team churned away on policy plans large and small. The leaders of the effort met with Meese over dinner at one point during the campaign but largely functioned on their own. When staffers from the Reagan campaign were asked what they had planned if they won, the answer was, es-sentially, "The Heritage folks are taking care of that."

Then, of course, Reagan won, and Republicans took over the Senate. Suddenly the idea of enacting a conservative agenda seemed a lot more plausible.

On the Monday after the election, Feulner and some of his Her-itage colleagues carried a box containing some seven thousand xe-roxed pages of text—the assembled work of the twenty-three teams of specialists—into the Hay-Adams Hotel, across the street from the White House. At a restaurant in the hotel basement, they handed the box over to four representatives of the nascent Reagan transition. The Reagan Revolution had its battle plan.

Heritage soon turned the recommendations into a book, *Mandate for Leadership: Policy Management in a Conservative Administration,* which shot to the top of the *Washington Post* bestseller list. It in-stantly became required reading in a capital city trying to figure out what in the world the conservative invaders from the West had in mind.

The book was three inches thick, a total of 1,093 pages. Its rec-ommendations ranged from the mighty to the mundane. The Pen-tagon should get to work building two hundred more B-1 bombers and four new nuclear aircraft carriers, one chapter proposed. The Department of Education should cease to exist. Half of all admin-istrative law judges appointed by the National Labor Relations Board should have private-sector experience. Airlines should have to bid to win more landing slots at airports.

The blueprint had not just policy proposals but also ideas on how to rewire government to give conservative ideas a better chance to succeed. For example, the plan advocated creating a new under-secretary for tax policy in the Treasury Department. Why? Because tax policy traditionally had been placed in the hands of an assistant secretary, and in internal policy debates that assistant secretary was too low-ranking to get anything done. He or she had to go head-to-head with a higher-ranking official at the Office of Management and Budget. If you want to cut taxes, you need an official arguing for tax cuts who can stand up against the official whose principal concern is balancing the budget, not reducing taxes.

Reagan was inaugurated on January 20, 1981, a day that turned out to be unexpectedly auspicious: Iran's leaders announced, just as Reagan was being sworn in, that they were releasing the remaining fifty-two American hostages that Iranian students had been holding in the American embassy over the past 444 days. Was that move a sign that the Iranians feared that the incoming administration would come after them militarily to free the hostages in a way the Carter administration wouldn't? Or was it an overture from Tehran to the new president in pursuit of a less hostile relationship? In any case, the move lifted a dark cloud that had hung over the last year of the Carter presidency—and seemed almost a sign that Providence had decided to shine on Ronald Reagan.

The end of the hostage drama also opened the door to a fast start on Reagan's new conservative agenda. Whatever its other accomplishments or failures, the Reagan team proceeded to illustrate the virtues of striking quickly and dramatically when you have political capital to spend—and the benefits of having some luck along the way. Franklin Roosevelt's famed first-hundred-days agenda remains the gold standard for opening an administration with a bang, but Reagan's first two months have been studied by incoming White House staffs ever since.

For those of us in Washington covering the new administration, those first weeks were head-spinning. George Will hosted Nancy and Ronald Reagan for dinner just before the inauguration. He recalls the electricity that was in the air as network television crews camped outside his house, correspondents tracking every move of the California conservatives who had arrived to shake the capital and its status quo to the core. "You can't imagine the turmoil in

Washington," he recalls. "The barbarians were inside the gates now."

On the day he was inaugurated, Reagan instituted a federal hiring freeze. Eight days later he decontrolled the price of oil. The day after that, he held his first press conference, said he wanted an across-the-board spending cut (something he never got), and announced a sixty-day freeze on new federal regulations. Sixteen days after taking office, he gave a televised address to the nation describing the state of the economy in catastrophic terms and laying the groundwork for his economic program. Eleven days after that, he proposed the cornerstone of his presidency, an across-the-board 30 percent tax cut. And a week after that, the Pentagon requested an immediate giant increase in defense spending.

At times, and despite the Heritage Foundation's preparations, the Reaganites moved so fast that the action had an almost improvised air about it. In the first week of March, when I was helping cover the Pentagon, the new administration unveiled a dramatic new defense-spending plan. Reagan's team was requesting $26 billion in instant defense-spending increases for the fiscal year that already was well under way, and then another $150 billion in new spending over the following four years, above and beyond what the Carter Pentagon had allocated. The defense budget would almost double in a span of five years.

But the Reagan team wasn't just asking for more money for this or that project; it was seeking more money for just about everything the Pentagon was buying. When reporters were summoned to the Pentagon for the briefing at which the initial defense request was unveiled, we were handed photocopied sheets of paper with the Carter administration's numbers for funding for Pentagon programs crossed out and the new figures written in by hand. The implication was clear: The urgency of ramping up defense spending to counter a Soviet threat was so great, there wasn't time to print up new budget pages.

The centerpiece of the Reagan Revolution agenda, though, was the tax cut. This was the initiative that put a conservative stamp not just on the tax code but on the whole Washington agenda. Reagan himself had, over time, talked repeatedly about what he considered the insidious effect of high tax rates, usually by harking back to his days in Hollywood. He proclaimed that the tax rates on big earners had gotten so high that stars would simply stop appearing in movies after their earnings had pushed them into the top tax rate, because they would be allowed to keep so little of the money they made. They were working, they claimed, for almost nothing. He had a legitimate point: In the early 1950s, when Reagan worked in Hollywood, the top marginal tax rate—the rate applied to each additional dollar of income after hitting the top tax bracket—was more than 90 percent.

By 1980, that top marginal rate had come down to 70 percent, but Jack Kemp, leading the supply-side charge in Congress, wanted to bring it down further—along with every other tax rate. By the time he took office, Reagan had become an ardent convert to the Kemp gospel, and he pursued it with a convert's zeal. The miserable shape of the American economy—which by the second quarter of 1980 had slipped into negative territory, meaning it was contracting rather than growing—actually was Reagan's secret weapon in pushing for this turn to the right. After all, the feeling went, how could things get much worse?

Rampant inflation was pushing people into ever higher tax brackets as employers increased pay to try to keep up. That meant average Americans were paying steadily higher tax rates even though, in inflation-adjusted terms, their effective pay was stagnant. "Bracket creep," it was called, a disease that was infecting millions.

So Reagan went before a joint session of Congress and asked for a 30 percent across-the-board cut spread over three years. Large as that tax cut was by any historical standard, he portrayed it as essentially the bare minimum: "Again, let me remind you that while this 30 percent reduction will leave the taxpayers with $500 billion more in their pockets over the next five years, it's actually only a reduction in the tax increase already built into the system." Reagan portrayed the sharp turn in American fiscal policy as both revolutionary, which was what his conservative brethren wanted to hear, and not really radical at all, which was the reassuring note that the White House knew everybody else wanted to hear.

It's hard to overstate how unorthodox and risky the Reagan tax cuts were at the time. Federal budget deficits had risen during the 1970s, and inflation was soaring. To many analysts, both conditions argued against tax cuts, not in favor of them. Most mainstream Republicans—including the two most important Republican senators at the time on such matters, Majority Leader Howard Baker and Finance Committee chairman Robert Dole—came from the traditional, small-town, Dwight Eisenhower school of thinking, which eschewed deficit spending more than anything and which held balanced budgets as a goal to be cherished. Cutting taxes, and thereby reducing government revenues, seemed a recipe for driving the federal deficit to intolerable levels in the short run. The supply-side dream that economic growth would make up the difference in the long run was only that—a dream. Indeed, Baker captured the fear of many Republicans when he called the whole idea a "riverboat gamble."

Moreover, even if cutting taxes did stimulate the economy, as the supply-siders promised, traditional economic theory suggested that the stimulation would fuel greater inflation. And inflation already had hit a shocking and intolerable 13.5 percent in 1980. The prime interest rate had reached its record high of 21.5 percent the month before Reagan was inaugurated. The risks in Reagan's strategy were significant enough that one reporter, *Time* magazine's Laurence I. Barrett, entitled his book about the times *Gambling with History*.

In the face of those problems, Reagan proposed to take the traditional conservative step of proposing to cut federal spending, while also cutting taxes by an even larger amount, and hope that the revenue loss and spending cuts would even out in the long run. There were two problems with that approach. The first was that, given the defense-spending increases he was seeking, the reductions in spending couldn't catch up with the tax cuts. And second, the rules of politics dictated that it would be easier to get lawmakers in Congress to cut taxes—who doesn't like making voters happy by cutting their taxes?—than it would be to cut spending.

There was another problem. Though Reagan's Republicans had taken control of the Senate, they didn't have control of the House. Not even close, in fact. Democrats held a 243-to-192 edge in the House, and the idea of a Republican president pushing a controversial Republican economic program through a chamber where he faced that kind of partisan deficit seemed implausible.

But here is where the fact that the country, and not just the Republican Party, had shifted to the right came to Reagan's rescue. The Democratic Party at that time had a conservative wing, populated principally by southern lawmakers who at that point were Democrats more by tradition than by philosophy. They already were uncomfortable with the Democrats' prevailing positions on social issues—abortion, opposition to the Vietnam War, sexual mores—and were growing disillusioned with their party's recent record on handling the economy. Their constituents back home tended to agree.

In short, they were there for the picking by a new, conservative president.

The task fell to Kenneth Duberstein, a thirty-six-year-old White House staffer with deep ties in Congress from his days working in the Ford administration and for moderate New York senator Jacob Javits. Duberstein was named Reagan's director of legislative affairs, an appointment made because, while he was a reliable Republican, he had good relations with Democrats as well. His challenge was considerable, and there figured to be hand-to-hand combat between the Reagan forces and the Democratic leaders running the House over every important vote. So Duberstein set out to visit, or have someone on his staff visit, the office of every one of the 435 House members, regardless of party. "We're the new guys from the White House," Duberstein recalls saying. "You're going to see a lot of us. We want you to come to us with your concerns."

As he courted new allies for the White House, Duberstein had two factors working in his favor. First, some Democrats hailed from districts where Reagan had beaten Carter, meaning they knew siding with the Republican president would be popular with many of their voters back home. Second, Duberstein had back in the White House a president willing to do the plodding job of getting on the phone to woo wavering Democrats one by one. Reagan had and maintained a reputation for being a bit lazy. He even joked about that rap, once quipping that while people said hard work never killed anyone, he didn't see any reason to take chances. In truth, though, on this score, he was willing to put in the work—a lot of it.

Duberstein had Reagan keep his message simple. He asked for support, not on a long list of items, but simply on the basic budget and tax initiatives. He also tried to have Reagan call House members when they were home in their districts, rather than in Washington, because word would get around in the district that the president had called, pumping up the local folks' estimation of their local lawmaker's importance.

Luck also helped. At one point, Duberstein was searching for moderate and conservative Democrats to recruit from the Northeast, to join those he was winning over from the South, and he heard that Representative Gene Atkinson of Pennsylvania might be open to persuasion. Atkinson was back in his district, so Reagan called him there—and happened to get Atkinson on the line while he was appearing on a live radio talk show. Reagan delivered his standard deal-closing line to the congressman—"You're going to be with me on the budget, right?"—to which Atkinson assented. Having promised the president of the United States on a radio broadcast that he would support him, the lawmaker was hardly in a position to back down later.

The work set up a series of seminal House votes in the spring and summer of 1981 that cemented the Reagan agenda in place. The first test was a budget resolution containing the broad outlines of the spending cuts and defense increases Reagan wanted. He won the vote in the House, with a stunning sixty-three Democratic votes. Next, and even more difficult, was the actual spending plan. The Democratic House Speaker, Tip O'Neill, tried to break the spending measure into six different pieces, presenting wavering Democrats with not one but six difficult votes, thus making it tougher to pass the plan. In a crucial victory, Duberstein lobbied just enough Democrats to defeat that procedural maneuver, making the spending bill itself easier to pass on a single vote.

Then, finally, came the vote on Reagan's signature tax cuts. Just as the push on that began, fate intervened. As Reagan left a routine speech to a labor conference at the Washington Hilton Hotel on March 30, 1981—a mere ten weeks after he took office—a mentally troubled young man named John Hinckley walked up to him. As the president was boarding his armored limousine, Hinckley shot him with a .22 caliber pistol. In fact, four men were shot in a matter of seconds: Reagan, a District of Columbia policeman, a Secret Service agent, and White House press secretary James Brady.

Confusion and drama fell over the capital for hours, a deep and foreboding uncertainty the likes of which I wouldn't feel again until terrorists attacked the Pentagon on September 11, 2001. At first, nobody, even Reagan himself, was sure whether he had been shot, or instead just injured as he was shoved into his limousine. And when it became clear he'd been shot, it was impossible for those of us trying to catch up with the story to know how badly. Was he even alive? The White House didn't know much more than the rest of us did, so there were no straight answers. Vice President Bush was in Texas giving a speech, so it wasn't clear who was in charge in the president's absence. Secretary of State Alexander Haig bulled his way into the White House press room to say that he was in charge, though, in fact, nobody actually had decided that beyond Haig himself. The Reagan team was new enough that it had no experience in crisis management, and it found itself in the midst of a genuine crisis that day.

Of course, Reagan did survive, and a kind of mythology emerged about his survival. He was brave throughout his ordeal, it was said. He never lost his sense of humor as doctors worked to save his life. He quipped to his wife, Nancy, that he forgot to duck when the shots were fired. He asked his doctors and nurses to reassure him that they were Republicans. Months later, when asked what he would have done differently in the opening phase of his presidency, he cracked that he wouldn't have gone to the Hilton.

There emerged a wave of popular sympathy and admiration for Reagan in the wake of the assassination attempt. His job approval soared to 68 percent, and his calls seeking support from members of Congress took on new resonance. In Washington, where public approval translates into political power, Reagan had a newfound source of power to push his economic program through Congress.

And by Washington standards, it happened at lightning speed. Within weeks of the shooting, the White House was in serious negotiations with both parties to tie down the tax-cut package. Amid mounting concerns that the size of the tax cut would send the deficit soaring too quickly, the Reagan team agreed to trim it back a bit; there would be a 5 percent cut in rates the first year, and 10 percent each of the following two years, so the total would be 25 percent instead of 30. But the cut still would be across the board, on all rates, and still would include a hefty cut for businesses in the form of accelerated deductions for depreciation of assets. Significantly, the package also eliminated the "bracket creep" problem by indexing the tax cuts to inflation, meaning taxpayers wouldn't automatically be bumped into a higher rate just because inflation pushed up their wages.

The tax-cutting fever that summer was such that Democrats were countering with their own tax-cut plans, far bigger than any they would have considered had Carter won a second term. But Reagan prevailed. At the end of July, the tax cut—officially called the Economic Recovery Tax Act of 1981—passed the Senate by a whopping, bipartisan 89–11 vote. It passed the House 238–195, with forty-eight House Democrats siding with the Republican president to pass the most conservative tax package in memory. Reagan signed both the tax bill and the associated spending-cuts package while on vacation on his California ranch.

Hyperbole is common in Washington, but the tax cut was genuinely a monumental act. "It is very difficult to describe the Economic Recovery Tax Act of 1981 without recourse to the grandiose," the Tax Foundation declared in an analysis a few weeks after the dust settled. In dollar terms, it was the largest tax cut in history. Within five years, the total reduction of the government's tax income as a percentage of the gross domestic product would be 5.6 percent, several times larger than any tax cut of the previous two decades. By contrast, a celebrated tax cut President Kennedy pushed through in 1962 cut tax receipts by 0.2 percent of GDP. As a result of the bill, the federal government's tax receipts would be 19.2 percent of GDP by 1986, rather than the 23.9 percent they would have been otherwise. Over the coming five years, the cumulative reduction in the federal tax intake would amount to $749 billion—roughly equivalent to the country's entire economy in 1966.

Yet the real significance of the Reagan tax cut lies not in these numbers, nor in the idea that it was some kind of unqualified immediate success. In fact, it was not an instant success. It didn't immediately cause an economic rebound. A painful recession, caused largely by the Federal Reserve Board's use of high interest rates to wring inflation out of the economy, would drag on for more than a year. In the meantime, the tax cut caused the federal budget deficit to mushroom well beyond the White House's cheery forecasts, compelling Republicans in Congress to lead a charge to trim it back a bit the following year. After rising, Reagan's popularity began to decline.

But the significance of the tax cut lay in the way it changed the paradigm of Washington. It was the single act that most clearly demonstrated that there was a new sheriff in town—a conservative one—and that the rules of the town would be different. Republicans had moved rightward, but so had Democrats. Something different was going on, and that would be the case for almost two generations.

CHAPTER 3

★ ★ ★

Growing Roots

rover Norquist was a young foot soldier in the Reagan Revolution, one of many who reported for duty in Washington
early and then stayed to fight the long fight. He and his contempo-
raries helped the conservative movement sink roots, ensuring it
would last beyond just one man and one presidency.

Norquist, a bearded, bespectacled bundle of energy, delivers
revolutionary rhetoric in a nasal tone, with a twinkle in his eye and
a smile on his face, often leaving listeners uncertain how much of
what he said was for real and how much was for shock effect. It's a
style he has been developing since youth. Norquist grew up just
outside Boston, the son of Rockefeller Republicans—that is, moderate Republicans who in the 1960s were drawn more to the liberal-
leaning governor of New York, Nelson Rockefeller, than to the
hard-edged conservative senator from Arizona, Barry Goldwater.
Young Grover inherited their interest in politics, though the road
he traveled eventually veered farther to the right.

At the age of twelve, he took the short train ride from his hometown of Weston into Boston to campaign for Richard Nixon in the
1968 presidential race. Later, when the local high school decided to
sell off many of its old books for pennies on the dollar, Norquist
swooped in and bought all the conservative tracts, which he now
believes the leftist faculty was only too happy to dump.

He read *Masters of Deceit,* the obsessively anti-Communist book written by former Federal Bureau of Investigation chief J. Edgar Hoover, and *Witness,* the account by Whittaker Chambers of his journey from Soviet spy to anti-Communist crusader. Norquist developed an antipathy toward Communism and the Soviet Union. Then he read the books of Ayn Rand, the libertarian thinker, which pushed him toward conservative economic beliefs. He developed a theory that the Republican Party, which was known to many voters largely as the most anti-Communist party, could have a broader appeal if it simply branded itself as *the party that won't raise your taxes.* Norquist was bright and brash, and in 1974 he went on to study at Harvard, where he relished his role as a conservative amid a student body made up of far more on the left. He worked on *The Harvard Crimson,* the student newspaper, engaging in arguments with fellow staff members he considered socialists. He joined the Harvard Libertarian Association and the Harvard Republican Club.

As he was leaving college, a friend told him there was a job helping run the National Taxpayers Union, an organization that styled itself as the lobbyist for taxpayers, pushing for lower taxes and lower government spending. He happened to arrive just as the premier taxpayer revolt of the 1970s hit: California voters were in the process of approving Proposition 13, which put a constitutional limit on property tax increases. It was, in retrospect, one of the early signs of a voter backlash from the right, and Norquist arrived just in time to take advantage of it.

In the wake of Proposition 13, Norquist, as representative of the National Taxpayers Union, traveled the country, pushing to convene a constitutional convention that could enact a balanced-budget amendment to the U.S. Constitution. The idea built steam but fell just short of the thirty-four states needed to approve it. Still, ideological seeds were being planted.

Norquist returned to Boston to attend business school. Then, when Ronald Reagan was elected president, the former lobbyist decided he wanted to get back into the political arena. He returned to Washington to work for the national Republican Party.

It was then that Norquist's most meaningful career turn took place, the one that would make him a key player in institutionalizing the conservative movement. White House officials, including the president and Treasury Secretary Donald Regan, had pushed for the creation of a sympathetic outside organization to advocate for lower tax rates in Washington and across the country. They figured the Reagan administration could use some outside help to preserve its cherished tax cuts. At their suggestion, the organization was launched, with private contributions, and called Americans for Tax Reform. As it happens, the incorporation papers were drawn up by an outside lawyer named William Barr, later to be attorney general for two Republican presidents.

The White House asked Norquist to run ATR, as the group came to be known. ATR specialized in not just creating pressure for low tax rates and reduced federal spending generally, but in applying pressure directly on candidates for office at every level to get them to promise they wouldn't raise taxes. This pressure took the form of "the pledge"—a simple written promise that the aspiring lawmaker would oppose any net tax increase. Norquist, a wizard at attracting attention to his cause, created an expectation among Republican candidates that all must sign the pledge by publicly shaming those who didn't. The pledge was offered to every candidate for state and federal office, as well as all incumbents. Eventually, the pledge would be signed by some 1,400 elected officials—including, as of 2019, 209 members of the House of Representatives, 45 members of the Senate, and just about every Republican who sought the presidency since its creation.

Norquist rapidly became known as a verbal bomb-thrower. He was catnip for reporters covering the conservative uprising. If Republicans were supposed to be bland men in boring suits uttering safe platitudes, Norquist saw himself as a rabble-rouser dressed for battle, saying the most outrageous things. He liked to say that his goal was to shrink the government in half, making it so small that "we can drown it in the bathtub." He infuriated the other side of the aisle with such rhetoric. When he wasn't campaigning for tax policies, he traveled to the Afghan border and Angola to illustrate his support for bands of anti-Communist guerrillas fighting the Soviet Union. He put some of the martial paraphernalia he picked up along the way on display in his office.

If the rap on Republicans entering the Reagan era was that they had become only too willing to go along with the idea that they were the permanent minority party, Norquist was precisely the kind of Republican determined to throw off those shackles. To be sure, he also annoyed Republicans with his threats to hurt them politically if they didn't sign and honor his pledge. The implication was that he was personally doing the work of Ronald Reagan. (In fact, his admiration for Reagan was quite real, so much so that he later launched the Ronald Reagan Legacy Project, which would, among other things, successfully lead a campaign to turn Washington National Airport into the Ronald Reagan Washington National Airport.)

The formation of ATR was part of a crucial front in the development of the conservative movement: the creation of institutions that put conservatism on a broader foundation that could not only help Reagan but outlive him. In short, starting in the late 1970s, the conservative movement built an actual political and policy infrastructure.

This build-out was crucial. Before it developed, conservatives tended to think they weren't just on the margins of the political system, but on the margins of their own party. The Republican Party in the 1970s saw them as slightly dangerous unguided missiles, a bit uncouth, standing in unfavorable contrast to the solid, gentlemanly approach of, say, President Dwight Eisenhower. The new wave of conservatives were edgier, less interested in getting along and more interested in throwing a few bombs into the system.

What they lacked was an infrastructure into which they could pour their energy and ideas and turn them into results. There was a real danger the Reagan Revolution could be a movement built around one man, only to dissipate when he was gone, just as the earlier conservative movement had withered after Goldwater suffered his ignominious defeat in 1964. Younger conservatives thought Republicans in general were too quiescent, too willing to go along with what had long been a dominant Democratic, liberal majority in Washington. And so they set out to create the machinery necessary to change that.

The effort had begun in the 1970s, with the birth of the Heritage Foundation. At about the same time, a group of young, hard-edged political operators figured out how to drive a truck through a loophole in a landmark campaign finance law made possible by the Supreme Court. The court ruled that the law couldn't actually limit the amount of money citizens and groups could spend on their own, independent of a formal campaign, to support candidates. Seeing a big opportunity, the conservative operatives created the National Conservative Political Action Committee, or NCPAC, and started spending money to boost conservative congressional candidates and, perhaps as important, attack their Democratic opponents.

Charlie Black, a young political operative from North Carolina who ventured into politics while at the University of Florida, was one of the founders. (Black later would become business partners with Paul Manafort and Roger Stone, who would achieve a different kind of fame as Donald Trump operatives convicted of crimes related to the investigation into Russian interference in the 2016 presidential campaign.) Black had worked on Reagan's 1976 presidential campaign and concluded, as it wound down, that conservatives needed a way to keep political activists occupied and employed in the cause between elections. NCPAC—almost universally called "nic-pac"—was the early answer to that need.

Black recalls getting Reagan to later sign a letter asking for contributions to NCPAC, which was sent out to a mailing list of Reagan supporters. "We raised almost a million dollars, which was an incredible amount of money in those days," Black recalls. The result was an early sign of both Reagan's power and the growth of a more meaningful and organized conservative movement. NCPAC's fundraising prowess and political activism would turn out to be key for a series of conservative Republicans who won races alongside Reagan. "We helped develop a professional political class and a policy class of people," Black says.

The other big gun in conservatives' national arsenal came in the person of Richard Viguerie, a wiry, balding activist who, more or less all by himself, invented the most important campaign funding tool at the time: the ability to raise millions of dollars through direct-mail campaigns.

Viguerie was a native of Pasadena, Texas, where he was born to parents who were rabid baseball fans—they attended a minor league game in Houston the night before Richard was born—and not particularly interested in politics. Yet as a youth, for reasons he couldn't quite explain later, Viguerie developed an intense interest in fighting what he saw as the Communist scourge. He joined the National Guard and then, upon release, went to work in the mid-1960s for a student group called Young Americans for Freedom, created by conservative writer and publisher William Buckley. One of his jobs was to help raise money for the organization. And he discovered that he intensely disliked the task of directly asking people for donations.

But he also discovered that he was good at finding ways to ask people for money another way: through mailed solicitations. Soon he decided to quit working for Young Americans for Freedom and set out to raise money for other groups as a contractor. His breakthrough came when he discovered that, in those days, presidential candidates had to file with the clerk of the House of Representatives a list of all donors to their campaigns who had contributed $50 or more—filings that happened to include mailing addresses.

Viguerie, carrying a legal pad and a pen, walked into the House office where the filings were kept and began writing down, by hand, the addresses of as many Republican donors as he could. He came back again the next day. And the next day. And then he hired six secretaries to help him do more. Within a few weeks they had collected the names and addresses of 12,500 donors to Barry Goldwater's presidential campaign—the first-ever conservative direct-mail list.

Viguerie began hiring his firm out to use his mailing list to raise money for Republican candidates and conservative causes. As he moved from client to client, he kept adding names to his list. By the end of his first year in business, he had 100,000 names and addresses. By 1970 he had more than a million. And by 1980 he had perhaps three million names and addresses.

Viguerie had, in short, the most powerful fundraising tool in the land, and he was putting it to use to help conservative candidates and causes. Oddly, though, it didn't endear him to many Republicans, as his work undercut the traditional Republican establishment and its leaders by stealing the fundraising clout they had previously enjoyed. Moreover, it empowered insurgent conservative groups and candidates who were too far to the right for many traditional Republicans.

"However, all of the criticism stopped within a few hours on Election Night, November 1980," Viguerie recalls. The Viguerie network had mobilized voters who would ultimately help elect Ronald Reagan and the conservative Senate candidates who swept into office alongside him. Eventually Democrats and liberals would catch up with the direct-mail machine Viguerie had built, but for years his work gave conservatives an advantage few appreciated.

Meanwhile, Delaware governor Pete du Pont created an organization called GOPAC to find and nurture conservative candidates for local and state office around the country, creating a kind of farm system for developing conservative candidates and sprinkling them throughout the political system. Within Congress, Representative Newt Gingrich, still a rebellious back-bencher, created the Conservative Opportunity Society, a group of like-minded young House conservatives interested in steering the party's legislative apparatus onto a more aggressive conservative path. "We wrote books, gave long special orders (speeches on the House floor) that were the equivalent of college lectures, crossed the country again and again giving seminars," Gingrich wrote later.

At the same time, the National Rifle Association was being transformed from a fairly sedate organization of hunters and outdoorsmen into a potent nationwide tool for conservative Republican causes. After eschewing politics for years, the group began to change that posture after the passage of the Gun Control Act of 1968, a bill to regulate the interstate transfer of firearms that grew out of the national anguish at the assassinations of President John Kennedy, his brother Robert Kennedy, and civil rights leader Martin Luther King. Ironically, the NRA's push into politics was propelled by a Democrat, Representative John Dingell of Michigan, an avid outdoorsman and hunter. He told the NRA's leaders that their members' access to guns would soon be at risk, and that the organization had to get politically active.

David Keene, a longtime Republican and conservative operative with the silver hair and baritone voice of a TV anchorman, who would later become president of the NRA, says that idea set off "a huge fight within the NRA, because the traditionalists wanted to move it to Kansas or someplace and turn it into a conservation organization, because they found politics tacky. And so there was a revolution within the NRA."

The forces in favor of taking on a political role won, and in 1975 the NRA created a lobbying unit, the Institute for Legislative Action, giving the organization an avowedly political tool. That tool became a powerful cudgel largely because of the work of Wayne LaPierre. LaPierre, a former schoolteacher, had joined the NRA as a field organizer and eventually rose to head its lobbying arm. He began raising its profile and forging connections to conservative political organizations. Crucially, the NRA also developed a campaign finance arm. Forty years later, in the 2016 presidential election, the group would spend an eye-popping $54 million, every penny of it to support Republicans or oppose Democrats, according to the campaign watchdog organization Center for Responsive Politics. LaPierre rose to become the NRA's chief executive officer, and along the way turned the organization into not just a vociferous defender of gun rights and opponent of virtually every effort to enact gun-control legislation, but also a force for conservative causes and candidates all across the country.

NRA membership proceeded to grow steadily and "organically" in the following years, according to Keene. It happened that the NRA's greatest political impact would emerge in a set of swing states crucial to determining the outcomes of battles for control of both the White House and Congress, a power enhanced by the fact that gun-owning Democrats in such states were prepared to cross party lines to follow NRA advice. "There's not a lot of cross-voting," says Keene. "In the NRA, there is. People cross party lines to vote. And the greatest influence that the NRA has politically has been in Michigan, Wisconsin, Pennsylvania, Ohio, the Midwest. That's where our membership is." Those also happen to be the states that, years down the road, would be decisive in Donald Trump's election to the White House.

None of these new shoots of conservative power, however, would have as much broad impact on American society as the one that sprouted in 1982, when a group of conservatives and libertarian legal experts launched the Federalist Society to promote conservative principles in the legal system and spread the conservative legal gospel more effectively through law schools. Over time, the most important task the society performed was to vet and recommend nominees for federal judgeships, creating a kind of team of jurists who held a conservative seal of approval.

In short, since its creation in the early 1980s, the Federalist Society has managed to own the process of picking Supreme Court justices nominated by Republican presidents. It has proven influential in building a squadron of like-minded younger and lower-level jurists from which future presidents could choose nominees to fill out the rest of the federal bench. It also became instrumental in driving those kinds of candidates onto the bench. When Donald Trump became president, his chief outside adviser on judicial picks was Leonard Leo, co-chairman of the Federalist Society, while, on the inside, the process was overseen by White House counsel Donald McGahn, a Federalist Society stalwart. To those interested in putting a lasting conservative imprint on American society, it's hard to think of a more effective way than to fill the judicial branch of the federal government with proven conservative thinkers who have been granted lifetime appointments.

As this network of new conservative organizations grew and matured, it was Grover Norquist who sought to tie it together and put a bright red bow on top. He began convening a regular Wednesday meeting of the leaders of all conservative groups in Washington, called, obviously enough, the Wednesday Meeting. More than one hundred conservative leaders—elected officials, activists, think-tank types—were on the roster, and the sessions became backroom planning sessions for keeping the Reagan Revolution rolling.

Norquist next took the movement outside Washington. His Wednesday Meeting in the capital would be replicated over time in forty states.

All this activity mattered because it amounted to the institutionalization of the conservative movement. Some of the biggest names to populate the movement in the decades to follow—Gingrich, Norquist, Black, LaPierre—found their places on the front lines during this period.

The build-out mattered for another reason: The eye-popping success of those early days of the Reagan term couldn't be sustained without some structure. Inevitably, a backlash would develop. Conservatives' failures and shortcomings would become more apparent, and the internal tensions inherent in any movement as it grows and takes more riders on board would become unavoidable. The foundation built on Reagan's road to the presidency, and in the first few years after he arrived in the White House, would allow the conservative movement to survive harsher winds. And those winds would start blowing soon.

CHAPTER 4

The Gipper

What do you need to carry out a political revolution?

A leader with some charisma. A message. An army that believes in the leader and the message, or is at least inclined to give them both a chance. A public ready for change. An opposition that is back on its heels. You need reinforcements and a logistical network that can keep feeding the generals and the soldiers. It also helps to have some good fortune.

In the early stages of his first term, Ronald Reagan had all those things. In a matter of months, he had moved all of Washington and its entire governing agenda to the right. The presidency no longer seemed paralyzed. Democratic voters had defected to the conservative cause in the 1980 election. Soon thereafter, one particularly prominent elected Democrat—Representative Phil Gramm of Texas, an increasingly outspoken member on the right wing of the party—threw in the towel by switching parties to become a Republican himself. Others would follow.

Reagan himself was an enigma. He had some harsh things to say about the Washington establishment. But unlike Donald Trump four decades later, he was shrewd enough to court that establishment as well. He and his wife dined happily at the home of Katharine Graham, the publisher of *The Washington Post* and the very embodiment of the Washington establishment. They made sure mainstream Washington movers and shakers were invited to the White House for social events.

To some in the capital, Reagan's conservative beliefs were a sign of simple but clear thought. To others, they were merely simplistic. Either way, Reagan seemed utterly unafraid of trying something different. He once asked the chairman of the Federal Reserve why the Fed couldn't simply be eliminated—a perennial fantasy of conservatives who distrusted central bankers as they distrusted all centralized power. When the nation's air traffic controllers went on strike in August, Reagan declared the walkout a threat to the public safety, even though the controllers' union had actually supported him in his presidential campaign. He ordered the controllers back to work. When they refused to go, he simply fired all eleven thousand of them and ordered supervisors and managers to control the skies in their stead.

Meanwhile, the president's popularity was buoyant. By the end of that first summer, his job approval had risen to 60 percent. The revolution appeared to be humming.

In fact, though, the whole conservative enterprise soon fell into serious jeopardy.

Contrary to the myth that would develop later, the economy didn't magically respond to the elixir of Reagan's tax cuts. It remained mired in a recession. The Reagan team's original economic predictions were wildly overoptimistic. The combination of tax cuts and a slow economy meant there would be billions less in tax revenue for the government, which meant the federal budget deficit soared. Unemployment actually continued climbing and would soon surpass the levels reached in those much-maligned Carter years. More unemployed workers meant more Americans collecting government benefits, which drove the deficit higher still. Interest rates, meanwhile, remained stubbornly high.

The Republican establishment hit the panic button. Most of the establishment players hadn't really been convinced that Reaganomics would work anyway. After all, Reagan's own vice president, George H. W. Bush, had called the whole plan "voodoo economics" at one point before taking office. In so saying, he spoke for most of the moderate centrists in the party. The party's old guard decided it had to save Reagan from himself.

So Republicans in Congress led a charge in 1982 to roll back some of the prior year's tax cuts. It was a transparent effort to reassure financial markets that the Republican Party, supposedly the party of balanced budgets and fiscal responsibility, wouldn't let the government's books get too far out of whack. The resulting effort, euphemistically called the Tax Equity and Fiscal Responsibility Act of 1982, took back some of the original tax cuts by ending some of the tax breaks in the original plan, adding some excise taxes, and closing various loopholes. Reagan was unhappy but professed to be assuaged by a promise that government spending would be cut by even more than taxes were being raised. Few people believed a Democratic-controlled House would actually carry out those spending cuts—and it didn't.

Almost lost in the uproar, though, was the crucial underlying reality: The new, lower tax rates Reagan had pushed into place remained in place, even while some of the surrounding bells and whistles were removed. The core of Reaganomics survived.

To conservatives, though, their revolution appeared in danger of being put out of business before it had really gotten rolling. It was their turn to panic, and they responded in a manner that would become familiar to those of us who were chronicling the conservative movement: They turned their guns inward.

Conservative activists began complaining that their hero, Ronald Reagan, was too soft and too willing to compromise. And they began attacking those around Reagan for somehow leading him astray, conniving to convince him to abandon his principles and bend to the ways of the political establishment. In the cry that would become commonplace, Reagan's aides refused to "let Reagan be Reagan." The most frequent target of these attacks was Jim Baker, who was serving as White House chief of staff and who sat precisely at the divide between the old moderates of the Republican Party and the new conservative rebels.

Baker stood out for two reasons. The first was his sheer competence. And the second was the fact that he had twice run campaigns
by party moderates dedicated to defeating Ronald Reagan, the first
for then president Gerald Ford, in 1976, and the second for George
H. W. Bush, in 1980. To say that this made movement conservatives
a little suspicious of him is like saying Boston Red Sox fans are a
little disdainful of the New York Yankees.

Baker himself had entered politics almost by accident, an act of
the fates more than a conscious decision. He hailed from a prominent family of Houston lawyers and became one himself. A good
tennis player, he became doubles partners with Bush, a fellow member of the Houston Country Club. The two had become close
friends by the time tragedy struck.

Baker's first wife died of cancer in 1970, a cruel blow to Baker
and his children. To help him recover from his grief, Bush suggested
Baker lend a hand in his campaign for a U.S. Senate seat in Texas.
Baker had no political experience and, in fact, was a lifelong Democrat. Baker signed up to help anyway and, although Bush's campaign would ultimately fail, it succeeded in hooking Baker on
politics. He became active in the Texas Republican Party, later was
offered a top job at the Commerce Department in Washington
under President Ford, and eventually was asked to run the Ford
reelection campaign. When his best friend ran for president in 1980,
it was inevitable that Baker would run the Bush for President campaign as well.

Baker rose so quickly because of the formidable arsenal of
personal skills he brought to the political game. He was smooth,
smiling, quick-witted, articulate, and something of a maestro at
handling the press. In the emerging world of Reagan advisers,
populated at the top by people who knew Reagan and California, but didn't know much about Washington and sometimes had
trouble making crisp decisions, Baker stood out. As Reagan entered the presidency, Baker, along with Ed Meese and Reagan's
advertising-and-communications impresario Michael Deaver,
became a troika of top advisers running the new White House.

Before long, it was clear Baker wasn't one of three equals, but the man really in charge.

But that didn't mean he was trusted by Reagan's conservative allies. In many ways, Baker's personal fate was a test of whether the two wings of the party—the old Ford moderates and the new Reagan conservatives—could hang together under new conservative leadership. When something didn't go the way the conservative forces on the outside liked, they tended to blame Baker for not being sufficiently loyal to the cause. That was particularly true when Reagan was compelled to make his painful partial retreat from his initial tax cuts. The resulting anger on the right is illustrated in an exchange of letters that can be found in the Reagan Presidential Library.

In mid-1982, a wealthy conservative from Texas, Clymer Wright Jr., sent a lengthy letter to fellow Reagan supporters around the country, declaring, "Our beloved President today stands alone under siege. His economic program is being undermined by White House Chief of Staff James Baker." The letter found its way to the White House, where it drew a peeved but revealing reply from Reagan himself. "Some in the media delight in trying to portray me as being manipulated and led around by the nose," Reagan wrote. "Clymer, I'm in charge and my people are helping to carry out the policies I set. No, we don't get everything we want and, yes, we have to compromise to get 75% or 80% of our programs. We try to see that the 75% or 80% is more than worth the compromise we have to accept. There has not been one single instance of Jim Baker doing anything but what I've settled on as our policy. He goes all out to help bring that about."

The exchange revealed something critically important about Reagan. His enemies tended to view him as an ideologue, but one secret to his success was his flexibility. "Look, I want to tell you something," Baker says now. "Reagan was a very pragmatic person. I can't tell you how many times I'd be sitting there with him in the Oval [Office], just the two of us, and we'd be debating a position we might have to take up on the Hill. And he'd say, 'Jim, I'd rather get

80 percent of what I want than go over the cliff with my flag flying.' Said it all the time. The movement conservatives wouldn't admit that, but he was a very pragmatic person."

Reagan's willingness in 1982 to beat a partial tactical retreat on his economic program bought that program a crucial bit of time. In fact, the move probably saved his tax cuts, his presidency, and the conservative revolution. The economy staggered through the rest of the year, with gross domestic product declining for all four quarters. Reagan's job approval had fallen to 35 percent by the beginning of 1983.

Then, a miraculous turnaround began. The economy began growing, slowly at first and then by gangbusters. In the first quarter of 1984, the economy grew at a staggering 8.6 percent, a rate not even remotely approached since then. That surge set the stage for the rest of Reagan's first term, including his reelection in 1984.

For a time, there was some doubt about whether the seventy-three-year-old president actually would run again. Nancy Reagan never quite recovered emotionally from the assassination attempt on her husband, and her dread that there would be another was so great that she was hesitant to see him serve a second term. "She was very reluctant to go through it again," recalls Stuart Spencer, a California political consultant who was at the Reagans' side from the 1960s on. "In his mind, he was going to do it. In her mind, there were always doubts." About a year before the election, Spencer says, he asked for a meeting with the First Couple to force a decision. He met them in the White House residence and told them they were running out of time and simply had to make a choice: In or out for reelection? Ronald prevailed over Nancy in that conversation; he would run again.

The economy's growth opened the door for the campaign to be run on the theme that it was "morning in America," and Reagan ultimately destroyed his Democratic opponent, former vice president Walter Mondale. He won forty-nine of fifty states. Meanwhile, Republicans maintained control of the Senate and picked up seats in the House.

That reelection victory opened the way for Reagan to pursue with more fervor the other, non-domestic half of his conservative agenda: his quest to become the man who brought an end to the Communist scourge. Reagan was the ultimate Cold Warrior, driven by an intense desire to end the nuclear threat posed by a powerful and ideologically driven Soviet Union. Spencer recalls flying with Reagan to the 1980 Republican convention, where the candidate would be nominated and set on the road to the White House. The consultant asked him the most basic of questions: *Why do you want to be president?* "I got an outline for the next hour about Russia, Communism, and nuclear capabilities," Spencer says. "He had a master plan to bring the nuclear thing to a halt."

Reagan was as animated by his hatred of totalitarianism, and as fixated on the Red Menace, as any conservative of his age and Cold War vintage. The difference between Reagan and many hard-liners, though, was his genuine belief that the virtues of capitalism and democracy were so obvious and so powerful that they would inevitably win out in the end. For him, the ideological struggle wasn't open-ended and needn't go on forever, because Communism inevitably would end up, in the phrase Reagan made famous in a speech to the British Parliament, on the "ash heap of history." In his view, all that was needed was a good, hard shove for Communism to fall into that ash heap. There was no better illustration of Reagan's optimistic view of conservative philosophy.

That view explains the arc of Reagan's approach to the Soviet Union, and to foreign policy in general. First, in his early years, came the hard shove. American defense spending shot up, as a warning to Moscow that its defense machinery could never outdo the capitalist juggernaut when it came to rolling out planes, ships, and missiles. Then came confrontations on the ground. If the Soviets thought they could make trouble in America's backyard by supporting leftist and Communist governments and insurgencies in Central America, Reagan would counter by giving direct American military aid to right-wing forces there, even if that meant supporting some truly unsavory thugs. When workers rose to challenge Communist orthodoxy in Poland, the Soviets' own backyard, the United States would lend rhetorical support and international succor. And if the Soviets wanted to try to intimidate American allies in Western Europe by placing intermediate-range nuclear missiles within range, the United States would counter by putting in a new class of intermediate-range, nuclear-armed missiles of its own, even if that effort brought into the streets of Europe hundreds of thousands of anti-nuclear protesters.

So it went through most of Reagan's first term, a period of rising tensions and genuine fears of superpower conflict. Then, when Soviet leader Konstantin Chernenko died—becoming the third Soviet leader to pass away on Reagan's watch—the chance to move beyond the hard shove to idealistic outreach materialized. It came in the form of Mikhail Gorbachev, a new general secretary of the Soviet Union and a new kind of Soviet leader who seemed to share Reagan's view that Communism was headed toward the ash heap of history. The two leaders met five times. They agreed to limit those controversial intermediate-range nuclear missiles, one of the most effective and consequential treaties the two sides ever struck, and—in a startling move entirely at Reagan's initiative during a summit in Reykjavík, Iceland—discussed whether they might even be able to eliminate all their nuclear weapons.

That idea itself was stunning, and left some of Reagan's conservative fans wondering whether he'd taken leave of his senses. The end-of-nuclear fantasy never came to pass, of course, but a drumbeat of criticism from conservatives over the chumminess their hero exhibited toward a leader of the Soviet state did emerge, and would never entirely go away. Reagan defended himself by insisting he had never given anything to Gorbachev without getting something in return, and by always insisting he was sure he could verify whether the Soviets were honoring their commitments.

Reagan's faith in the power of Western ideals simply outstripped that of his critics. The ultimate illustration came late in Reagan's second term when he traveled to the Berlin Wall. Berlin, like Germany as a whole, was still divided between a Communist East and a democratic West, and the wall was the most poignant symbol of the divide. Reagan was to give a speech at the wall, a dramatic setting that was a dream for White House image-makers. But for Reagan it wasn't just a speech; it was a chance to say something he was itching to get out. He put a line in the speech in which he would declare to the Soviet leader, who by now was his negotiating partner, "Mr. Gorbachev, tear down this wall." Almost everyone involved thought it was a bad idea: too provocative, an invitation for a popular uprising that the Soviets would have to crush in the streets, and simply too wildly unrealistic an idea to state outright. State Department officials kept trying to take the line out of the speech. Reagan kept insisting that it be left in, a debate that continued until the president climbed into the limousine to be driven to the speech.

He delivered the line, of course. Just over two years later, the Berlin Wall fell.

The fervor of his anti-Communism led Reagan into the one serious scandal of his presidency, the Iran-Contra scandal. It created a serious constitutional crisis, and almost brought the house crashing down around him. Reagan's desire to help anti-Communist rebels in Nicaragua was so deep that his aides were intent on sending them military aid even after Democrats in Congress, wary that Reagan was heading into a Vietnam-like military morass in the region, forbade the provision of arms. This effort to circumvent clear congressional intent took the form of a bizarre scheme in which the administration secretly sold missiles to Iran—which at the time was fighting its own war with Iraq and needed the help—and then used the proceeds to finance the provision of military equipment to Nicaragua's rebels from private arms dealers. Under the elaborate scheme, Iran would in turn use its power to free Americans being held hostage by friendly groups in Lebanon. That also appealed to Reagan, who was genuinely anguished about the idea that Americans were being held, in some cases shackled to radiators in the Beirut slums.

When news of the scheme broke, there was an uproar in Congress, where Democrats saw the enterprise as a brazen effort to break a clear and simple law. To liberals, the Iran-Contra affair was an example of conservative zealots run amok, in the process trashing the Constitution they professed to love. Reagan himself never made very clear how much he knew and didn't know about the scheme, which, to some extent, only made things worse: Was he dissembling about what he actually did, or was he so detached he didn't know that an unconstitutional plot was being hatched beneath his nose? There was even talk of impeachment. Eventually, Reagan cleaned house at the White House, bringing in an entirely new staff for his last two years, and appointed an independent commission to investigate.

His job approval slumped again, falling to 43 percent. But the furor eventually subsided after a congressionally appointed independent committee issued a lengthy report on Iran-Contra and Reagan appeared to accept responsibility. The economy continued to hum, and Reagan finished his term on a popularity upswing.

In the end, what did the Reagan presidency bring to the country, and to the world? Well, the conservative change was considerable, though certainly not complete. Tax rates were lowered and would stay low for decades to come. But despite years of rhetoric about shrinking the size of the government, and various efforts to do so (some of them fairly half-hearted), the government didn't really shrink on Reagan's watch. Government spending grew by more than $300 billion annually. The share of government spending as a portion of the nation's gross domestic product was changed only a little; it stood at 19.1 percent as Reagan entered office, and at 17.8 percent as he left. As a consequence, what did grow was the federal budget deficit. It basically doubled in aggregate size, and as a share of GDP it grew from 2.5 percent to 2.7 percent.

If the goal of all this was to make the economy grow faster, that certainly happened as well. Economic growth was flat when Reagan took office but was expanding at roughly a 4 percent annual growth rate when he left.

Yet there also were early signs of what would become a corrosive problem over time: the rise of income inequality in the United

States. Critics on the left complained that the Reagan tax cuts were a "sop to the rich," and that the spending cuts he championed, such as they were, fell disproportionately on the poor and the working class. The deeper problem, though, was that Reagan's arrival marked the beginning of a long period in which wealthier Americans would begin to steadily pull further and further ahead of their less prosperous countrymen. This phenomenon has been chronicled most definitively in research done by economists Thomas Piketty and Emmanuel Saez, among others. Their research shows that when Reagan arrived in office, the wealthiest 1 percent of Americans earned about 11 percent of the nation's income. By the time he left office it had risen to 15 percent, and it would keep rising. The bottom 50 percent of earners, by contrast, saw their share of national income fall, from about 20 percent to 17 percent. Those trend lines would continue for years to come, haunting the conservative cause.

It's fair to say Reagan set the stage for the demise of the Soviet Union and the fall of the Berlin Wall, though it's hard to say how much of that was the work of Reagan himself, how much was due to the pressure on Moscow produced by the giant military spending increases he ordered, how much was the costly and disastrous consequence of the Soviet invasion and occupation of Afghanistan, and how much was the handiwork of Mikhail Gorbachev, who saw history's handwriting on the Soviet wall.

Domestically, the most significant, lasting impacts of the Reagan Revolution may have been more subtle. Reagan's administration, over the course of eight years, empowered and credentialed an entire generation of conservative thinkers, bureaucrats, and, perhaps most important, federal judges. Reagan saw three Supreme Court nominees—Sandra Day O'Connor, Anthony Kennedy, and Antonin Scalia—seated during his tenure and, all told, appointed 402 federal judges, more than any president before or since. And for the following three decades, until the arrival of Donald Trump, virtually every Republican political candidate and elected official at every level of government would profess to be a disciple of Ronald Reagan.

For those of us assigned the task of watching him and chronicling his administration, Reagan remained an enigma and a study in contradictions. He harnessed much of the anger that had been building up on the political right yet never really conveyed that anger himself. It's hard to overstate just how momentous and implausible his agenda seemed at the time. He cut taxes more than most thought possible, and increased defense spending by more than many thought necessary.

On a personal level, Reagan was old-fashioned and, in many ways, just plain corny. He refused to take off his suit jacket in the Oval Office, a sign of respect for the office that would have been schmaltzy or phony for others. The Reagans gave grand Christmas parties where the hundreds of guests got not just trinkets but real gifts: White House–embroidered mittens and scarves, for example. (Green, with WHITE HOUSE knit in red, they still sit in storage in our house.)

White House reporters would watch for a particular couple of suits Reagan would wear, and snicker among ourselves when he appeared in them. One was a shiny brown suit, the other a blue plaid one, both of a color and pattern that we figured had gone out of style a quarter century earlier.

Reagan carried out of office the same simple but clear definition of conservatism that he carried in. This was true, in a particularly striking way, with immigration. Reagan believed in immigration as a life force that gave new vitality to America, and he rhapsodized about that belief regularly. He held to a particular view of immigration as part of the American Dream, and immigrants as part of the American fabric.

That belief was enshrined in one of the most significant pieces of immigration legislation ever enacted, the Immigration Reform and Control Act of 1986. The bill sought to strike a grand bargain: to reduce illegal immigration, enhance security along the U.S. border, and penalize employers who hired unauthorized immigrants. But in return, the law offered a path to legal status for unauthorized immigrants in the United States, and created some new avenues for

legal immigration. It may have been the best and most balanced effort to solve the immigration puzzle in recent times; it led to legal
status for some 2.7 million undocumented immigrants, and some
increase in border security. But its potential never was realized, in
part because the border security steps weren't as robust as promised,
and because the employer sanctions weren't as effective as expected.
Better execution of the law might have saved the country, the conservative movement, and the Republican Party from a lot of agony
later.

Legislative maneuvering aside, there was little doubt that Reagan's views of the virtues of immigration hadn't changed. That was
abundantly clear when, just over a week before leaving office, he
gave a farewell address to the nation and offered a kind of bookend
to his 1980 campaign speech at the Statue of Liberty. He spoke again
of America as a "shining city upon a hill" and elaborated in words
impossible to imagine being used by one of his Republican succes-
sors, Donald Trump: "In my mind it was a tall, proud city built on
rocks stronger than oceans, windswept, God-blessed, and teeming
with people of all kinds living in harmony and peace; a city with
free ports that hummed with commerce and creativity. And if there
had to be city walls, the walls had doors and the doors were open to
anyone with the will and the heart to get here. That's how I saw it,
and see it still."

The president came into office a sunny and optimistic man, and
left the same way. In January 1989, just two days before Reagan
finished his two terms, I was one of a handful of reporters who sat
down with him in the Oval Office for a farewell interview. He
knew who I was, for I had, by happenstance, gotten some presidential attention earlier in his presidency.

In the mid-1980s, my wife, Barbara Rosewicz, and I spent some
time as Middle East correspondents for the *Journal,* based in Cairo.
In early 1987, after months of futile efforts, I secured a visa to visit
Iran, a country usually off-limits to American journalists. Along-
side a couple dozen other Western journalists, including a few
Americans, I visited the front in Iran's then raging war with Iraq,

where we dodged bullets and shells and spent a tense night in an Iranian military bunker. Upon returning to Tehran, we were invited by Iranian officials to stay for a press conference, called specifically so they could boast of having received direct messages from Reagan as part of his administration's secret sales of missiles to the Iranian military. The press conference would keep us beyond the time allowed on our visas, so I turned over my passport to Iranian officials to get a visa extension.

Mysteriously, the officials then refused to give it back to me so I could leave the country. I spent a frantic day shuttling from government ministry to government ministry in the company of a Swiss diplomat assigned to oversee American affairs in Tehran, trying futilely to find out why Iranian officials wouldn't allow me to leave. As darkness descended, we returned to my hotel, followed all the way by a mysterious sedan. At the hotel, we discovered that I had been locked out of my room without explanation. Realizing that something truly bad was going down, the Swiss diplomat and I turned to each other, agreed it was time to get out, fast, and headed back to the parking lot to jump into his car and flee to safety in the Swiss embassy. At that point, the mysterious sedan that had been following us sped up alongside, and four men in camouflage uniforms jumped out, pinned my arms behind me, shoved me facedown on the back seat of the car, and sped off. They pulled a blindfold over my eyes while screaming at me in Farsi.

After careening through the streets of Tehran, the car came to a stop at the gates of Evin Prison, notorious as the repository for Iran's political prisoners. I was hustled inside and planted, blindfold still in place, in front of an interrogator, who informed me that I was accused of being an Israeli spy and should confess to the charge if I hoped to avoid dark but unspecified consequences.

There followed four days of interrogation, some of it intense and some of it simply silly, and a shifting set of accusations about my supposed spying activities. I asserted, of course, that I was nothing but the journalist I claimed to be, though I assumed I would be housed in Evin Prison for a good, long while. But then, after some harrowing time in a brightly lit prison cell, I was advised by interrogators that my case had been "successfully" resolved. I spent one more night in the prison, made a video designed to show that I hadn't been tortured, and was escorted to the prison's gates. At that point, I whipped off my blindfold to at last have a look at one of my interrogators. He promptly reached out to shake my hand and asked whether he could visit me if he ever made it to America.

That episode put me on the front page of newspapers around the world, coming as it did amid the raging controversy over the Reagan administration's Iran-Contra arms sales to Tehran. It also landed me on Reagan's personal radar screen, as seen now in entries in the presidential diaries available at the Reagan Presidential Library. So he knew who I was, vaguely, as we walked in for that farewell interview, even if, for him, most journalists were anonymous, interchangeable extras on the White House set.

Ever mindful that he'd be remembered as an actor who became a president, he began reeling off from memory a poignant passage from a long-ago column he'd read: "When we approach the final curtain," he recited, "all men must bear in their arms that which they have given in life. The people of show business will march in the procession carrying in their arms the pure pearl of tears, the gold of laughter, and the diamonds of stardust they spread on what might otherwise have been a rather dreary world. And when they reach the final stage door the keeper will say, 'Open, let my children in.'"

When the conversation turned more political, and more substantive, he was asked whether he had tried to emulate any previous president during his time in office. His answer might have seemed boastful from anybody else, but, delivered by him in that classic, aw-shucks Reagan style, it didn't.

No, Reagan said, he didn't try to copy anybody else. His views, he said, were formed "over the years, and long before I ever thought of public life . . . when I was out there on, as I've called it, the mashed potato circuit and speaking on the things I believed in. I came here with a pretty set program in my mind of what government should be and what it was intended to be by the Founding Fathers and where it had violated those precepts, and my determination to change it."

Reagan recalled supporting Franklin Roosevelt in 1932, the first election in which he could vote. And why? Because at that point Roosevelt "had a platform of reducing federal spending by 25 percent, returning to states and local governments and to the people the authority and autonomy that had been unjustly seized by the federal government, and the elimination of useless boards and commissions."

As usual with Reagan, his view of FDR was part reality, part myth. Roosevelt did want to cut spending by some government departments, but that was to free up money to go toward financing his New Deal programs, which were surely government spending under a different name. But never mind; the point is that Reagan had known for more than half a century what he believed—and what he thought a true conservative should believe—and that was that government spending should be cut; that less power in Washington and more in the states was a good thing; and that there were always wasteful government programs that could be cut or eliminated.

He dismissed criticism by some conservatives that he had been too quick to embrace Soviet leader Mikhail Gorbachev, arguing that Gorbachev was quite a different leader from those who came before him. (Those other Soviet leaders, he quipped, "kept dying on me.") Thus did Reagan, the conservative anti-Communist, defend the Russian who would essentially end Communism, the threat that had done so much to unite conservatives for so long.

He spoke as someone who knew he had carried the conservative torch farther than had anyone previously in American politics. But he also spoke as someone who fully intended to hand it over to others, with no intention of either trying to take the crusade any further himself or prodding others on from the sidelines. No, he said, he had no particular plans to return to the speaking circuit. And he certainly wouldn't go back into the movie business. That, he said, would amount to trying to "cash in on this honorable position."

What none of us knew was that Alzheimer's disease was creeping in around the edges, and soon it would start to envelop the Gipper. His brain would grow increasingly clouded in the years ahead, the decline perhaps accelerated by a serious fall from a horse just six months after leaving office.

Thus, Ronald Reagan wouldn't be the one to carry on the Reagan Revolution, or to guide the conservative movement onward. That journey would be left to others. In the next three decades, it would prove to be an eventful and deeply consequential journey.

CHAPTER 5

Turning Over the Reins

Just past noon on January 20, 1989, Ronald Reagan rode out of Washington on a U.S. military helicopter, having watched his vice president, George H. W. Bush, sworn in as his successor. The transition would pose a real test of the durability of the Reagan Revolution. Ultimately, it opened a deep schism among conservatives that served as a preview of the rise of Donald Trump a quarter century later.

At the moment of the Reagan-to-Bush handoff, though, none of those implications were clear. It simply was an emotional end to an important personal chapter for many people in Washington, including Marlin Fitzwater.

Fitzwater, a Kansas native, worked as White House press secretary for the last two years of Reagan's term. He is genial and self-deprecating, two traits that held him in good stead with both his bosses and the reporters with whom he dealt. When Fitzwater—balding and, at the time, a bit hefty—was appointed Reagan's press secretary, he quipped, "I think that it's obvious that the president wanted an anchorman type, thin, with a lot of hair."

Fitzwater was one of the few top officials who bridged the Reagan and Bush administrations. He had worked for a time as Bush's vice presidential spokesman and, as a result, had close ties to both the outgoing and incoming Republican presidents. Bush asked him to remain and become his presidential press secretary, and Fitzwater agreed. He had grown fond of both Reagan and Bush.

After Bush was sworn in on the west steps of the Capitol Building that cold January day, Fitzwater stole away for a few moments of reflection on his own. He traversed to the opposite side of the Capitol, to its east steps, at the foot of which waited the helicopter that would carry Reagan to Andrews Air Force Base for his flight back to California. Fitzwater talked his way past the Secret Service agents on duty, slipped into the back seat of the helicopter, and sat inside, alone, for a few minutes. Then he went back to the steps to await the departing Reagan.

"I was really kind of broken up about it," Fitzwater recalls. "So I'm standing there on the top steps and out comes President and Nancy Reagan and, with them, George and Barbara Bush. And right behind them was Jim Baker." Fitzwater watched the two presidents, old and new, walk together down the steps and onto the short red carpet that led to the helicopter door. They shook hands.

"President Bush turned around and started back up the steps, and he was crying," Fitzwater recalls. "And he pulled out of his back pocket the big white handkerchief he used to carry and started dabbing at his eyes. Jim Baker was right beside him. And I walked over and fell in with the two of them to go back up the steps." Soon Baker and Fitzwater were crying as well. "So all three of us were in tears and trying to control it," Fitzwater says. "Everybody in the damn world was looking at us."

The scene said much about the personal bond that Bush had worked to develop with Reagan. It wasn't a natural bond, because they were quite different men. Reagan was a true conservative, Bush more a moderate. Before coming together, they disagreed on taxes and abortion, the two hottest buttons in the conservative world. The men had battled each other, hard, for the Republican presidential nomination eight years earlier. In the process Reagan thought that Bush had shown signs of personal weakness. Yet Bush was the one who had been a legitimate war hero in the Pacific during World War II, while Reagan served his country by making propaganda films in the safety of a Hollywood studio. Reagan, genial but reserved, never made many close friends in Washington, while Bush, gregarious and outgoing, had a wide circle of loyal friends throughout the capital. Bush had a large and boisterous family around him, while Reagan often seemed distant from his own children. Bush's family periodically felt that Nancy Reagan was cold and unwelcoming toward them.

But Bush had been intent on bridging such differences. Baker, who was both Bush's closest friend and Reagan's chief of staff, made sure that each week's schedule included a private lunch between the president and the vice president. Bush ordered others on his staff to never say anything suggesting there was a gap between his positions and Reagan's.

It worked. Reagan embraced Bush, at least as much as Reagan's independent and somewhat aloof nature would allow. When the time came, as his second term was nearing an end, Reagan had, for all intents and purposes, blessed Bush as his successor.

Other conservatives weren't persuaded.

At the outset of the 1988 presidential campaign, many in the conservative movement preferred Jack Kemp over George Bush as Reagan's successor, considering him the true conservative most likely to faithfully continue the Reagan Revolution. Part of their discomfort with Bush was cultural. He hailed from—was the ultimate product of—the eastern establishment that many conservatives mistrusted. His father, Prescott Bush, was a Wall Street financier who lived in Greenwich, Connecticut, and won a U.S. Senate seat as a prototypical northeastern moderate, at a time when the Republican Party still had a phalanx of such lawmakers.

George Bush himself went to an elite boarding school, Andover, and then on to an Ivy League university, Yale. He served as U.S. ambassador to the United Nations, an institution widely hated on the right, and as an early American envoy to Communist China, and seemed to thoroughly enjoy both jobs. Like his father before him, Bush was an enthusiastic supporter of Planned Parenthood, which implied support for abortion rights. Every element of that biography was cause for mistrust among conservatives, who had long felt belittled by the establishment Bush personified.

In truth, such a view of Bush was misleading and overlooked important aspects of his personal story. He had consciously not followed his father into a safe spot on Wall Street but struck out on his own, as an oilman in Texas, surely the kind of entrepreneurial move that should have appealed to conservatives. It's true that Wall Street money, provided via family connections, helped him get started, but there were few parts of the country, and few businesses, where rugged individual initiative mattered more than being a wildcatter in Texas, as Bush was at the outset of his career.

Moreover, at the time Bush arrived in Texas, the state was deeply Democratic. Yet Bush proudly declared himself a Republican. In 1964, as he unsuccessfully sought a Senate seat from Texas, Bush proved a visible and enthusiastic supporter of Barry Goldwater's presidential campaign, the most important litmus test on the right before Reagan's arrival. While serving as vice president, he took on a job near and dear to conservative hearts, running a task force dedicated to striking down federal regulations deemed onerous or unnecessary.

More dramatically, Bush was demonstrably deferential to Reagan during the most traumatic hours of Reagan's presidency, after the attempt on his life. Bush was out of town when Reagan was shot, and hurried back to Washington. Upon arriving, he ordered the helicopter carrying him into Washington from Andrews Air Force Base to land not at the White House but several miles away, at the vice presidential residence, lest it appear he was trying to take over while Reagan was disabled.

Later, when he had secured the presidential nomination in 1988, Bush made an overt appeal to conservatives by picking as his running mate Senator Dan Quayle of Indiana, a rising young star on the right wing of the Republican Party. Quayle, in turn, would bring along other trusted young figures in the conservative movement as members of his staff, including William Kristol and Spencer Abraham.

Perhaps most important, in the convention speech he gave upon accepting the 1988 Republican nomination, Bush delivered a line that was designed to give complete reassurance to conservatives on the issue that mattered most to them: protecting and preserving the Reagan tax cuts. In that passage of his speech—one that would prove fateful—Bush predicted that, once he was in office, Democrats would push him repeatedly to raise taxes. His reply to those tax-hike demands, he pledged, would be "Read my lips: No new taxes."

Bush's opponent in that 1988 general election was Democrat Michael Dukakis, the governor of Massachusetts, who began the fall campaign ahead in the polls. To overtake him, Bush needed to energize the conservative GOP base that supported Reagan through two elections. To make that happen, he relied, above all, on his chief political strategist, Lee Atwater. Atwater was a young, hard-edged South Carolinian, the opposite of Bush in background, age, and ideology.

Atwater knew how to push hot buttons on the right, and Bush allowed him to do just that. Atwater steered the campaign's advertising toward red-meat issues that would appeal particularly to cultural conservatives: love of the flag, toughness on crime. The most notorious political ad of the campaign featured a grainy and frightening picture of Willie Horton, an African American convict serving a life sentence, who had been released on a weekend furlough program supported by the Dukakis administration in Massachusetts, only to attack a young man and rape his girlfriend. The point was to show that Dukakis was soft on crime, but it struck many as an overtly racist appeal to white voters. Though the ad was run by an independent political committee separate from the Bush campaign, much of the blowback hit Bush personally.

Those of us who followed Bush around the country in that campaign saw a generally nice man sometimes trying hard to play the part of political attack dog. He knew he was battling the perception that he was, in the words of his critics, a "wimp" compared with Reagan, a label *Newsweek* actually put on its cover in a story about the campaign. That charge deeply and visibly angered the candidate's wife, Barbara, who let it show in her occasional encounters with journalists. Bush himself seemed more anguished by the idea than angered by it, and could never bring himself to punish the poor *Newsweek* reporter who wrote the cover story but certainly not the offending cover headline.

In the end, Bush defeated Dukakis fairly easily in the 1988 general election. In doing so, he officially became guardian of the Reagan Revolution.

Yet conservative doubts about Bush were reinforced at the very outset of his term, when the ranks of the new administration were being filled. Feulner recalls that his Heritage Foundation proposed a list of conservatives for jobs on the new team. "We had hundreds of names," he says. "We were told those names were ditched as soon as they were submitted."

The tension grew when Bush's aides promptly dismissed some Reagan appointees already in government and replaced them with Bush loyalists. Incoming White House chief of staff John Sununu—who had been well trusted by conservatives while governor of New Hampshire—moved most of Reagan's appointees out of the White House, outside of Fitzwater. Cabinet members did the same. Jim Baker insists this wasn't a purge of Reaganites, but merely a need to show "a new beginning."

Once Bush's term got rolling, it became clear the new president's real passion was foreign affairs, not domestic policy. He had been influenced heavily by his time at the U.N. and in China, and in the brief stint he served as head of the CIA. He found that the big problems of the world fascinated him, and also were a good distance removed from the petty internecine warfare that defined domestic politics. More than that, those previous jobs allowed Bush to build a wide network of foreign contacts that, inveterate networker that he was, he maintained through the years. In the White House, Bush worked that network relentlessly, turning his Oval Office telephone into a kind of international hotline for picking up intelligence about what was happening around the globe.

But it wasn't only foreign leaders Bush sought out. He knew I had been based in the Middle East for *The Wall Street Journal* before returning to Washington and becoming a White House correspondent. So, one day early in his term, when inclement weather forced him to cancel a domestic trip and remain in Washington, he invited me and Thomas Friedman of *The New York Times,* who also had been a reporter in the Middle East, to have lunch in the small, private President's Dining Room, just off the Oval Office. We were joined by Brent Scowcroft, Bush's trusted national security adviser. The purpose of the meeting was an off-the-record discussion of the state of affairs in the Middle East, especially the endless conflict between Israel and the Palestinians—though it soon became clear Bush was as interested in asking questions of us as we were in quizzing him.

Conservatives could hardly complain about his success on global affairs, in particular how he steered to a conclusion the journey started by Reagan in bringing down the curtain on the Soviet Union. The most dramatic early test of Bush's feel for diplomacy came in Berlin, where young Germans in the eastern sector of the city began clamoring for an exit from the Soviet sector and reunification with their brethren in West Germany. Their protests centered on the wall that cut Berlin in two.

Finally, in early November 1989, the East German authorities, sensing that the tide of history had turned, relented and stopped protecting the wall. Young Germans from both East and West began climbing over it and hammering pieces of the concrete. Reagan's cry to "tear down this wall" had been heeded, by the German people themselves.

It was a genuinely dramatic and historic moment, and Bush handled it brilliantly. He was, by nature and rearing, a gracious man who genuinely disliked braggarts—a character trait perfectly suited for this occasion. As the wall fell, Bush resisted the urge to celebrate what amounted to victory by the West, and insisted those around him do the same. His goal was to avoid embarrassing Gorbachev, thereby allowing him the time and space to work out a plan to peaceably let go of East Germany, the crown jewel of the Soviet empire. All that dialing for diplomacy Bush had done paid big dividends as he worked closely with West German chancellor Helmut Kohl on a plan for German reunification.

With that, the end of the Soviet empire was inevitable. Bush reassured Gorbachev the United States wouldn't cause him problems as he let Russian satellites go their own way and allowed reforms to begin internally. The two leaders also agreed to a giant arms-reduction plan, fulfilling another Reagan dream. By the end of 1990, the two Germanys were formally reunited into a new state that fell firmly into the Western camp. By the end of 1991 the Soviet Union itself was dissolved.

In effect, the Cold War had ended without a single battle, and Bush deserved a considerable amount of the credit. The end of the American-Soviet competition carried enormous consequences—for foreign policy, defense spending, diplomatic calculations, and Americans' sense of security. All that was clear at the time.

Less clear was the impact the change would have on the conservative movement. When the Soviet Union fell, it meant the demise of the one threat that held conservatives together when they disagreed on other, less weighty matters. For years conservatives were the Americans most committed to defending America against the Soviet bear; Reagan's 1984 campaign, in fact, had devoted an entire TV ad to showing a bear lurking in the woods. After the collapse of the Soviet Union, "there wasn't any bear in the woods anymore," says Jim Baker. The ripple effects of that change on domestic American politics would take years to play out, but they were significant.

Momentous as the end of the Cold War was, it amounted to just one of two enormous national security successes Bush enjoyed. The second came in the tiny Persian Gulf state of Kuwait. The ruthless strongman next door, Iraqi leader Saddam Hussein, sent his army into Kuwait in August 1990, ostensibly because of a dispute over exploitation of oil fields along the two countries' border. In fact, it was a blatant attempt to take over those oil fields and wipe little Kuwait off the map. In the early hours of the invasion, Bush, egged on by British prime minister Margaret Thatcher, declared, "This will not stand."

And it didn't. Over a period of months, the Bush administration organized a fearsome international fighting force, anchored by half a million American troops massed in Saudi Arabia and the Persian Gulf. Bush's personal diplomatic skills again proved crucial in convincing Russia and China to stand aside and let the American effort to liberate Kuwait proceed. In early 1991, a fierce American aerial campaign bombarded Iraqi forces, disrupting their command structure and frightening the poorly trained troops in the trenches. Then the American-led ground forces moved into Kuwait. In four days, it was effectively over. Iraqi forces fled in a mad rush, freeing Kuwait and humiliating Saddam Hussein.

At that point, with the rout complete and Kuwait liberated, Bush decided to end the hostilities rather than send American forces into Iraq itself to take down the regime. It was a controversial decision, because Shiite and Kurdish insurgents within Iraq, heeding American calls for Iraqis to rid themselves of Saddam, had risen up. In fact, the United States' calls for an anti-Saddam movement were meant for Iraqi military leaders who were capable of effecting change, not Iraqis on the street.

Bush felt strongly that his pledge to allies and the international community had been that he would lead a campaign to free Kuwait, and no more than that. Getting Saddam wasn't part of the deal, and he wasn't going to double-cross his international partners now. More than that, Bush and his top White House advisers—National Security Adviser Brent Scowcroft and his deputy, Robert Gates— felt strongly that overreaching by going into the morass of Iraq, with its tangled web of sectarian groups, was a recipe for disaster. Scowcroft, a former Air Force general, remembered all too well what happened when the United States overreached during the Korean War and sent its forces all the way through North Korea to the Chinese border, provoking a brutal Chinese counteroffensive.

Their view on Iraq was "If you break it, you own it." That strong conviction was driven home to me in an interview with

Gates about a month before the U.S. strikes began. We sat in his office in the West Wing of the White House on a bleak winter's day, and he forecast what was to come: The United States would prevail militarily in Kuwait, and there would be pressure to keep going, into Iraq and on into the capital, Baghdad. That wasn't the plan, Gates said, and it wasn't going to be the plan. Smashing Iraq itself would only open the door for greater influence by the power next door, Iran, and that wouldn't be a good outcome. I wrote a *Journal* story saying precisely that: The Bush plan was to free Kuwait but go no further. Gates was trying to send a signal, to manage expectations. It was a controversial decision, but one vindicated over time.

Bush wasn't the president conservatives wanted, but he turned out to be the one America needed in these two historic moments. His critics on the right still weren't entirely pleased. They complained he had given away too much in arms-control deals with Gorbachev, and should have taken out Saddam Hussein—a neoconservative dream that would be realized, with disastrous consequences, years later.

The bigger problem for most conservatives lay on the domestic side of the Bush agenda, where his instincts were simply different from theirs. He imposed a ban on the importation of semi-automatic rifles. He championed the passage of the Americans with Disabilities Act, a far-reaching law to make it easier for disabled Americans to navigate everyday life, but one that conservatives considered a case of regulatory overreach. He oversaw the passage of a new Clean Air Act, which environmentalists applauded but many businesses saw as another set of government-ordered burdens.

Far and away, though, the subject on which Bush and conservative activists fell out most dramatically was the core issue of taxes. By June of 1990, economic growth was flagging and government spending climbing as Washington spent heavily to bail out a savings-and-loan industry that had run into deep trouble. The federal deficit was climbing to levels that alarmed the financial markets, and Congress was flailing in its attempt to come up with a budget that would reduce the red ink. There was a real chance government would shut down over the impasse.

Amid a crisis environment, Bush agreed to Democratic demands that he hold a "no conditions" conversation about a new budget plan, and sat down with congressional leaders from both parties in the Family Dining Room of the White House. In that conversation, it became clear to Bush that there was no way to get Democrats—who held majorities in both houses of Congress—to limit spending without a Republican agreement to produce more tax revenues. Fatefully, Bush agreed in that meeting to say taxes could be raised, if Democrats agreed that spending on programs they loved, including entitlement programs such as Medicare and Medicaid, would be addressed, too.

The bipartisan group committed its agreement to writing, and Sununu summoned Fitzwater. The room was quiet when he arrived, Fitzwater recalls. Bush handed his spokesman a statement laying out the deal just struck, indicating that a new budget package would include "tax revenue increases." Fitzwater knew trouble when he saw it: The statement would be read as a complete reversal of Bush's "Read my lips" pledge, the most high-profile position he had taken in his entire presidential campaign.

Fitzwater felt that it was inappropriate to raise his concerns in the room with the bipartisan negotiators gathered around the president. So he stepped outside and asked a White House usher to summon Sununu to meet with him. "Sununu came out and I said, 'John, this is just going to be a disaster. The press is going to be all over this, the public is gonna say he went back on his promise. Is this absolutely final?'" Fitzwater recalls. "And he said, 'Absolutely it is. Quit arguing about it and go do it.'"

So Fitzwater went back to the White House press office and posted the statement, including its reference to "tax revenue increases," on the press room bulletin board, where reporters viewed announcements. Administration officials euphemistically referred to tax increases as "revenue enhancements," which fooled no one.

The reaction, as Fitzwater suspected, was immediate and, among conservatives, scathing.

Crucial as it was, the statement didn't end the debate. It merely opened the door to three more months of haggling over the details of a budget plan. In the meantime, Iraq had invaded Kuwait, and Bush was eager to get the budget and deficit problem off the front burner to focus on the crisis halfway around the globe. He and the Democrats finally struck a deal—and his problem with conservatives only got worse. As congressional leaders gathered at the White House to bless the final budget plan, Representative Newt Gingrich, then a young member of the Republican congressional leadership team and a favorite on the right, said he couldn't assent to the agreement because it included tax hikes.

"I was the junior person in the room," Gingrich recalls. "Everybody else committed to vote for it. When it got to me, I said, 'I can't vote for it, and I'm really afraid this may end your presidency.'" When the assembled group of leaders walked out to the Rose Garden to announce the deal, Gingrich was conspicuously absent. The most outspoken conservative involved in the negotiations had turned thumbs down—a step Bush never forgave, and from which he never really recovered.

Even worse for Bush, voters weren't convinced the budget deal did the trick. The budget deal was completed, and, in fact, the economy did pick up afterward. Growth was declining by a shocking 3.6 percent at the end of 1990, when the tax increase was signed into law; by the beginning of 1992, when Bush was running for reelection, the economy was growing by more than 4 percent. That robust economic growth was the kind rarely seen in the years since, but voters are slow to believe in an economic turnaround. The unemployment rate, a more politically sensitive indicator, wasn't responding as quickly; it actually rose through the middle of 1992.

That left the president open to two populist challenges—the first from the right within his own party, and the second from an emerging radical center.

The internal Republican challenge came from a former Reagan

aide, Pat Buchanan, who so loves the former president that his email address is a variation on "Gipper." In retrospect, if anyone represented a warning sign of the populist tsunami that would hit the Republican Party two decades later, it was Buchanan.

Buchanan is one of those uniquely Washington figures who traverses the boundaries between journalism, government positions, and outspoken advocacy. He started out as a newspaper editorial writer, became a campaign and White House aide to Richard Nixon, returned to journalism as a columnist, worked in the Reagan White House, and then developed a national following as a columnist and TV commentator. Along the way, he developed a reputation as a conservative pugilist, one with a particular affinity for the downscale, working-class Reagan Democrats who had moved from their traditional moorings in the Democratic Party and became Republicans because of Ronald Reagan.

By contrast, Buchanan had little natural affinity for Bush. "It was cultural, it was ideological," Buchanan says now. "There's just a gulf between George H. W. Bush and the people who I spoke for and represented." He fumed as the Bush administration agreed to the tax increase and pursued what he saw as big-government domestic policies. The last straw for Buchanan came in 1991, when Bush signed a new version of the Civil Rights Act that made it easier for workers to sue employers if they felt they had been discriminated against on the basis of race, which Buchanan felt made employers guilty of discriminatory practices unless they could prove themselves innocent.

Buchanan recalls driving home from the taping of his regular show on CNN after that act was signed and saying to himself, "Look, if I'm supposed to be a leader of this movement and George Bush is taking us in the other direction totally, and if you're a leader, then go out and give it a shot."

But it wasn't just Bush's actions that spurred him on. Buchanan himself had changed, developing views that ran counter to traditional conservative positions, a sign that the seeds of Trumpism already had been planted within the Republican Party. Having once shared traditional Republicans' support for free trade and relatively liberal immigration policies, he no longer believed in them. Trade deals, he felt, were leading to the shutdown of factories all across the country, victims of unfair foreign competition. And the same workers suffering from foreign imports were also being hurt by illegal immigrants flowing into the American workforce, he believed. At one point he was taken to the Mexican border by Representative Duncan Hunter and told that illegal immigrants were simply walking across by the thousands because of the lack of border security. In another precursor to Trumpism, Buchanan decided that Bush's interventions in Europe and the Middle East amounted to global overreach that distracted the government from helping working-class Americans.

"I was converted to a new form of conservativism, more populist, more nationalist, less ideological," Buchanan says.

So Buchanan decided to run for president as a populist, against the sitting president of his own party. He called the angry voters who followed him into battle "the pitchfork brigade," because, metaphorically, they were like farmers who took on the entrenched powers that threatened their land armed with nothing but the tools at hand. And for a time it appeared he might pose a formidable challenge. He won more than 30 percent of the vote in a handful of early primaries, including the key states of New Hampshire, Georgia, and Florida. But the power of Buchanan's populist message wasn't as great as it would prove to be later. He could never overtake Bush.

Yet by revealing weaknesses in the president's political standing, as well as showing the potential power of a populist message, the Buchanan campaign had a more enduring impact on the 1992 campaign: It helped persuade billionaire Texas businessman Ross Perot to run as an independent candidate, pushing a similar anti-establishment message.

Initially, the Perot campaign focused on the federal budget deficit, and his contention that the dysfunctional major parties were both responsible for and incapable of stopping a flood of red ink in Washington. Eventually Perot wound around to the issue that would come to define him: opposition to the North American Free Trade Agreement with Canada and Mexico, which was in its formative stages. The idea for NAFTA was hatched by Reagan, nursed along by Bush, and cheered by most Republicans, who fancied themselves free traders. By contrast, Perot maintained, in the phrase he made famous, that he heard "a giant sucking sound" of manufacturing jobs being pulled toward Mexico.

That was an early version of the critique Donald Trump would use, but it wasn't the only way in which Ross Perot looked and sounded like a trial run for Trump's eventual candidacy. He used his wealth to fund his own campaign. He had no particular friends in the establishment of either party. He eschewed the advice of political pros and instead relied on his own gut instincts. He used frequent appearances on cable TV to propel himself. Critics thought he was obsessed with his own image. He displayed little trust in anyone except a few longtime aides; other staffers came and went with regularity. He was mercurial, getting in the race, then out of it, and then back in all during the course of mid-1992. He attacked the news media.

By the summer, Perot was cruising along with about 20 percent of the support of voters in nationwide polls. Then he plateaued. In the end, he failed to win a single state in the general election.

Still, Bush was fatally weakened by the combination of a Buchanan challenge from within, a well-financed Perot insurrection from the outside, and a malfunctioning economy. He lost to Clinton, 43 percent to 37 percent, a shockingly low percentage of the popular vote for an incumbent president with a significant record of international achievement. Perot won 19 percent of the vote, easily the best performance by a third-party or independent candidate since George Wallace won five states in 1968.

Bush's aides were bitter, and they tended to blame Perot more than Buchanan for the defeat. Baker, in fact, is unequivocal in pointing the finger of blame at Perot for siphoning away votes that should have gone to Bush: "The reason we lost was a little jug-eared prick named Ross Perot."

In truth, though, both Buchanan and Perot had put their fingers on an emerging populist strain within the Republican Party, made up of voters unhappy with its economic policies, including its traditional belief in the virtues of free trade and immigration. The anger they displayed at the "system" was no passing fancy; it would grow ever wider in coming years. Bush's challengers, more than his presidency, were the best indicators of what was to come.

For his part, Bush was as gracious in defeat as he had been in victory. That was no surprise to those of us who covered him, for we had become familiar with the basic decency of George H. W. Bush. He respected the press, even when he was irritated by its coverage of him. When we and our families trekked north to cover him during his regular vacations at his family compound in Kennebunkport, Maine, he regularly hosted the press corps at the compound. Kids were welcome, and often got rides off the shore in the Bush speedboat, driven by the president of the United States—much to the consternation, we assumed, of the Secret Service agents trying to keep up with the man they were pledged to guard. With Bush's loss, the capital lost a bit of simple graciousness that has been hard to find since.

Meanwhile, the reaction of a lot of conservatives to Bush's loss was, essentially, "I told you so." They were unhappy Republicans had given up the White House, of course. Yet they weren't bereft, for they had found a new champion to turn to in this hour of distress. He worked the other end of Pennsylvania Avenue, in Congress, and his conservative credentials, unlike Bush's, were impeccable. A new chapter in the conservative revolution was about to open.

CHAPTER 6

Newt Steps In

Newt Gingrich has a penchant for bold ideas and audacious behavior, and he knows how to get media attention for them.

As it turns out, those are traits he came by naturally, and early in life.

As an eleven-year-old living in Harrisburg, Pennsylvania, little Newtie went off one afternoon to the movies and saw a double feature that included footage of the African jungle. Excited by the sight, Gingrich left the movie knowing what needed to be done: Somebody needed to start a zoo in Harrisburg, which, sadly, had none.

Outside the theater, Gingrich spotted a sign pointing to city hall, which, he says now, was "almost divine guidance." So, instead of catching the bus home, he detoured to city hall, where he announced he was there to talk about a zoo. A receptionist, presumably either puzzled or amused, directed him to the parks-and-recreation office, where a kindly assistant director humored the lad by disclosing that the city once had a zoo but had lost it, and that the way to bring it back was to go to the city council and make the case. He put Newtie in a cab and sent him home.

Sure enough, though, the young Gingrich returned for the next meeting of the city council and made his case for creating a zoo within an existing city park. The spectacle was enough to attract the attention of the local newspaper and, subsequently, the Associated Press, which reported in a dispatch, "Young Newton Gingrich told Mayor Claude Robins and four city Councilmen that he and a number of youthful buddies could round up enough animals to get the project started if granted use of the park."

From there, Newtie continued his campaign by visiting a mayoral candidate, and then the publisher of a local weekly newspaper. The publisher told Gingrich that if he wrote a column making the case, the newspaper would publish it. Young Gingrich didn't know how to type, so he sat down at a manual typewriter and wrote a column by pecking out one letter at a time.

Alas, the great zoo crusade failed. Still, it marked the birth of Newt the political activist—and future conservative hero.

From Harrisburg, Gingrich moved around, following his adoptive father, a career Army man, who eventually planted the family in Georgia. While many baby boomers of his vintage went leftward and liberal as they grew up, Gingrich did the opposite, going right and conservative. One big political influence was a favorite uncle, a rock-ribbed Republican precinct worker back in Pennsylvania, who instilled his leanings in young Newt. Gingrich's first real political role model was Richard Nixon. The longest night of his young life, Gingrich says now, was Election Night in 1960, when Nixon lost to John Kennedy. It's a loss that Gingrich still pointedly and bitterly attributes to Democratic vote stealing in Illinois and Texas.

Like Reagan before him, Gingrich went on to read *The Conscience of a Conservative,* by Barry Goldwater, whose ringing embrace of conservative principles represented the Rosetta Stone for young conservatives. "For a whole generation of people, that clarified a way of thinking and a way of questioning the established thought that was very powerful," he says. In 1964, the year Goldwater sought the presidency, Gingrich dropped out of college for a year to help run a Republican congressional campaign in northern Georgia. He also got his first long-distance introduction to Ronald Reagan, listening to Reagan's classic televised speech making a case for the Goldwater candidacy.

A decade later, this introduction to Reagan became real and firsthand. Gingrich was an ambitious young college professor by then, and was running a long-shot campaign for Congress in a Georgia district, a hopeless task in an area still heavily Democratic and in a year when Nixon's Watergate scandal was pulling Republicans under the waves all over the country. Still, Reagan himself came through the region to help out fellow GOPers. Gingrich was a relative unknown, and almost certainly a loser that year, yet party leaders were so grateful to have somebody running as a Republican that they rewarded Gingrich by letting him drive California's governor back to the airport after his appearance.

"This was, as you can imagine, a more primitive era," Gingrich recalls. "[Reagan] had one California Highway Patrolman with him. He was flying commercial, so I drove back to the airport, and his plane was like an hour late.

"So I sat and chatted with him, and after a few minutes he got bored with me and he said, 'Would you like to see how I give speeches?' And I said 'Sure.' And he pulled out his cards, and his technique was that he had a whole series of four-by-six cards that had key phrases on them that would trigger an entire riff. He had about seventy of these cards, and just before a speech he'd go through and pick out ten or fifteen or twenty he wanted to talk about that day. And he would then shuffle them. And his theory was 'If I give the same speech every day, I will get bored. And if I'm bored, you'll get bored. But if I'm not sure what the next topic is, I'll have an adrenaline flow, be leaning forward, because I'm going to go from whatever I'm now talking about to this new topic. And you'll sense that I'm focused and then you'll stay focused.'

"And from that point on, I used a pattern that was a little bit like him."

Rhetorical lessons from Ronald Reagan weren't enough to save Gingrich's candidacy that year, and he lost. But one characteristic never in short supply for Gingrich was his irrepressible self-confidence. He kept trying until he finally won a House seat from Georgia in 1978.

From the minute he arrived in Washington, Gingrich was seen, depending on whom you asked, as brilliant, audacious, or annoying. He was a font of ideas—a six-point plan for this, a manifesto for that—and not long on humility. Yet none of those things explains why Gingrich was crucial to the expansion and maturing of the conservative movement. He was pivotal because he brought two attributes the movement needed badly.

The first was an absolute conviction that there could be a conservative, Republican majority in the country, one that could live on beyond Reagan and sink deep roots. Most conservatives, suffering from a bit of an inferiority complex, didn't dare to think that.

Second, Gingrich was a master at generating publicity for himself—and whatever cause or vendetta he was pushing at the moment.

Many conservatives are deeply distrustful of the mainstream media, which they consider hopelessly liberal and naturally hostile, and therefore steer clear of it. By contrast, Congressman Gingrich, much like young Newtie trying to create a zoo out of thin air, ran straight for reporters and television cameras. And, much like Donald Trump a generation later, Gingrich became a master of the art of attacking the mainstream media even while feasting off the coverage it gave him.

Also like Trump, Gingrich seemed to operate on the belief that a story about him, even a controversial or critical one, was better than any story about his foes. The approach worked. At one point when he was ascendant, *The Wall Street Journal* conducted a survey of readers and found that any story that had "Gingrich" in the headline, or was illustrated with one of the *Journal*'s iconic line drawings of Gingrich, would instantly jump in readership.

These attributes became crucial in extending the conservative revolution, and they were on display from the moment Gingrich entered Congress. At the time, House Republicans had been in the minority for more than two decades, and most in the party simply assumed that was the natural order of affairs. Gingrich decided that he, personally, would do something about that.

So he approached Michigan representative Guy Vander Jagt, a well-established leader among House Republicans who had seen something in Gingrich early on, and told him the party needed a plan to become the majority party, and a committee to develop that plan. *Fine,* Vander Jagt told him. *You're now the chairman of it.*

Gingrich rounded up a few young, like-minded back-benchers and began making noise. As it happened, a conservative revolution was bubbling just below the surface—not just in the United States but also in Great Britain, where, in 1979, Margaret Thatcher had been elected prime minister as a union-busting conservative activist. So the young Gingrich brought her political advisers in to brief House Republicans on how they pulled it off.

From Thatcher, it was a natural leap for Gingrich to become a Reagan supporter the next year when the Gipper ran for president. At one point, he was asked to help organize an event for the Republican presidential nominee when he appeared at the Capitol to link arms, figuratively at least, with fellow Republicans running for Congress. Gingrich, never one to walk past an opportunity to stage a big scene, set out to create a big one for the former actor. He decided to use the Capitol steps—a setting he would put to good use again later in his career—and set a tableau consisting of every available Republican House and Senate candidate gathered around Reagan.

And, rather than have them simply be extras in this scene, Gingrich thought all those Republicans should do something to advance the conservative cause and, at the same time, their own candidacies. So he drew up a set of five conservative governing principles everybody on the steps would sign on to, along with Reagan. The principles were fairly standard Reagan fare, drawn from his campaign speeches and position papers.

But the apparatchiks from the Reagan campaign didn't see it that way. Two staffers appeared in Gingrich's office and said they thought it risky for the presidential candidate to associate himself with a specific agenda. They would prefer that he simply give a nice speech and be on his way. Gingrich thought that absurd, and said so. In a huff, he set out to cancel the event.

"Two hours later I get this call, the only call I got all year, from Bill Casey," who was managing the Reagan campaign, Gingrich recalls. "I pick up the phone and he says, 'Young man, I assume you wanted my attention.' I said, 'Yes, sir . . .' He said, 'I believe within two hours you'll be happy.' Two hours later, the two guys come back and go, 'This is great. We're going to do everything we can to make this work.' "

The event went off, and was considered a success. What nobody, including Gingrich, could realize at the time was that it was a forerunner of the precise strategy he would use more than a decade later to seize control not just of Congress, but of the conservative movement.

By 1982, Gingrich appeared on the cover of *Conservative Digest,* under a headline reading "A New Conservative Leader for the '80s." He also became a burr under the saddle of both the Democratic leadership and the more quiescent members of his own party. His message was not just that the liberal welfare state that had evolved since the days of Franklin Roosevelt had become bloated and inefficient, but that the entire political system that supported it was corrupt.

Perhaps more important, he discovered a tool lying at the side of the political road, unused by others but ready to be exploited. It came in the form of the then sleepy operation known as C-SPAN.

C-SPAN was created when the Congress's Democratic leadership, under popular pressure to move the chamber's proceedings more firmly into the twentieth century, agreed in early 1979 to position television cameras in the House chamber and make its proceedings available for broadcast. C-SPAN was the network that the cable television industry, at the behest of a farsighted broadcaster named Brian Lamb, created as a public service to carry the legislative proceedings.

It wasn't much to watch at first. Under the tight restrictions congressional leaders imposed on the new service, the cameras in the chambers were fixed in place, showing only the presiding officer at the big dais up front and whichever member happened to speaking on the floor. And as anybody who has experience watching Congress work knows, the proceedings are, about 90 percent of the time, roughly as thrilling as watching paint dry. Things got especially boring later in the afternoon, when the day's scheduled work was done and the floor lapsed into a period called "special orders," which meant that speakers were free to come to the floor and talk about whatever pet project or issue they had on their minds. It was, essentially, downtime.

But Gingrich realized that the downtime was, for him, hidden gold. He and his conservative compatriots began plotting ways to use the free airtime provided by C-SPAN, and the blank slate provided during special orders, to begin preaching their gospel to the American public. They would take to the floor in turn, attacking liberal programs and pushing their alternatives. As word started spreading among their adherents across the country, voters began tuning in. To the annoyance of Democratic leaders, Gingrich had begun using the very television platform they had created to attack them.

At about the same time, Gingrich used another cutting-edge technology to expand his network and spread the conservative gospel. It seems almost crude now, but this technological revolution was the cassette tape. And the machine he used to amplify his message was a once sleepy conservative organization called GOPAC.

GOPAC was the brainchild of Delaware governor Pete du Pont in 1978, born of the pre-Reagan frustration over the inability to get more Republican conservatives elected to Congress. The organization was doing a decent job giving candidates useful practical advice when du Pont decided, in 1986, that he was going to run for president and shouldn't try to do so while running the organization. So he turned the organization over to Gingrich, who, in typical fashion, decided to turbocharge it. It occurred to him that political candidates spent a lot of time driving in cars, traversing their districts and moving from event to event, and that it would be great to get training messages to them during those downtimes.

So he came up with an idea: to record messages candidates could listen to while driving around, getting tips on how aspiring conservative politicians down at the grassroots level should approach and talk about issues of the day. Leading conservatives in Congress, or in offices at the state and local levels, recorded what amounted to pro tips on tape. At one point, Gingrich says, GOPAC was distributing 75,000 tapes a month to aspiring conservative political leaders.

What Gingrich was doing, through C-SPAN and GOPAC, was building something conservatives had never had before: a farm team of rising new leaders, and a grassroots support system for them. Conservatives are by nature not great believers in centralized power, so they had never done much to build national networks. Thanks to Gingrich, C-SPAN and GOPAC effectively gave them two such networks, steps that would prove crucial in keeping the revolution rolling in the years ahead. Perhaps most important, they were steps that in coming years would help produce a surge in conservative governors and state legislators around the country.

Ironically, Gingrich was doing all this to extend the Reagan Revolution even though some on the right harbored quiet concerns that he might at any time wander off the conservative reservation. As I would write of Gingrich years later, "He is intellectually promiscuous. As someone who fancies himself a powerful intellectual, Mr. Gingrich often seems unable to resist a new idea." He actually liked government activism in some areas, particularly favoring big funding for health research and science, and would come to support a cap-and-trade system to combat global warming, which would allow companies to buy and sell the right to emit gases into the atmosphere, a concept that made some conservatives nervous.

Over time, though, Gingrich became the party leader best able to articulate in pithy sound bites what conservatives believed. On top of that, he endeared himself to the right by going after, and then capturing, one of the biggest Democratic fish in the sea: House Speaker Jim Wright.

Wright opened himself up to attack by arranging a sweetheart book deal for himself, under which he got exceptionally high royalties for sales, in turn using the book as a platform to earn high speaker's fees. All of that looked like a backdoor way for supporters to bend the House's rules to help the Speaker enrich himself. His scheme raised questions that might have simply evaporated in the hubbub of Washington business had Gingrich not gone on the warpath—using, among other things, the C-SPAN platform he had discovered for himself and his allies to keep pounding away at Wright. Eventually there was an Ethics Committee investigation, and in May 1989 Wright was forced to resign.

Gingrich had done the unthinkable within the clubby world of the House of Representatives: He had toppled the most powerful man in Congress. He also had become the darling of the cadre of young conservative House members who had ridden the Reagan wave into Congress. Their support helped him get elected as Republican whip, the second-ranking GOP member in the House.

It was a remarkably swift rise, though there was an element of luck involved. Other Republicans who might have advanced— Dick Cheney, Trent Lott, Jack Kemp—all had left the House for various reasons, clearing the way for Gingrich.

So it was that, after just a decade in the normally plodding House, Gingrich was one step from the top. It was from that perch that he again, in 1990, did the unthinkable by going after the president of his own party over that fateful decision to raise taxes. As the GOP whip, Gingrich was in the room for much of the haggling that went into the budget deal that carried the tax increase. Bush aides believed that, by being present in the room, he was obliged to go along with whatever compromise emerged. "By their standards, they think I lied," Gingrich concedes now. When it became clear he wasn't inclined to support the deal, Gingrich recalls, the White House had Cheney, who had become defense secretary, call Gingrich from the Pentagon to lobby him to fall in line. Gingrich turned their time as fellow House conservative warriors against Cheney. "I said, 'Dick, I was just reading your brilliant speech against the Reagan tax increase of '82.' He said, 'Got it,' and hung up," Gingrich recalls.

With Gingrich at the lead, House back-benchers rebelled against the Bush tax hike, making the final budget deal an uphill battle for the president and his team. Gingrich became persona non grata to the Bush White House—and, in the process, even more of a hero to young conservatives in the House.

He stood, at the time, second in line in the House Republican hierarchy behind Representative Robert Michel of Illinois, who was of a different generation and style—Michel was a decorated veteran of World War II, while Gingrich got a family deferment that kept him out of the Vietnam War. Bob Michel was to Newt Gingrich roughly what Bruce Wayne was to Batman: one a genteel gentleman moving in polite society, ready to do a deal, the other a crusader tearing through the streets of Gotham, ready to do battle. In his fights against both Jim Wright and President Bush, Gingrich had signaled the arrival of a new kind of conservative leader. Michel came from the old school, where Republicans stuck to conservative principles, but not too hard; they debated Democrats, but at the end of the day they were prepared to have drinks and share a round of golf with them. Gingrich was willing to slash, to arouse grassroots anger and turn it to his advantage.

After Bush lost his reelection bid to Bill Clinton, it was clear that many in the House were ready to adopt the Gingrich style of leadership, and jettison both Michel and his brand. So Michel announced he wouldn't run for reelection in 1994, effectively handing the reins of the House Republican leadership over to Gingrich.

All that was left for Gingrich to do at that point was make good on his declaration that conservatives and Republicans could, in fact, become the majority party in Washington by taking over the House. That ambition may sound simple now, but in 1994 Democrats weren't in charge by just a little; they held an eighty-two-seat advantage. For most people in Washington, the idea that Republicans could take over just didn't compute.

But that didn't deter Gingrich. In fact, President Clinton helped make the goal attainable. Clinton, sensing the country had moved to the right, had won the White House by running as a "New Democrat," one who had moved away from the party's New Deal liberalism and staked out ground more in the center of the political spectrum. He delivered NAFTA, completing a dream launched by Ronald Reagan and pushed along by George H. W. Bush, despite some doubts among Democratic liberals.

But on other fronts, Clinton moved away from the center and back to the left early in his term. He had campaigned promising a middle-class tax cut, but abandoned that during his transition because of rising deficit numbers. He ended up proposing a tax increase, not a cut, as part of a budget package designed to reduce federal deficits. His White House began considering a broad-based energy tax, too. Perhaps most damaging, the president's wife, Hillary Clinton, presided over the construction of a new healthcare program that was widely attacked for its cost and complexity. Beyond matters of policy, the White House was plagued by mini-scandals and self-made controversies, particularly one involving insiders from Clinton's home state of Arkansas moving in on the business of booking travel for the White House press.

Clinton's job approval slumped below 40 percent early in his term, and the door was open for Gingrich and the Republicans. As Gingrich set out to develop a winning message, help arrived in the unlikely form of a brash young message-meister named Frank Luntz.

Luntz, a genial young man given to rumpled khakis, tennis shoes, and colorful socks, was a graduate of the University of Pennsylvania and Oxford University. At an early age, he earned a reputation as a pollster, a student of public opinion, and a master at helping politicians speak to voters in terms that would resonate. He had worked for Pat Buchanan's insurgent, populist campaign for president, as well as for Ross Perot and Rudy Giuliani, who had just run an unconventional campaign of his own for mayor of New York. Luntz also had studied the Reform Party of Canada, a populist, western movement of breakaway conservatives who wanted to bring authentic voter voices into the political debate.

After the 1992 election, Luntz was speaking at a conference sponsored by the conservative *National Review* magazine, at which he excoriated the losing Bush presidential campaign and explained what he had learned from the Canadian Reform Party's efforts to channel grassroots voter anger at the political establishment. As it happens, one audience member was Gay Gaines, who was running GOPAC for Gingrich at that point. She invited Luntz to meet with Gingrich.

Gingrich pulled in Luntz to address House Republicans at a retreat, and was impressed. They met again in November 1993, after Canada's Reform Party had scored a significant breakthrough in elections there, proving the power of an insurgent movement with a populist, grassroots message. Among other things, Luntz urged Gingrich to convince his comrades, in their eagerness to belittle Clinton's healthcare plan, to stop saying there was no healthcare crisis. That, he argued, simply made Republicans look mean. At their second meeting, Gingrich asked Luntz to go to work for him, starting immediately. Luntz demurred, saying he was already committed to depart to conduct focus groups of consumers for the Disney movie studio. "Fine," Gingrich responded as he turned away. "Some people are serious, some people aren't." Luntz relented and went to work for GOPAC.

The key moment, though, didn't come until months later, amid an ice storm at a retreat of Republican House members in Salisbury, Maryland. In an early-morning walk to breakfast, Gingrich asked Luntz what he would do to prove Republicans were different from typical politicians. Gingrich was particularly focused on winning over independents and unhappy Democrats who had been shaken loose from their moorings by Buchanan and Perot. Luntz had brought along a copy of a "compact" with voters that he had drawn up for a candidate for attorney general in Massachusetts, which told voters exactly what the candidate would do if elected. It was a gimmick, but, because the compact was addressed directly to voters, it signified that they were in charge, not the candidate. And that was Luntz's goal: to make Republicans show they were willing to give power to voters.

Gingrich liked the idea, and it evolved in the coming months into a "Contract with America"—a simple and specific list of ten pieces of legislation that Republicans pledged they would pass if given control of the House. It was, in a way, a conservative manifesto, turned into simple and bite-size nuggets that voters could more easily digest than politicians' typical promises. It also consisted of conservative ideas that were safe and broadly popular to voters in the ideological center. The rule Gingrich and Luntz followed was that every item had to attract at least 60 percent support in public polling. Notably absent were items on abortion and school prayer; Gingrich didn't want the document attacked by enemies of the religious right as some kind of fringe religious-right declaration.

Luntz recalls, "What was special about this document was the goal: expand the base beyond just Republicans to capture the independent Perot constituency. And the only way to do that was to be nonpartisan." It was precisely the constituency Donald Trump would corral two decades later.

More than proposing ideas, though, the contract included specific legislative bills that Republicans promised to vote on within the first hundred days after taking control of the House. Those proposals included a balanced-budget amendment and line-item veto; a tough-on-crime bill that included longer sentences and more prisons; reform of the welfare system; a bill beefing up enforcement of child support payments and providing more education choice; family-friendly tax cuts; more defense spending; a bill allowing senior citizens to earn more income without losing Social Security benefits; business tax breaks as a way to create more jobs; a tort-reform plan to reduce lawsuits; and term limits for lawmakers. The contract also promised reforms in how Congress works, including a guarantee that all laws Congress passed would apply to lawmakers as well as the rest of America, and cuts in the numbers of committees and staffers.

Some of the ideas—term limits, tort reform, the balanced-budget amendment—were evergreen proposals, often discussed in Washington but never given a serious chance of passage. Others—

business tax cuts, welfare reform—were straight out of the standard conservative playbook. Still others—stronger enforcement of child support payments, family-friendly tax cuts—were designed to show that conservatives had new ideas for supporting women and families. Equally important, the document never used the word "Republican." It was designed to attract those who were disgruntled with both parties.

The contract was identified, then and forevermore, with Gingrich, as it should have been. But it had an undeniable flavor of Ronald Reagan as well. In fact, Reagan biographer Lou Cannon later wrote that more than half its proposals "were taken verbatim from Reagan's 1985 State of the Union address."

Gingrich made sure the contract was at the center of every fall campaign. He staged a showy signing ceremony on the steps of the Capitol at which hundreds of Republican lawmakers and candidates walked up to the table, three by three, to sign the contract, essentially giving their word of honor it would be implemented. Gingrich used the network of supportive conservative organizations to spread word of the contract everywhere. His supporters paid to have a printed copy of the contract placed in *TV Guide,* on the theory that the popular magazine of TV schedules was picked up not once in a week but seven times in every household that received it, multiplying the chances recipients would actually read it. The printed contract had a checklist so voters could track the progress of legislation, a toll-free phone number to call for details, and a clause that invited voters to toss out Republicans if they didn't follow through.

The contract, when compared with the occasional chaos that seemed to prevail in the early days of the Clinton White House, helped convince Americans that there actually was a Republican plan for governing that involved things conservatives were for, not just things they opposed. Worse for Clinton, the economy, though recovering from the recession that had killed his predecessor, Bush, wasn't recovering fast enough to convince voters that improvements were under way.

By Election Day, it was clear the outcome would be good for conservatives and Republicans generally, but few foresaw the landslide that took shape. Republicans flipped fifty-four Democratic seats in the House, to take command for the first time since 1954. They also claimed eight new seats in the Senate, to take control there as well. The night's success was especially sweet for conservatives because the tide carried a notable group of strong conservatives into the Senate: Spencer Abraham of Michigan, James Inhofe of Oklahoma, and Rick Santorum of Pennsylvania. Congress hadn't merely gone Republican; it had moved decisively to the right.

Something else changed as well, something that wouldn't serve the cause over time. The face and tone of conservative leadership had shifted from the sunny, optimistic, and gentle approach of Ronald Reagan to the much harsher, angrier, and more pugilistic approach of Newt Gingrich. Rahm Emanuel, an adviser in the Clinton White House who worked both with and against Gingrich, thinks the change in style and approach was so significant that the ascension of Newt Gingrich, rather than the arrival of Donald Trump two decades later, marked the end of the Reagan Revolution. "Newt Gingrich is the beginning of the modern new Republican Party, which was manifested in Donald Trump," Emanuel says.

It's certainly true that Gingrich did wear out even some friends and admirers with his intensity and his seemingly endless embrace of ideas and plans. Conservative writer and commentator Lee Edwards summarized it this way:

Before there was the Contract with America, there was a 1990 lecture by Newt Gingrich at the Heritage Foundation listing five goals for the United States. And before Heritage, there was an eighteen-day retreat in the Colorado Rockies during which Gingrich declared that the welfare state had to "be blown up and replaced." And before the Crested Butte, Colorado, retreat, there was a 1986 series of Gingrich speeches suggesting six points for America's future. And before the 1986 speeches, there was a 1983 memorandum by [Gingrich friend and ally] Judd Gregg outlining nine conservative programs. And before the Gregg memo, there was a 1981 meeting in Racine, Wisconsin, at which Gingrich set forth a 12-year plan for a conservative majority in America. And before Racine, there was the October 1980 rally on the steps of the U.S. Capitol where Republican members of the House and Senate stood proudly behind their presidential candidate, Ronald Reagan, and pledged to support his conservative presidential platform.

Still, in retrospect, one can make a good case that the conservative movement actually reached its peak with the Contract with America, the Republican takeover of Congress in 1994, and the significant conservative advances at the state level made throughout the country that year. All of those developments had real and significant impact on public policy, and Newt Gingrich had more to do with them than anybody. Moreover, they showed that Gingrich was right: There was, at least for that moment, a genuine conservative majority in the country.

All of which, for conservatives, made what followed over the next few years all the more bittersweet.

CHAPTER 7

The Best of Times,
the Worst of Times

In retrospect, perhaps it was inevitable that Newt Gingrich and Bill Clinton would collide.

At the height of their powers, they were like two comets streaking across the American sky, running hot and bright and sometimes out of control. They were so big they couldn't really avoid each other. When the collision came, it shook the country, its political system, and Washington's new conservative power structure to the core.

Bill Clinton was born in the summer of 1946, three years after Newt Gingrich. That meant Clinton was at the front edge of the baby boom and Gingrich technically just ahead of it, but for all intents and purposes they were the first children of the post–World War II generation to lead the country. Watching them go head-to-head was a bit like watching a 1960s college dorm-room fight spilling out onto a national political stage.

Gingrich was nerdy and conservative, while Clinton was more hip and liberal, but they had more in common than not. Both were draft age during the tumultuous years of the Vietnam War, but both avoided the fight. Both were brilliant and precocious, and taught college before launching their political careers. Both were, politically speaking, sons of the South—Clinton from Arkansas and Gingrich from Georgia. Both made their first run for political office in the same year, 1974, in the midst of the Watergate scandal. Both have, to this day, big personalities, the kinds that fill a room. Both were endowed with prodigious political skills, as well as, most observers would agree, some notable character flaws.

To those of us who covered them both in the 1990s, they were irresistible—stimulating and impossible to walk past. They were smart and articulate, they loved being in the political arena, and they enjoyed the give-and-take with journalists even as they complained about it.

Clinton read voraciously; he would occasionally call in columnists for chats about the issues of the moment, and pay them the ultimate compliment of remarking knowingly on what they had written. Unlike some presidents, he enjoyed engaging both columnists who liked him and those who disagreed with him. There was a touch of hubris involved there. Clinton could articulate both sides of a political argument—the side he agreed with as well as the one with which he disagreed—more adeptly than just about anyone, and he knew it. He would have made a great newspaper columnist himself. He had a mind so nimble that he occasionally worked on a crossword puzzle while listening to his aides debate an issue, without missing a beat in the argument as it played out.

Clinton was the most naturally talented politician I ever covered. He had the complete skill set: He could—and, at political conventions, regularly did—deliver a speech that captivated thousands in an arena. But he also had the ability to walk into a room of just a few people, engage any of them in conversation on any topic, and convince each of them that he or she was, at that moment, the most fascinating person Clinton had ever met. Politicians have to be able to suffer fools gladly, but nobody did it better than Bill Clinton. In fact, he didn't merely suffer them; he set out to seduce them.

Both men knew they were engaged in an epic battle of ideas and ideologies. For his part, Gingrich took office as Speaker of the House in 1995 determined to oversee a conservative reversal of what he and his compatriots saw as the essential liberal trend lines of the 1960s: a growing government that intruded on ever broader parts of Americans' daily lives from Washington. "The essential lesson of the sixties was the politics of dependence—turn your problems over to the government and they can be solved," Representative Dick Armey of Texas, Gingrich's second in command, told my colleague David Rogers and me early that year. Clinton, for his part, sought to save the core of the Great Society's liberal programs by pulling the Democratic Party toward the center, seeking to trim the liberal agenda to make it more sustainable, lest it be washed away en masse by the rising conservative tide.

The battle between these two escalated after the stunning Republican and conservative advances in the 1994 election. "Gingrich had proved to be a better politician than I was," Clinton wrote later in his autobiography. "The nationalization of midterm elections was Newt Gingrich's major contribution to modern electioneering."

Gingrich entered this battle with an array of powerful new forces deployed to support him, helping him attain a kind of reach that no Republican or conservative leader had ever enjoyed before. One of the most powerful was also the most unlikely: a onetime baseball marketer who took a flier as a radio commentator, caught the conservative wave, and then, in time, played a key role in driving it higher.

His name was Rush Limbaugh. He had spent the early years of his career bouncing around—and sometimes being bounced from— jobs as a radio disc jockey in his native Missouri and in Pittsburgh. Eventually he took a position in the marketing and sales department of the Kansas City Royals baseball team. "I was in charge of ceremonial first pitches, national anthem singers, group sales," he recalls now. "I was the producer of the game every night."

After five years, he lost that job when his boss, the club's marketing director, left the Royals. So Limbaugh returned to radio, his first love—though this time not as a disc jockey but as a host on a talk radio station in Kansas City. Suddenly he was free to express his own opinions, something he had never been able to do before.

The one time he had tried to was during a gig in Pittsburgh, when he was hosting the morning show at an oldies station. When he dared to question on the air why Democrats, under a new innovation, were being allowed by television networks to respond to a State of the Union speech by President Richard Nixon, "I was told by management to shut up about politics," he recalls. "That was the extent of it."

Now, at the post in Kansas City, Limbaugh was allowed, even expected, to air his opinions, which turned out to be quite conservative. More than that, he was entertaining in presenting them.

Limbaugh was heard by a consultant who steered him from Kansas City to a station in Sacramento, California, which wanted more of what Limbaugh was delivering. He began hosting a show there in 1984 and found that he flowered as a genuine conservative radio talk show host. His first goal, Limbaugh insists, was to host a good and successful radio show rather than to become a political figure. "Everybody puts it in political terms, which makes sense," he says. "But the bottom line was: it's radio, it isn't politics. It's got to be a good show. It has to be compelling." There were no guests. There was no script. There was just Rush Limbaugh, doing what amounted to political commentary and political satire, which was both funny and rude.

His reputation grew, and eventually, with the help of a media management firm, he was hired by a big New York radio station, WABC, under a deal in which he would produce a radio show to be syndicated nationally. The deal kicked off in July 1988, just as Reagan was halfway through his final year in office.

"It was provocative, compelling, never boring," Limbaugh says. "All the ingredients for media success. The politics in it was supplemental. . . . I started this to be the number one most listened-to radio person in the country."

Yet, like Ronald Reagan and Newt Gingrich, Limbaugh soon discovered there was a bigger market for conservative views than had been imagined previously. "It's not that I converted a bunch of people that didn't know what they are. I validated what a lot of conservatives already were and already thought. They just finally had something to attach to and somebody to believe in and somebody to associate with, and to help grow this. So I was originally portrayed as the Pied Piper misleading a bunch of mind-numb robots. It wasn't that at all."

The Limbaugh show took off, faster and higher than anyone could have predicted. By 1994, Limbaugh was heard on 636 radio stations, was being telecast simultaneously on C-SPAN, had a separate television show, and was mailing out a regular newsletter to listeners. Limbaugh was becoming a cottage industry, yet the cottage was pretty big. While much of what he said in his thousands of hours of airtime was designed to drive a conservative message, some of it was simply offered for shock value, and some of it was just silly. Mocking liberals, Limbaugh found, was one pursuit that conservatives of various stripes could agree was worthwhile.

In a typical broadcast in early 1994, he offered a series of what he described as irrefutable truths. They included: "No nation has ever taxed itself into prosperity," "Evidence refutes liberalism," "There is no such thing as a New Democrat," "The most beautiful thing about a tree is what you do with it after you cut it down," and, most simply, "Ronald Reagan was the greatest president of the 20th century."

Limbaugh had known back in Sacramento that something big was starting when he happened to mention one day that he was attending a charity function that night. When he showed up for the event, the venue was overrun with people—most of whom had come out simply to meet and talk to Limbaugh. Much later, after moving to New York, he recalled flying on a plane along with CBS television personalities Ed Bradley and Charlie Rose. When the plane arrived and the three men were waiting at the baggage claim, the fellow passengers rushed to talk with Limbaugh, not the CBS stars. "There was an actual connection being made," Limbaugh concluded. "And by the way, it was really sobering." By 2019, he had a weekly audience of 24 to 26 million listeners.

Limbaugh's success opened the door for the emergence of what conservative communications consultant Greg Mueller refers to as a series of "mini-Limbaughs": radio talk hosts who picked up Limbaugh's style and conservative views and made their own imprints on the debate all across the nation. One of them was Sean Hannity, who would rise from radio talk show host in the South to become, two decades later, one of President Trump's most vociferous media champions.

But Limbaugh may have paved the way for the emergence of another, even bigger force. At first this new creature on the media landscape was regarded as something between a curiosity and a surefire failure. It proved to be much, much more.

This new creation was Fox News, the brainchild of Australian media magnate Rupert Murdoch. Murdoch was a newspaperman at heart, and a shrewd businessman who had parlayed his earnings into a much bigger fortune by buying the 20th Century Fox movie studio, as well as a string of local television stations, and welding them into a giant and profitable new-age media company.

But as anybody familiar with Murdoch knows, he is, at his core, a news junkie. He loves nothing more than wandering into the newsroom of one of his properties to find out what's up and swap political gossip. He had watched with interest—and probably a bit of jealousy—as a fellow media titan, Ted Turner, broke with convention by launching an all-news cable network, the simply and aptly named Cable News Network, in 1980, and saw NBC create CNBC, a business network that also was delivered via cable systems. NBC, in tandem with Internet giant Microsoft, was preparing to launch a third cable news network, MSNBC. Murdoch was convinced there was room for another cable offering with a completely different rationale, which could reach an audience he was convinced was being either ignored or scorned by those in the media centers on the East Coast: conservatives in the American heartland.

Murdoch believed the news media in general, and the television news media in particular, tilted to the left, whether they realized it or not. Fox News's opening, as both a business and a journalistic proposition, was that it would provide a counterweight on the right. Fox News also would be different in style and tone—as the media critic Ken Auletta has noted, while CNN prospered by taking the style of all-news radio and converting it to television, Fox News would do something different: It would attempt to take the more brash and opinionated style of talk radio and convert that to television.

Murdoch had nursed along the idea for some time, but the mission didn't crystallize until he connected with Roger Ailes. Ailes was a strange sort of hybrid. He was a television guy, and a political guy, but not really a news guy.

Ailes hailed from the small factory town of Warren, Ohio, near Youngstown. His father was a factory worker—blue-collar all the way—and his mother a housewife who embroidered handkerchiefs for extra money. Roger himself would work summers for the state highway department, doing various manual-labor tasks, including digging ditches. He enrolled at Ohio University, and when he came home for Christmas break his first year he discovered that the family home had been sold and his mother had moved away with a new man. Ailes, already pretty tough and independent, became more so.

He spent a lot of his time at the college radio station, where he worked as a disc jockey and sportscaster. That led to an interview at a Cleveland television station, which hired him. There came the crucial break in Ailes's career: The station was launching a local television talk and variety show, *The Mike Douglas Show,* and Ailes signed on as a production assistant.

Douglas's show took off, was syndicated nationally, and soon was landing nationally famous guests. In 1967, Richard Nixon was one of them. The twenty-seven-year-old Ailes, brash and self-confident, began talking to Nixon about how television should be regarded by a political candidate—a conversation that led to a job with Nixon's presidential campaign. Ailes, who had previously been vaguely Republican but not especially serious about it, had crossed over into the world of politics.

After that campaign, Ailes formed his own communications

company, which helped draft communications and ad strategies for Ronald Reagan's reelection campaign in 1984 and then began advising George H. W. Bush's 1988 presidential campaign. He got to know the candidate, and, inexplicably, they bonded—the patrician, well-mannered Bush and the blue-collar, brash Ailes. Some saw Ailes, along with campaign manager Lee Atwater, as forming the darker side of the sunny Bush; they were the ones who could convince him to embrace nasty attacks on his political opponents. That idea was enshrined by cartoonist Garry Trudeau, who, in his *Doonesbury* cartoon strip, portrayed Bush as invisible, but with an evil twin. Bush and Ailes bonded, and the bond outlasted the campaign. In fact, I first met Ailes when Bush was president and I walked into the Oval Office for an interview. There, standing alongside the president, was Ailes.

In the next few years, though, Ailes put politics behind him and went back into television, joining NBC to run its new CNBC channel and to launch an "America's Talking" channel, which would become MSNBC. But he and NBC's corporate chiefs had a falling-out—among other things, Ailes's style was way too brash for them—and Ailes left.

Murdoch seized the moment. He invited Ailes to lunch, which brought together a couple of swashbucklers who both grated on the establishment and were happy to do so. They talked about Murdoch's idea for a new news channel, and Murdoch became convinced that Ailes was the man who could help him pull it off.

On January 30, 1996, Murdoch announced the launch of the Fox News Channel. Years later, he described his rationale this way: "If you look around the world, there is a crying need for more alternative news programs, different news organizations. We've had a sort of a monolithic view of the world, and we ought to give a more fair and balanced view, something quite different that people weren't used to."

It was an audacious gamble by Murdoch. For his part, Ailes was confident enough to believe he could create an entirely new network, which had to be built from the ground up in a building near

Rockefeller Center, in a matter of months. "About two or three weeks before the launch," he recalled later, "our engineers came to us and said, 'I think we can launch with one control room, one studio, no graphics, or we'll have to push the launch back.' I remember calling a 4 A.M. meeting for the executives and explaining to them that we were going to launch with all the studios, all the control rooms, and all the graphics. We went into a crash mode in the last few weeks."

Fox News launched on October 7, 1996. Fox host Shepard Smith recalls, "We didn't have the systems in place." Alan Colmes, who survived for years as one of the few liberal voices on the network, recalled that the general initial response was "Fox what?" Ailes said simply, "Everybody laughed at us."

They wouldn't laugh for long. Fox was available in 17 million homes at its birth. As more cable systems began picking up the new channel, the number rose to 20 million in six months. Ten years later, it had nearly quintupled to 91 million. In 1997, Fox averaged 23,000 viewers during the daytime and 37,000 in prime time. A decade later, those numbers had exploded, to an average daytime viewership of 814,000 and an average prime-time viewership of 1.5 million. Fox News passed CNN in total daily and prime-time viewership in 2002 and has been number one in cable news viewership ever since. By 2016 it was the most watched network not just in news but in all of cable. By 2019 it was reaching 90 million homes.

Around the same time he was greenlighting Fox News, Murdoch sponsored the launch of another conservative media voice, *The Weekly Standard* magazine. For years, liberals had felt they had their own weekly organ, *The New Republic*. Bill Kristol, who had worked for Vice President Dan Quayle, was out of power in the Clinton years, and searching for a way to have an impact. He hit upon the idea of a new conservative magazine that would be more overtly political than the typical stuffy intellectual conservative publications that had long predominated. "Why shouldn't we have our own *New Republic*?" he recalls thinking.

Kristol set out to find wealthy conservatives to invest in the idea.

When he got to Murdoch, however, he recalls that he got a different response. *I already run a media company,* Murdoch said. *Why should I invest in somebody else's magazine? I can just start it myself.* So Murdoch sat down with Kristol and journalist Fred Barnes in his office in Los Angeles and simply agreed to launch *The Weekly Standard* as part of his media empire. It was up and running in months.

In sum, a new conservative megaphone had been crafted. Conservatives were thrilled. Yet they also couldn't have appreciated now how that megaphone might be used in ways they disliked over the years.

Limbaugh and Fox News were as much populist as traditionally conservative. As successful mass-media institutions, they were more in tune with their audiences' attitudes than with political theory, and over time they would come to take on, and then amplify, the grievances of their listeners and viewers, and their scorn for the establishments of both parties. The targets of that scorn happened to include, frequently at least, the establishment of the Republican Party. For its part, meantime, *The Weekly Standard* would become a platform for neoconservative foreign policy thinkers, as well as their drumbeat for a war with Iraq after the 9/11 terrorist attacks. That war had disastrous consequences for the country, the Republican Party, and the conservative movement, which was in some measure blamed for starting it. The conservative movement's megaphone would play a part in bringing the movement down.

But those problems lay in the future. From the perspective of Newt Gingrich, his governing phase of the conservative revolution couldn't have started any better. He and his fellow Republicans, newly in charge of the House, set out at the beginning of 1995 to systematically pass legislation enacting the Contract with America, thereby fulfilling the most high-profile campaign promise in recent history. By the fall, all the bills they had promised, except for a constitutional amendment imposing term limits on lawmakers, had passed the House. Three of those bills whisked through the Senate and into law: a provision subjecting Congress to the same laws it applied to other employers; one putting limits on federal mandates that order state and local governments to take actions or spend money; and a third that reduced federal government paperwork.

Those were relatively uncontroversial, though. Even Clinton said he supported them. Other initiatives ran into difficulty. An early warning sign appeared in March, when the proposed balanced-budget amendment to the Constitution, after quickly passing the House, failed in the Senate. It fell a single vote short of the two-thirds majority needed for a constitutional amendment when one Republican, Senator Mark Hatfield of Oregon, voted against the measure. Hatfield was one of the dying breed of moderate Senate Republicans, and he considered a balanced-budget amendment a gimmick. In truth, so did a lot of his Republican colleagues, though they weren't willing to buck the conservative movement by saying so or voting so.

The vote on the balanced-budget amendment illustrated the practical problems the Gingrich revolution still faced, despite the enormous success it had experienced just months earlier during the 1994 election. The Republican Party in those days still had a meaningful bloc of moderate legislators who hadn't really bought into the full Contract with America, and who were turned off by the combative style of Gingrich and his lieutenants. The most important group of these skeptical Republicans, unfortunately for Gingrich, resided in the Senate, where the rules of the chamber, the existence of a legislative filibuster option, and the power of committee chairmen all made pushing through legislation difficult under the best of circumstances.

To navigate the Senate, Gingrich had to rely on Senator Robert Dole of Kansas, who had taken over as majority leader, with a small majority, as a result of the 1994 tsunami. Dole himself had once been considered something of a conservative slasher, but by the mid-1990s he was mistrusted by many in the conservative movement. His willingness to work with Democrats to pass tax and budget legislation, honed during a long and distinguished stint on the Senate Finance Committee, had led Gingrich years earlier to brand him derisively as the "tax collector for the welfare state." To younger conservatives, Dole personified the old go-along-to-get-along attitude that had doomed Republicans to a seemingly perpetual minority status in Congress.

In fact, that rap was inaccurate and unfair to Dole. True, he was an old-fashioned, Main Street, midwestern conservative, one who happened to place great stock in balancing the books. But he also liked tax cuts. After all, he was already planning to run for president in 1996 and, as a shrewd political operator, understood that the conservative tide was running high within his party. He wasn't foolish enough to think he could win the nomination by swimming against that tide, especially when conservative darlings such as Jack Kemp were available to run against him for president.

Above all, though, Dole was a realist. He knew better than almost anyone what could and could not pass the Senate and what was needed to make the possible become reality. That meant compromises, and Gingrich and the younger conservatives pushing the Contract with America had explicitly chosen a no-compromises strategy. Gingrich would later wonder whether that was the right approach, but at the time it wasn't in doubt within the House leadership. That inevitably meant trouble in the Senate.

So Dole did what he could, but the Senate was always a problem. The other problem was President Clinton. As the House's conservative troops soon discovered, the challenge at the other end of Pennsylvania Avenue wasn't that Clinton would fight them at every turn. To the contrary, he seized upon a strategy, impressed upon him by onetime Republican pollster Dick Morris, to engage in "triangulation": He would position himself somewhere between his party's own liberal wing and the Gingrich conservatives. It was a simple but brilliant strategy, one that allowed him to co-opt the conservative movement by actually embracing much of what it offered. He even agreed to do a joint town hall with Gingrich in mid-1995 to show he wasn't going to adopt a just-say-no posture.

By doing that, he also positioned himself to successfully resist some parts of the conservative agenda by declaring that they were too radical for the sensible people, like him, who were firmly in the ideological center. If the president couldn't live with some ideas the House conservatives were throwing out, it must have been because they were too radical. After all, hadn't he embraced the more reasonable parts of the conservative agenda? It was a strategy designed to get Gingrich to overreach—and it worked.

Clinton moved to the middle in a variety of ways. He embraced the Bush administration's market-based plans to reduce air pollution over rigid federal mandates. He cut the federal workforce. He cleared the way for at least some prayer in public schools. He put himself on record favoring curbs on affirmative action programs. He was tough on crime, following up on a 1994 violent-crime act that he had championed. On these and other counts, he signaled that he wasn't resisting the country's move to the right, but rather trying to direct it down reasonable paths.

This battle of wits played out above all in an epic battle over federal spending. In mid-1995, Clinton proclaimed that he, like the Republicans, was in favor of a balanced budget, and offered his own ideas on how to get there. He just didn't propose getting there quite as fast as Gingrich did, or with as much crimping of popular social programs, particularly Medicare, along the way.

Having laid that predicate, Clinton figured he was well positioned to stand against the first real budget plans Republicans offered from their new congressional perch. He vetoed one early spending bill midyear, and then dug in for a big confrontation in November. Gingrich offered a budget that would balance the books on his timetable and his terms, which included raising Medicare premiums and cutting funding for some education and environmental programs. In doing so, the House Speaker tried to create leverage over Clinton: If the president didn't sign the Republicans' budget package, he said, the government would shut down and the nation's debt ceiling wouldn't be raised, sending the United States into default with its creditors around the world.

Clinton vetoed the Republicans' budget plan anyway. Funding ran out and the federal government shut down, first for five days and then for twenty-one days, idling some 800,000 government workers and shuttering national parks. Government agencies fell dark through the Christmas season and into the new year, 1996.

The key question, politically, was who would be blamed. At that point, Gingrich made a key tactical error. As the budget battle reached its climax, he appeared at a press breakfast and complained that Clinton's White House had stuck him in a seat at the back of Air Force One when he was part of the official U.S. delegation to the funeral of slain Israeli prime minister Yitzhak Rabin, and then made him exit the plane from the rear. He further complained that Clinton didn't schedule a time to negotiate on the budget with him during the flight, and implied he had made the Republicans' budget demands tougher as a result. Those complaints sounded petty and made Gingrich's stance on the budget appear to be based on pique rather than principle.

Sure enough, public polling showed that Americans blamed the Republicans—now in charge of all of Congress—for the shut-down. Panicky Republican legislators saw that and ultimately ac-cepted most of Clinton's budget terms to reopen the government. But the damage was done. Conservatives had taken charge in Con-gress and, in the eyes of a lot of Americans, shown they couldn't govern effectively and smoothly. Congressional job approval in the *Wall Street Journal*/NBC News poll fell to 23 percent. Clinton's job approval also dropped initially during the government shutdown but then started to rise steadily, hitting 60 percent by mid-1996.

The irony is that, in losing politically, conservatives actually won substantively. They had forced a Democratic president to commit to balancing the federal budget, a goal that, in the end, was realized. Thanks to both an improving economy and the greater budget discipline Gingrich and his party inspired, the federal bud-get moved out of deficit and into surplus in 1998, for the first time in almost three decades, and then stayed that way for four straight years. The new debate in Washington was about the best way to handle a budget surplus.

More than that, Clinton, in the immediate aftermath of the shutdown showdown, moved even more decisively to the right, thereby further co-opting the conservatives and their agenda. In his State of the Union address in January 1996, he declared, "The era of big government is over," a remarkable statement from the Democratic descendant of Franklin Roosevelt and Lyndon Johnson. By the spring he had signed a bill, passed by the Republican Congress, giving the president a line-item veto, allowing him to strike out individual spending items without killing an entire appropriations bill. Another item in the Contract with America had become law.

Most striking of all, in August 1996 Clinton signed into law a welfare-reform bill. Welfare reform was another key to the Contract with America, but just months earlier Clinton had vetoed a welfare-reform plan. Now, as he headed toward a reelection race, he signed a new version, thereby positioning himself to get the credit with moderate voters who liked the idea. The reform moved some control over welfare benefits and requirements out of Washington and to the states, just as conservatives had been demanding, and put limits on the length of time families could get financial assistance. It also blocked many legal immigrants from receiving aid and cut spending on food stamps. Requirements that welfare recipients be working or seeking work were strengthened.

Clinton argued that he had signed this new bill to "end welfare as we know it" because he had succeeded in making such provisions less harsh than in the Republicans' original version, while putting more money into programs such as childcare for single mothers. Still, it was a classic Clinton triangulation move: In a year in which he would be running for reelection, he now would be able to get credit both on the left, for vetoing what he called a harsh Republican welfare-reform plan, and on the right, for signing a similar version.

In short, conservatives had moved the country, and the Democratic president was positioning himself to get the credit for it.

To see just how far Clinton moved Democrats to the center, it's instructive to look back at the platform Democrats adopted at the 1996 national convention. It was an ode to the virtues of middle-class and small-business tax cuts. It was tough on crime. It repeated

Clinton's assertion that "the era of big government is over" and added, "Big bureaucracies and Washington solutions are not the real answers to today's challenges. We need a smaller government." And the Democrats sounded positively Trumpian on immigration:

> We cannot tolerate illegal immigration and we must stop it. For years before Bill Clinton became President, Washington talked tough but failed to act. In 1992, our borders might as well not have existed. The border was under-patrolled, and what patrols there were, were under-equipped. Drugs flowed freely. Illegal immigration was rampant. Criminal immigrants, deported after committing crimes in America, returned the very next day to commit crimes again. President Clinton is making our border a place where the law is respected and drugs and illegal immigrants are turned away. We have increased the Border Patrol by over 40 percent; in El Paso, our Border Patrol agents are so close together they can see each other.

The platform also offered a full embrace of free trade; indeed, it boasted that the Clinton administration had signed more than two hundred agreements to lower trade barriers, a sign of just how much conservatives' love of free trade had become a bipartisan idea. There were two significant dissenting voices on that front, though, providing early signs that animosity toward free trade was starting to seep into both the Republican Party and the general electorate. Pat Buchanan ran for the Republican nomination again, still in full-throated populist mode. He was anti-immigration and hostile to free-trade agreements and, if anything, even more outspoken on those views than he had been four years earlier.

The second dissenting voice belonged to Ross Perot, who, like Buchanan, was back for a second run with his populist message. This time, Perot's focus had shifted substantially, from a relentless cry for balancing the budget (it was, after all, on its way to being balanced) to a harsh critique of free-trade agreements, particularly NAFTA. Where he had famously declared that the agreement was creating "a giant sucking sound" pulling American jobs into Mexico, this time he tried to put an actual political organization behind his message. He turned his one-man show into a third party, the Reform Party, and declared that the party's nomination was open to anybody its members chose. In fact, almost nobody believed that, because the Reform Party was about Ross Perot, full stop.

During the 1996 campaign, I traveled to Wind Gap, Pennsylvania, to profile a group of Perot supporters. They were charming in their idealism, but also conscious that they were following a flawed leader. They felt the nation's trade strategies had left them behind and believed strongly that the political systems of both parties in Washington had rotted out. They were desperate for a third party yet wished that somebody other than Perot, with all his personal eccentricities and excesses, were available to lead it. Their movement badly needed Perot's money and fame, however, so they were prepared to throw their support his way despite their misgivings.

"Regardless of how I might have disagreed with Perot on strategy, man, the guy is persistent," said Nicholas Sabatine III, a leader of the local Perot group. In short, they sounded a lot like the radical centrists who would throw their votes to Donald Trump two decades later.

At one point, the Perot and Buchanan rebellions came together when Perot asked Buchanan to speak to a meeting of his Reform Party. The potential for a populist movement was on full display. "We tore the roof off the building with the populist stuff," Buchanan says. As he recalls it, his message was *"When I take that oath of office, their new world order is coming down.* Everybody was on their feet. My sister, Bay, said, 'Look, Pat, there were guys in wheelchairs standing up.'"

In fact, Buchanan put a deep scare into the Republican hierarchy when he won the party's New Hampshire primary by a single percentage point over the establishment favorite, Bob Dole. But the populist anger he stoked had its limits in 1996; the economy was going strong, and the insecurity created by trade shifts still was limited to pockets of the country. Within the Republican Party, Gingrich and his conservative army at that point were, as Reagan had been, firmly behind free trade. They harshly criticized Buchanan as an apostate to the true conservative cause.

Dole, the elder party statesman who had run for president twice before, was the clear favorite for the Republican nomination. Traditional conservatives were uncertain, but their hostility to Buchanan helped swing many of them behind Dole. Crucially, Jack Kemp had decided not to run, meaning the alternative to Dole around which conservatives might have coalesced wasn't available. The front-runner still faced a challenge from a true darling of conservatives, publisher Steve Forbes. But Forbes was seen as a kind of fringe figure, a one-note candidate who pushed the idea of a low, flat income tax.

Dole, who is nobody's fool, had tacked toward the Gingrich conservatives. He signed Grover Norquist's no-new-taxes pledge and crafted a tax-cut plan of his own. Perhaps most important, he ultimately picked Kemp to be his running mate. In so doing, he continued a pattern that would hold for decades: Republicans would nominate the leading establishment candidate whose turn had come, usually disappointing conservatives in the process. Then that establishment candidate would try to energize conservatives by picking a running mate they liked. George H. W. Bush did it with Dan Quayle, Bob Dole did it with Jack Kemp, and George W. Bush would do it with Dick Cheney, as would John McCain with Sarah Palin, and Mitt Romney with Paul Ryan. Even Donald Trump, unconventional as he was in every other way, fell in line by picking as his running mate Mike Pence, well regarded across the conservative movement. If conservatives never quite got the next coming of Ronald Reagan at the top of the ticket, they repeatedly settled for seeing his would-be heirs in the number-two spot.

Sadly for Dole, who had spent decades eyeing the White House, there was really no way for him to beat Clinton in 1996, even with conservative support. Clinton had planted his flag so firmly in the center of the political spectrum that he owned that territory. The economy was good, the country was at peace, and the incumbent in the race had made it appear he was the reasonable man in Washington when compared with those rabble-rousers on the right. Perot, who became the Reform Party candidate for the general election, remained on the warpath on trade, but Clinton's support for free-trade agreements was at that point a thoroughly bipartisan position. Indeed, in one telling picture, Clinton had held a ceremony at the White House to sign the NAFTA trade accords, and behind him as he did so was an array of past presidents from both parties: Jimmy Carter, Jerry Ford, George H. W. Bush. In 1996, Perot was the one who seemed on the fringe on free trade, and he faded as the election approached.

Dole was a "lifelong conservative" who nonetheless was hurt in the Republican primaries by the challenges from Forbes and the "Pitchfork Pat Buchanan brigade," says Scott Reed, who managed Dole's campaign. "Dole had the skills and the muscle to navigate and win the nomination, but the path took a toll on his general-election chances of victory."

Clinton won reelection easily. Republicans maintained control of the House, though with a smaller majority, and Gingrich remained Speaker. Still, both Clinton and Gingrich were headed for trouble, though neither quite realized just yet the full magnitude.

For his part, Gingrich continued in the second Clinton term to put a conservative imprint on national policy, sometimes working with the president, sometimes forcing his hand. The two sides came together on a formal plan to balance the budget, and Gingrich's troops pushed through a capital gains tax cut while trimming Medicare spending.

But beneath the surface, the conservative troops were starting to fume at Gingrich. They thought he was too willing to compromise with Clinton and hadn't pushed hard enough for more tax cuts. They considered the Speaker too imperious and unpredictable in his decision-making, and too attracted to the national spotlight at the expense of the daily work of Congress. In the House's back rooms, the same conservative firebrands who had cheered on Gingrich earlier began plotting his ouster in mid-1997. They were aided by some members of Gingrich's own leadership team. As Ronald Reagan could have testified, conservatives have a preternatural ability to form a circular firing squad and begin to shoot at one another. In 1997, that's what they began to do.

Worse for Gingrich, who had paved the road to the majority and his own speakership by stirring charges of ethical lapses by Democrats, he soon became enmeshed in an ethics scandal of his own. It centered on a series of college classes and town hall meetings he had hosted, paid for by donations to a tax-exempt group that allowed donors to get a tax write-off of their own. To critics, the setup looked like both a backdoor way for supporters to funnel undeclared political contributions to Gingrich and a tax-evasion scheme. Gingrich blamed the problem on a faulty explanation from his own lawyer, but the House Ethics Committee reprimanded him, and the full House followed suit.

Gingrich survived both the coup attempt and the ethics embarrassment. He even wrote a book about it all, entitled *Lessons Learned the Hard Way*. Still, he emerged from the fight damaged.

Clinton, meanwhile, was headed toward serious damage of his own. In January 1998, *The Washington Post* reported that special counsel Kenneth Starr, who was charged with looking into Bill and Hillary Clinton's financial dealings back home in Arkansas, had begun examining whether Clinton had encouraged a young White House intern named Monica Lewinsky to lie about having an affair with him. Clinton was being sued by an Arkansas woman, Paula Jones, for sexual harassment, and testimony of a young woman lured into an affair with Clinton would have been deeply harmful.

That disclosure set off a long and tortured investigation by Starr, during which Clinton admitted to giving misleading answers under oath about his relationship with Lewinsky when he was deposed in the Jones case. Clinton admitted as much in a speech to the nation in August 1998, with that year's midterm elections less than three months away. But Clinton denied he actually lied, and denied asking anybody else to lie. Within a month, Starr had released his report, which directly accused Clinton of lying under oath—essentially inviting Gingrich's House to impeach him.

Much as shutting down the government proved to be a trap for Gingrich, so did impeachment. Under his leadership, the House charged ahead with impeachment hearings, convinced that the picture of a president lying under oath and potentially suborning perjury from others and obstructing justice required action. To many of their countrymen, though, the impeachment quest seemed more about sexual immorality and Republicans' thirst to even scores politically with Clinton. The country was actually doing quite well. Clinton's womanizing was a problem voters had long since baked into their feelings about him, and impeachment seemed to many to be more a Washington game than some kind of constitutional imperative.

That was the backdrop for the 1998 midterm election. In the second midterm of a two-term president, the president's party usually loses ground as voters grow weary of the power structure—and one might have thought that would be especially true for a president in the midst of an impeachment process. Yet the opposite happened. Democrats gained five seats in the House and held even in the Senate—though it wasn't enough to take control of either chamber.

The results were seen as a rebuke to Gingrich, who responded by stepping aside, both as Speaker and as a member of the House, shortly after the election. He was done in as much by the mutiny among fellow conservatives as anything. Even Clinton, in his autobiography, asserted that conservatives had exhibited a striking lack of gratitude to Gingrich, given that "they were in power only because of his brilliant strategy in the 1994 election and his years of organizing and proselytizing before then."

With Gingrich on the way out, the House Republicans decided to proceed with impeaching Clinton, which they did shortly after the election, on a largely party-line vote. Then, utterly predictably, the Senate refused to convict Clinton. So the outcome of months of attacks on the president was that Clinton kept his job and Gingrich lost his. Ralph Reed, a longtime leader of the religious right and a fellow Georgian who had worked on Gingrich's campaigns, recalls visiting Gingrich not long afterward back in their home state. "I don't understand what happened," Reed recalls Gingrich saying. "Clinton lied under oath, and he's in office, and I'm down here."

Clinton wasn't just in office; he finished his term with job approval over 60 percent and for much of the next two decades would remain the most popular figure in the Democratic Party.

Gingrich himself is philosophical about how things collapsed so quickly around him. Among other things, he believes a deal he had made with Clinton would have paved the way for more progress. They had agreed privately that Clinton, in his 1998 State of the Union address, would propose reforming the politically explosive Medicare and Social Security programs, and that Gingrich then would support him. That would have carried the budget changes they had brought about forward. But the deal fell apart after the Monica Lewinsky story exploded.

Beyond that, Gingrich cites three additional problems. First, his Republican troops ran out of gas because they had exhausted their stockpile of "large ideas" in the trying quest to pass four consecutive balanced budgets. Second, and crucially, "we didn't have a Reagan" to lead the movement. "I wasn't a Reagan." And, third, "I burned people out. I pushed them so hard in so many different directions, we got so much done, they were just tired of it. They wanted an ability to relax."

On one level, it's a mistake to measure the Gingrich era solely by what happened in the nation's capital, even though that encompassed a lot of action in a short period of time. Those of us in Washington rarely appreciate the deep conservative roots that were sunk out around the country in those years. Those roots were grown in no small measure because of the work Gingrich did, with the help of powerful forces including Fox News, Rush Limbaugh, and the NRA, to build conservative majorities in state after state.

A few simple numbers tell the tale. In 1980, before Ronald Reagan arrived in Washington, Republicans had full control of fourteen state legislatures. By 1996, after the Gingrich revolution, that number had grown to twenty-five. By 2017 it had climbed to thirty-two. Similarly, the number of Republican governors in 1980 was twenty-four. By 1996 it had risen to thirty-one. And by 2017 the number had risen to thirty-three.

Together, those numbers spell Republican and conservative statehouse majorities at the grass roots, reversing years in which Democrats enjoyed similar dominance. That translated into state legislatures that drew congressional districts favorable to Republicans; to state legislatures that passed, and governors who signed, laws restricting abortion rights; and to state legislatures that passed, and governors who signed, bills cutting taxes and regulation. This legacy is at least as important as anything Newt Gingrich accomplished with the Contract with America and his tenure as House Speaker. The rise and reign of conservatives was a national phenomenon, not just a Washington one. Yet on another level, Gingrich had blown a golden opportunity for conservatives to consolidate their control in Washington, an opportunity that would never quite reappear.

Beyond that, the Gingrich period is important because conservatives—and everybody else, for that matter—also missed some warning signs of building populist ferment. One such warning sign, of course, was the sustained Buchanan/Perot attack on free trade. The second was antipathy toward immigration, which began in California. In 1994, just as Gingrich was leading to a conservative takeover of Congress, voters in California approved Proposition 187, a ballot initiative blocking illegal immigrants from receiving social services. The measure provided an early indication of the way illegal immigration could start tearing apart both the Republican Party and the conservative movement. California's Republican governor, Pete Wilson, championed Prop 187 in his successful reelection campaign that year, and carried it in the 1996 presidential campaign, when he entered that race. Ultimately, Prop 187 died in the courts, and Wilson's presidential bid died an early death as well.

In California, the ballot initiative's political effects were clear.

Prop 187 turned the state's significant bloc of Hispanic voters hard against Republicans, helping to morph California from a competitive state into a deeply Democratic one. Republicans have never recovered. Yet the initiative survived as a subject of debate long enough to deeply divide Republicans on the subject of immigration. In 1996, the party wrote a platform that supported Prop 187, while nominating for president a man lukewarm about it (Bob Dole) and for vice president another who flatly opposed it (Jack Kemp).

Classic conservatives and Reaganites were full-throated supporters of both free trade, as embodied by NAFTA in particular, and liberal immigration. Yet the trade and immigration debates were starting to open up. Conservatives ended the twentieth century not only in need of a new leader, but on the road toward some big divides.

CHAPTER 8

Conservatives Ride Again

Automakers have the Detroit Auto Show. Aircraft manufacturers have the Paris Air Show. And conservatives have the Conservative Political Action Conference.

CPAC, as it is universally known, is a kind of national trade show for those engaged in conservative politics in America. It's an annual gathering in the nation's capital that has grown steadily from a small and obscure event into a giant, multi-day extravaganza that fills a hall at the giant Gaylord National Resort and Convention Center, just outside Washington.

It isn't a place for the faint of heart. The CPAC roster of speakers tends to be peppered with hardcore, outspoken figures on the right who express their views in no uncertain terms. The audience is heavily populated by people who share those views and like that tone. Conservative radio hosts set up shop at the hotel where the gathering is held, and activists who like guns, hate abortion, and abhor taxes roam the hallways outside the convention hall proclaiming their messages.

Liberals are attacked roundly, as is the news media. The halls of CPAC were where the late Andrew Breitbart, founder of the conservative news site that bears his name, famously got into shouting matches with reporters. "Are you insane?" he yelled at one, on camera. Participants aren't shy about airing intramural disagreements, either. When former vice president Dick Cheney appeared after leaving office, he was applauded wildly after being introduced—and then met by shouts of "war criminal" from a libertarian in the crowd who was unhappy over the war in Iraq. "The usual spirited exercise," Cheney replied.

The young conservatives in attendance are famous for arguing hard during the day, then partying hard at night. "Some people do take a break from morals," a former head of CPAC once said.

For a long time, CPAC wasn't a particularly welcoming place for the Bush family. It drew the kinds of activists who never really considered George H. W. Bush part of their crowd. The feelings were mutual. In his four years as president, Bush never appeared at a CPAC gathering; in his stead, he sent Vice President Dan Quayle, a man significantly more comfortable with the conservative movement.

The CPAC gathering in 2000 was a different story, however, because now the assembled conservatives were thinking about a different Bush. George W. Bush was in his second term as governor of Texas, and he had emerged as the favorite to win the Republican nomination for president in that year's election. Unlike his father, George W. Bush got the benefit of the doubt from the CPAC universe.

He was more comfortable with movement conservatives, and knew better how to speak their language. After a young adulthood marked by at least some carousing and too much alcohol, he became a devout Christian. His opposition to abortion seemed, to pro-life supporters, far more genuine than his father's. All told, he looked and sounded more like a CPAC kind of guy.

Equally important, in the wake of Newt Gingrich's fall from grace—and from office—the conservative movement was desperate for a leader who could pick up the pieces, spin the conservative movement forward, and defeat Bill Clinton's vice president, Al Gore, in the 2000 election. "Republicans said, 'We gotta win,'" recalls Karl Rove, Bush's top political adviser. "And Bush was an acceptable conservative—he was the conservative governor. He got

all of his mother's friends and fans, and most of his dad's fundrais-
ers."

So when Bush spoke to CPAC by satellite hookup, his remarks
were a hit. He sounded all the right policy notes and got a laugh
when he said CPAC should, for this year, be renamed "See Bill
Clinton Pack." *Human Events,* a magazine beloved by the right, reported later that "Bush's speech was well received, with some attendees expressing the opinion that Bush's tone and demeanor
reminded them of Ronald Reagan." More to the political point,
Bush won a straw poll among CPAC attendees when they were
asked to name their top choice in that year's presidential election. A
year earlier, the choice had been Gary Bauer—a well-regarded figure on the religious right but hardly a household name.

The love affair wouldn't last. Bush didn't speak to CPAC again
until eight years later, during the last year of his presidency, when
his remarks seemed designed to burnish his legacy among disillusioned conservatives. A year after that, after Bush left office, some
nine thousand gathered at CPAC, and the mood was summarized
by the headline of a *Politico* story: "Bush a Four-Letter Word at
CPAC." The story explained, "If there's one thing those attending
the annual Conservative Political Action Conference this week
agree on, it is this: They don't want another George W. Bush. . . .
Indeed, for a president who publicly embraced conservative principles, there is little evidence that the movement returns the sentiment."

What happened in the intervening years? That tale is a story of
some meaningful achievements, followed by some bad luck, significant mistakes, and a dose of conservatives' seemingly endless ability
to see a glass as half full. Mostly, though, it is a story of how history
intervenes in ways nobody can anticipate.

To understand the George W. Bush era of the conservative
movement, it's necessary to start much earlier. Midland, Texas, is a
good starting point. That's the oil town in West Texas where
George W. spent his early years. He grew up there while his father
established himself in the oil business, and from there he began a

lifelong journey in which he would, at various and alternating times, admire his father, break away from his father, emulate his father, and seek to show that he was different from his father.

The elder George Bush had grown up in the leafy, wealthy suburbs of Greenwich, Connecticut. Culturally speaking, Midland is about as far from Greenwich as one can travel while still staying within the United States. The young George W. Bush went to Midland public schools, where he absorbed West Texas mannerisms, attitudes, and speech patterns—all attributes that would stick with him throughout his life. Unlike his father, he had not just a Texas address, but a Texas swagger that conservatives tended to like.

Before long, though, George W. Bush moved onto the same path his father had traveled. He followed him to the Phillips Academy prep school, in Andover, and to Yale University, got a business degree from Harvard University, and then returned to Midland to get into the oil business. Along the way—and, as critics would later charge, to avoid active-duty service in the Vietnam War—he became a pilot, as his father had, though he served in the Texas Air National Guard rather than on active duty. He married a lovely young Texas girl, Laura Welch. He ran for a House seat in the delegation from Texas, just as his father had, and lost, to Kent Hance, a conservative Democrat who later turned into a Republican. Over the years, he moved in and out of his father's political world, just as he moved between the worlds of West Texas and the eastern establishment.

Bush was, in short, a hard guy to pigeonhole, and, like his father, not one to lie down on the couch and allow himself to be psychoanalyzed. I know; I tried once. The first time I met George W. Bush was in 1987, when he had moved from Texas to Washington to help lead his father's then nascent campaign for president. The campaign was housed in a suite of offices, half of them still empty, in a building not far from the White House. Bush was, as he always would be, outgoing, personable, and approachable. As Rove observes, "He was the guy who you'd look at over the back fence, and he'd be barbecuing and invite you over for a beer."

When I walked in for my appointment with Bush, I found him seated in his small office, leaning back on his chair, his cowboy boots propped up on the desk. It was an easy conversation. At one point, trying to draw him out a bit more, I observed that he seemed to have spent a lot of his life following in his father's footsteps: Andover, Yale, military pilot, oil entrepreneur in Texas. I wondered whether that was a conscious choice, and what it meant. Bush looked back at me with a blank expression and replied, *It's funny, but I never thought about it that way.* He seemed to mean it. I saw in that initial encounter what I always felt I saw in the younger Bush: an instantly likable man with a quick mind and an air of self-assurance. He was edgier than his father, but a bit more wary of a national press corps that his family felt hadn't been entirely kind to the senior Bush.

After his father was elected president, George W. Bush returned to Texas as a part owner and operating partner of the Texas Rangers baseball club. He was perfectly positioned to run for governor of Texas—to catch the rise of Republicans there and the rapid decline of Democrats. In 1994, he beat Democratic incumbent governor Ann Richards, a fiery politician who had famously insulted both the Bush father and son.

As governor, Bush was determined to be a new kind of conservative, in hopes of redefining the movement for the Republican Party nationwide. He pushed what amounted to a conservative reform agenda: welfare reform, education reform, juvenile-justice reform, and tort reform. The first three of those initiatives were designed to show that government activism could be combined with the conservative principles of individual responsibility and freedom of choice to improve people's lives—even those on the lower rungs of the socioeconomic ladder.

It was a tough-love approach. If a poor single mother was in poverty, the government wouldn't ignore the problem—but it wouldn't just provide a handout, either. Instead, the Bush approach moved more of the tasks of providing help and training over to private contractors and religious organizations, on the theory they would do the job more efficiently and effectively than would government agencies. If a minority child was getting a rotten education, the state would neither walk away nor just throw money at the bad school; rather, it would provide an alternative by paving the way for the opening of independent charter schools outside the traditional system. If a teen got into trouble, Bush's reforms made the penalties harsher, as a way to scare juveniles away from the corrections system.

In the terminology of Bush and his advisers and supporters, it added up to a new "compassionate conservative" agenda, one that showed that conservatives were worried about more than delivering tax cuts and deregulation for the prosperous. "The language was a different kind of language than Republicans normally deployed," Rove says. "Suddenly they had somebody who made them feel better about themselves, inspired them to believe, 'Yes, our conservative values will make life better for every single American, not just comfortable white couples in the suburbs.'"

Not everybody was pleased, of course. Liberals didn't see all that much compassion in a system that was as tough on juvenile offenders as Bush's was, or that laid work requirements on single welfare moms. And some conservatives grumbled that by declaring a new era of "compassionate conservatism," Bush was not-so-implicitly saying that other conservatives had been uncompassionate. They saw compassionate conservativism as a fancy way of caving in to liberal demands for government activism.

Still, it worked politically in Texas. In fact, Bush had a big wave of momentum behind him as he rode into a reelection campaign in 1998. He also turned out to be a good retail politician. During that campaign, I once rode with him to an event at a town in West Texas. Before the proceedings began, a local resident walked up to Bush and said, "You probably don't remember me, but we met when you campaigned here before." Bush not only remembered the man; he remembered his wife's name and how many children he had, and he inquired about them.

For Republicans, there was one other piece to the Bush proposition—one that looks especially ironic in the rearview mirror. He thought the health of the party in the long run rested in part on improving its standing among the nation's mushrooming population of Hispanics, and that getting right on that front meant, among other things, adopting a posture that seemed less hostile to immigrants.

Bush argued that Hispanics tend to be socially conservative and, as such, should be a natural audience for Republicans. He pursued them hard. The first appointment he made as governor was Tony Garza, a grandson of Mexican immigrants, as secretary of state. Bush opposed California's Proposition 187 and sometimes spoke in Spanish when addressing Hispanic voters. In return, he won a far larger share of the Hispanic vote than most Republicans did nationally. The figures are debated, but Bush probably won more than a third of the Hispanic vote in his first run for governor, and then half of it in his reelection bid.

All that helped Bush ride to a landslide thirty-point reelection victory in 1998, and the stage was nearly set for him to run for president carrying the conservative banner. Only one piece was needed to complete his résumé: a giant tax cut. If George W. Bush was going to prove himself to conservatives, that step probably was essential; after all, he had to exorcise the ghosts of his father's famous and fateful decision to reverse the "no new taxes" pledge.

In his first term as governor, Bush had pushed for a $4 billion cut in property taxes and gotten only a piece of what he wanted out of the state legislature. Undeterred, he tried again at the outset of his second term, proposing a $2 billion property tax cut as part of a complex tax package. In truth, a governor isn't particularly powerful in the Texas governmental system, so Bush had to mostly nudge and cajole as the state legislature sliced and diced his proposal. In the end, he didn't get the full tax cut he sought, but he got to sign a big one nonetheless.

So George W. Bush sailed into the 2000 presidential campaign as both the Republican establishment's choice and a candidate with plenty of backing among conservatives. He wasn't necessarily their favorite; for many, that would have been Steve Forbes or, more so, Jack Kemp. But Kemp had decided not to run and bestowed his endorsement on Bush. Bush benefited among conservatives simply by not being Senator John McCain, the media darling of that year's campaign, who was an iconoclast in policy terms and scathing in his criticism of the religious right.

After winning the nomination, Bush further endeared himself to conservatives by picking Dick Cheney as his running mate. Cheney, a Gingrich sidekick from the House and the defense secretary in the cabinet of Bush's father, was seen as having helped guide the United States to victory in the first Persian Gulf War. George W. Bush was, as a result, very familiar and comfortable with Cheney, and initially put him in charge of finding a vice presidential choice for him. In the end, Bush decided Cheney shouldn't help pick a running mate; he should *be* the running mate. Cheney was thoroughly acceptable on the right.

The general election was an uphill struggle. The country was at peace and prosperous at the end of the Clinton presidency, so turning the reins over to his vice president, Al Gore, seemed a logical choice. And besides, the wounds of the Gingrich period had left people doubting that conservatives could govern effectively.

Yet Clinton's scandals had left plenty of scars too, and Gore couldn't seem to decide whether to embrace the Clinton record or distance himself from it. Bush and Gore fought that 2000 political campaign to a virtual draw. The election came down to a contested count in Florida, which the Supreme Court eventually threw Bush's way. Gore had won the popular vote, but Bush had won in the Electoral College. The White House moved back to the Republicans.

In retrospect, what really propelled Bush toward victory was all the work conservatives had done for years at the grass roots, turning large swaths of the country, particularly in the South, to the political right. Just four years earlier, Clinton had won Kentucky, Tennessee, Arkansas, Louisiana, and Florida. Gore, though himself a son of the South, didn't win any of those states, even his own home state of Tennessee. In the narrowest sense, the election was decided by the recount in Florida and the U.S. Supreme Court decision that tipped Florida's Electoral College votes to Bush. But in a broader sense, the outcome was determined by the long-building conservative wave across the South.

That conservative wave was pushed along by some big new sources of political funding that had entered the scene just as Bush was rising to the top of the Republican Party. In particular, a pair of brothers who lived up Interstate 35 from Texas—Charles and David Koch of Wichita, Kansas—were in the process of becoming mega-donors to Republican and conservative causes. The Koch brothers ran a giant petrochemical and industrial firm that bore their name, and they were known over the years more for guarding their privacy than for playing a high-profile political role.

Yet they had strong views, particularly about the evils of government regulation, which had caused them headaches in their own business, and over time they decided to do something about it by trying to influence the political process. In truth, the Koch brothers were more libertarian than conservative—believers that better government almost always means less government. That meant they didn't always agree with Republicans—particularly on social issues, where their libertarian instincts were more hands-off—but by the 1990s they had decided their business interests and personal beliefs compelled them to get involved on behalf of the GOP.

As a result, millions of dollars flowed toward Republicans and conservative causes. Between 1989 and 2010, the Koch Industries Inc. Political Action Committee donated almost $6 million to federal political causes, 83 percent of it to Republicans. And the Koch brothers as individuals gave another $2.58 million to Republican campaign committees. Millions more would come in the years ahead.

So George W. Bush had some conservative winds at his back as he followed his father's footsteps into the White House. On the other end of Pennsylvania Avenue, Republicans had maintained control of the House, and the Senate was evenly divided between the two parties. Against that backdrop, Bush set out to make "compassionate conservative" more than a catchphrase or intellectual notion.

The opening phases of that effort were quite successful. In fact, the Bush administration moved methodically down a kind of compassionate-conservative checklist. The new president chose to start at a spot where small-government conservatives and religious conservatives intersected. In his first two presidential executive orders, he established a White House Office of Faith-Based and Community Initiatives, as well as similar offices in five cabinet agencies.

These offices were charged to connect the federal government with religious organizations around the country so Washington could help them set up programs to provide social services. The idea was that faith-based groups were better at helping people on the ground; they just needed an administration that would clear away the legal barriers that stopped them from receiving government grants to do the job. "When we see social needs in America, my administration will look first to faith-based programs and community groups, which have proven their power to save and change lives," Bush declared in a speech just days after taking office.

The second item on the Bush compassionate-conservative checklist was education reform. That came in the form of a "No Child Left Behind" education package. In a nutshell, No Child Left Behind dangled federal funds before state and local school systems but in return required them to set standards in math and reading, create annual assessments to measure how students were meeting those standards, and report the findings publicly and in detail. If states or local school districts wanted to create alternatives to the traditional public school system, they could get federal grants to set up charter schools. On the other hand, states with schools that weren't performing could lose federal funds. In short, No Child Left Behind used federal funds as both carrot and stick, and embedded the federal government more deeply into the business of local education. Though not everybody on the right agreed, Bush considered it a conservative plan, because it still left decisions on how to meet the new standards to local leaders.

The third item on the new agenda was an even bigger departure from the conservative norm. It was an expansion of the Medicare health program for the elderly—and a significant expansion at that. Late in his presidency, Bill Clinton had begun trying to add a prescription-drug benefit to the standard Medicare coverage of costs for doctors and hospital visits. This was no small idea; it represented the biggest expansion of Medicare since its creation. Bush, the newly minted Republican president, decided to take the baton from his Democratic predecessor and carry it forward.

The irony was significant. A conservative Republican president, working with a Republican House and—after the 2002 midterms—a Republican Senate, would drive through a significant expansion of the Medicare program that Ronald Reagan had once decried as socialized medicine. There may have been no clearer sign that, while Republicans continued to sing odes to the Reagan Revolution, the revolutionary precepts had evolved. Still, considering the way healthcare had evolved, most everybody agreed that Medicare Part D was necessary. Certainly it was popular. It also was successful: The costs of the program actually turned out to be less over time than many had forecast.

Some conservatives still considered the compassionate-conservative agenda basically big-government growth in a conservative disguise. That analysis seems unfair and shortsighted in light of later self-critiques among some conservatives, who came to believe that their movement lost some of its power and appeal because it failed to adequately connect conservative policies with real-world problems for average Americans. Compassionate conservatism was, at its base, an attempt to do exactly that. Still, there was grumbling, and some opposition among true believers. A rising young conservative star in the House named Mike Pence, of Indiana, voted against both No Child Left Behind and the creation of Medicare Part D, for example.

But Bush's fourth big initial proposal was one that no conservative disagreed with: a giant tax cut. The new president didn't mess around on this front. Three weeks after taking office, he sent off to Congress his proposal: a blueprint for a $1.6 trillion, ten-year tax cut. It was the most ambitious tax proposal since Reagan's big tax cut, exactly twenty years earlier. The Bush plan would cut tax rates, which had crept up since Reagan's time, by reducing the lowest rate to 10 percent and the highest to 33 percent. The "marriage penalty" in the tax code, under which married couples paid more in taxes than they would if they were single, would be eliminated. So would the estate tax, over time. The tax credit families got for each child would go up.

Bush had campaigned on such a tax proposal, so he could claim a mandate for it. And the political landscape was favorable. Republicans controlled the House and, effectively, the Senate. Though the Senate was evenly divided between the two parties, fifty to fifty, the vice president could cast the deciding vote in a tie—giving the president control there, too. Perhaps more important, the federal budget actually was continuing to run a surplus, so a tax cut was harder to portray as fiscally irresponsible. Bush made the simple argument that a federal surplus should be returned to taxpayers, and his plan was designed to do exactly that.

On top of that, the conservative machinery that had been built so steadily around the country since Ronald Reagan's inauguration kicked into gear to support the tax cut. Grover Norquist's Americans for Tax Reform organization ignited efforts at the state level to support a federal tax cut, and by April, eleven state legislatures had passed pro-tax-cut resolutions. A coalition of 790 business organizations and conservative groups from around the country began meeting to push Bush's initiative. They ranged in size from the giant American Bankers Association to the Catoosa, Oklahoma, Chamber of Commerce. One of the targets of this grassroots pressure was a conservative Democrat, Max Cleland of Georgia. The effort worked; in the end, Cleland was one of twelve Senate Democrats who supported the plan. The tax-cut campaign was the practical result of years of grassroots conservative labors.

With that momentum behind it, the plan moved briskly through Congress. It didn't emerge entirely unscathed. The total tax cut, in the end, came to $1.35 trillion rather than the requested $1.6 trillion. The top tax rate was reduced from 39.6 percent to 35 percent, not to 33 percent, as Bush had requested. The estate tax would go away for a while, but then, in a nod to fiscal responsibility, it was to return.

Still, it was a big tax cut, by anybody's reckoning. Beneath the surface, both parties were a little nervous that, because of a gimmick to make the package palatable under congressional budget rules, the tax cuts were to last for ten years and then go away. Republicans worried they hadn't made some of the reductions permanent. Democrats wondered whether Congress really would have the guts, in a decade's time, to bounce back to the old, higher rates, which would look like a giant tax increase. Republicans also were uneasy about getting their big tax cut passed only in the nick of time, just before Vermont senator Jim Jeffords switched parties to become a Democrat and cost them control of the Senate.

But none of that seemed to eclipse the happy smiles in the White House East Room on June 7, 2001, when Bush signed the tax cut into law. In his remarks, he invoked the godfather of tax cuts, Ronald Reagan, noting that this was the first across-the-board tax cut since the one the Gipper had engineered. And Bush, as was always his wont, invoked his compassionate-conservative brand as well: "Tax relief is compassionate, and it is now on the way." The Bush 2001 tax cut wasn't just a big deal at the time it happened; it also provided the template for the big tax cut President Donald Trump and a Republican Congress would pass sixteen years later.

Something else of deep, long-term significance unfolded early in the Bush term, though it got considerably less attention. At the end of 2001, after fifteen years of negotiation, and with the enthusiastic endorsement of the U.S. government, China was formally admitted to the World Trade Organization. This amounted to giving the Communist giant a ticket into the club of world capitalism. Bush punched that ticket immediately thereafter when he signed a congressional proclamation granting China permanent normal trade status with the United States. Together, those steps gave China access to first-world markets on a par with other developing countries (which China was considered at the time). In return, the understanding was that China would begin to dismantle the state controls and subsidies that dominated its economy and let a free-market system take over.

In Washington, the move was thoroughly bipartisan; indeed, during the 2000 presidential campaign, Bush had singled out his support for normalizing trade relations with China as an area in which he agreed with the Democrats in the Clinton administration. To the extent the move was controversial, it was only because critics thought China should have to do more to improve its human rights practices before being granted such an economic prize. Economically, almost everybody assumed that letting China into the free enterprise club would inevitably lead it to play more like the club's other members, economically and politically.

In reality, as the years unfurled, China didn't do nearly as much as was expected to turn its economy over to private enterprise and free markets. The state continued to play a heavy role, steering help and advantages to its own firms as they moved out to compete in the world market. In short, China played far less fair than was expected. In 2001, when the Asian giant joined the WTO, the United States had a trade deficit with China of $83 billion. By 2016 it had ballooned to $350 billion. A ticking time bomb was planted, one that would be exploded down the line by Donald Trump.

Bush punched some other buttons that pleased conservatives. For example, he curbed federal support for research using stem cells extracted from human embryos, a top priority for anti-abortion forces. Whatever their misgivings about other parts of the Bush vision, conservatives were thrilled. There is no more conservative fiscal idea than a big tax cut, and no social issue more important to conservatives than abortion, and the new president had made a priority of both and taken action—fast. "George W. Bush was a rock star among the conservative right for most of the first term," says Pete Wehner, a political adviser and speechwriter in the Bush White House.

"And," he adds, "that changed in the second term."

CHAPTER 9

The High Price of Terror

September 11, 2001, dawned bright and crystal clear in Washington—not just a beautiful day but a spectacular one, the kind that makes it worth having endured the miserably hot and humid preceding month of August in the nation's capital.

Pete Wehner went to work that morning at the White House, as he had done since the outset of the still young Bush administration. Wehner was a veteran of the Reagan and first Bush administrations, and now was the deputy speechwriter to George W. Bush. On that morning, as it happened, Wehner attended the 7:30 A.M. senior staff meeting, the daily gathering of the president's top aides. Normally that seat was filled by Mike Gerson, the president's chief speechwriter, but on September 11 Gerson had figured it was a safe day to stay at home and work on a big upcoming speech.

Wehner was an intellectual, and very much on board with the idea that George W. Bush could modernize the notion of what it meant to be a conservative in the twenty-first century. Wehner was born in Texas but had moved to Washington State when he was six years old. As he grew up there, he came to realize he was more instinctively conservative than many of his compatriots. In a grade school debate, he spoke in favor of Richard Nixon's bid for reelection in 1972.

Yet he also was enraptured by the idealism and soaring rhetoric of John and Bobby Kennedy, and spent time in the university library listening to their speeches. He was taken with their talk of the common good, social concerns, and compassion for one's fellow man. In those college years, Wehner also grew increasingly religious.

All those impulses would combine in his political career. He worked for a time in the Washington State legislature, then moved to that other Washington—D.C.—to work for a conservative think tank and at the State Department. Thanks to an article Wehner wrote for *The Washington Post,* he caught the eye of a man who would be a kind of mentor and guide, the conservative social thinker William Bennett. The two came together in one of those odd ways in which alliances are born in Washington, when personal and political lives intersect. Bennett invited Wehner to join his touch football team. On one game day, when their squad was playing a team that included several former pro football players, Wehner went up for a pass against some bulky defenders, got knocked to the ground, and came up with a bloody lip. If the guy was that tough, Bennett decided, he was worth hiring.

Wehner worked for Bennett at the Department of Education in the first Bush administration and, after that, at Empower America, a think tank Bennett launched with Jack Kemp to advance conservative ideas and the belief that conservative social policies could help minorities and the poor as much as the wealthy. That was the gospel that Kemp preached fervently. Wehner embraced it.

Wehner worked alongside Gerson at Empower America, and they grew close. Then they went to the Bush White House as a kind of team, two like-minded young conservatives moving in unison to put into words Bush's belief that the Reagan Revolution should be renewed but updated. As it happened, the speech Gerson had stayed home to write on September 11 was on a new conservative idea for which he and Wehner had high hopes. The theme was to be "Communities of Character," a notion foreshadowed in a line in Bush's inaugural speech, in which he called on "responsible citizens" to build "communities of service and a nation of character." The idea was that Americans shouldn't rely on the federal government to improve the lives in their towns, cities, and communities, but should band together more, in good faith and with the best of intentions, to improve life for one another. The role of government, in this vision of conservatism, was to *inspire* more than to *do*.

As the senior staff meeting broke up that morning, Wehner sent an email to Gerson summarizing the session. "Very little of note happened," he wrote. The president was out of town. The biggest news at the White House was the plan to host a barbecue that night on the South Lawn for members of Congress. It was a good day for Gerson to get some work done on that speech.

The speech would never be given. Five minutes after Wehner sent the message, an airliner that had been hijacked by al-Qaeda terrorists flew into the North Tower of the World Trade Center. Seventeen minutes later, a second airliner flew into the South Tower. Thirty-four minutes after that, an airliner flew into the Pentagon. And roughly half an hour after that, an airliner that had been hijacked by terrorists crashed in Pennsylvania.

In a little over an hour's time, everything had changed. At the time of the attacks, President Bush was visiting an elementary school in Florida, in pursuit of not just his education-reform initiative but the idea that his would be a presidency focused on the home front. From that morning until the moment he left the White House after two terms, his administration had a new and different focus. Domestic initiatives would take a back seat to fighting terrorism and evildoers abroad. Spending would go up, because the war on terror would be mightily expensive. The government would grow, not shrink, because governments have to grow new appendages to fight wars, particularly long wars.

The first big change was a shift of power inside the Bush administration: Power moved to the neoconservative national security thinkers. A generation earlier, Reagan had brought traditional conservatives, driven mostly by their belief in a small government and a modest view of executive power, together with the neoconservatives just coming into prominence. In those days, the two camps could easily agree on the need for an aggressive approach to a common enemy, the Soviet Union. Now the Soviets were gone, and on 9/11 a new enemy, radical Islam, had appeared. The neocons didn't merely move from the back seat to the front seat of the conservative world; they would shortly take over the steering wheel, and would have it in their grip for the remainder of Bush's two terms.

That meant Vice President Dick Cheney and Defense Secretary Donald Rumsfeld were the new power centers. Just as important, two of Rumsfeld's underlings at the Pentagon, Paul Wolfowitz and Douglas Feith, also took on newfound prominence.

The Bush team's first challenge after the 9/11 attacks was to go after those who were immediately responsible: Osama bin Laden, the leader of the al-Qaeda terrorist group, and the Taliban leaders of Afghanistan, who had given him and the organization safe refuge. That mission was obvious, and there was a national consensus that it needed to be done. U.S. Special Forces led the way into Afghanistan shortly after 9/11, and by the end of 2001 American forces had chased bin Laden out of Afghanistan, disrupted al-Qaeda's operations there, and taken control of the country away from the Taliban.

The neoconservatives then shifted their sights to another, far bigger target: Iraqi leader Saddam Hussein. "The overthrow of the Taliban had come almost too quickly and too easily," wrote veteran American diplomat William Burns in his memoir. "For 'neoconservatives' like Deputy Secretary Paul Wolfowitz and Undersecretary Doug Feith at the Pentagon, Saddam's forcible ouster was not just a message, it was an opportunity to create a democratic model in Iraq, begin the transformation of the whole region, and reassert American hegemony after a post–Cold War decade of naïve attachment to the promise of a peace dividend." The Bush administration, in short, set out to begin doing exactly what the president had said in his campaign he wasn't interested in and what many other conservatives would have preferred to avoid. The Bush administration began engaging in nation-building abroad.

Actually, it was nation-building on an epic scale, and done badly to boot. It started with the attempt to remake Afghanistan, but it kicked into overdrive with the 2003 invasion of Iraq to topple Saddam Hussein. Middle East professionals in the government warned repeatedly that overthrowing Saddam, while feasible as a military matter, would produce a giant mess the United States would then own. Iraq has a complex society divided among Sunni Muslims, Shiite Muslims, and Kurds, which had been held together not because of any natural cohesion but by Saddam's brute force. Break up the regime and Iraq itself would explode into feuding parts. In a memo that became known internally as the "Perfect Storm" memo, senior State Department professionals, including Burns, warned of civil unrest, looting, collapsing institutions, and meddling by Iraq's neighbors—all of which would come true.

Yet *The Weekly Standard,* which had become the bible for neoconservatives, pushed hard for an invasion of Iraq, as did others on the neocon right. Neocons inside the government ignored or belittled the advice of actual Middle East experts who knew something important: Saddam Hussein was such a control freak that the idea he'd let terrorist groups run free within his country to plot trouble for the United States was a stretch.

In fact, Saddam ran a police state. I traveled there periodically while based in the Middle East in the 1980s, and Saddam's heavy hand was everywhere. Because Saddam had begun his rise to power as a political pamphleteer, he kept an iron grip on communications. Computers were suspect devices, and even a typewriter was considered a potential tool for subversives. I carried one in on a reporting trip, only to have it taken from my hands by a security guard upon exiting my airplane; it was tossed into a bin with other communications devices that had been seized. On that trip, I interviewed a businessman who had hired a guard to keep watch on his office photocopier twenty-four hours a day, lest he be accused of allowing it to be used for reproducing dissident materials. The idea that Saddam would allow extremists to run free as the Taliban leaders had in Afghanistan was simply implausible.

War advocates hit harder on the idea that Saddam Hussein was pursuing a broad program to build chemical, biological, and nuclear weapons. They began building a dossier of evidence to support that charge, almost all of which ultimately would be discredited by facts on the ground.

Cheney gave speeches pushing for the overthrow of Saddam. He downplayed the need for any formal international endorsement of American action. At one meeting of top administration aides, he declared, "The only legitimacy we really need comes on the back of an M1A1 tank."

The United Nations Security Council, under heavy American pressure, authorized action anyway, and Bush ordered an invasion of Iraq to oust Saddam Hussein. That operation itself went smoothly and quickly, proving again that the American military is better at what it does than anybody in the world. By contrast, the neoconservatives' dream of remaking Iraq into a democracy—and, crucially from their point of view, one less hostile to America's friends in Israel—turned into a nightmare almost immediately.

In part because of the Iraq conflict, Bush managed to push through a second round of tax cuts, which were sold in part as a way to ease any damage to the economy from aftershocks of the 9/11 attacks. This $350 billion package of tax cuts was designed to complement the 2001 tax cuts by focusing on reducing taxes for business and investment. Taxes on capital gains and dividends were lowered. The phase-in of some of the tax cuts in the 2001 package was accelerated. By encouraging businesses to invest more capital, and by putting a bit more money into the pockets of consumers a bit faster, Bush's aides argued, the package would both speed recovery from a relatively mild recession and smooth out any terror bumps in the economy.

Meantime, some other conservative initiatives continued to cross the finish line. In 2003, Bush signed legislation banning late-term abortions, fueling the belief that he was more of a believer in curbing abortions than even Reagan was.

As the shock waves from Iraq played out, the nation paused in the summer of 2004 for another reason: Ronald Reagan died, quietly, in California. His public voice had long been silenced by his dementia, but his presence was never far from public life. "Ronald Reagan's moment arrived in 1980," President George W. Bush said in a eulogy delivered in Washington's National Cathedral. "What followed was one of the decisive decades of the century, as the convictions that shaped the president began to shape the times." Yet it wasn't just Reagan's beliefs or convictions that led Americans to remember him fondly at his passing; it was as much the humane way in which he conveyed those beliefs, with a touch others who followed his value system often failed to emulate. Bush recounted the story of a boy who once wrote Reagan a letter seeking federal assistance to clean up his bedroom. "Unfortunately, funds are dangerously low," Reagan wrote back. "I'm sure your mother was fully justified in proclaiming your room a disaster. Therefore, you are in an excellent position to launch another volunteer program in our nation."

Reagan died just as the ties that held together his movement were fraying. Bush won reelection over Senator John Kerry in 2004, but only narrowly. Though it seemed only a footnote at the time, Bush's reelection success leaned heavily on the growing bloc of Republican populist voters. Bush couldn't claim victory until it was clear he had won the crucial swing state of Ohio, by the narrowest of margins—so narrow, in fact, that there was a recount. And Bush won Ohio only because of a big turnout in conservative, rural districts, driven in part by religious conservatives' support for a ballot measure designed to block gay marriages. Those decisive Republican voters "were nothing but Trump voters," says Steve Bannon, Trump's own political strategist. "In 2004, the inkling was, you could not win unless you really mobilized those working-class voters."

In Bush's second term, the Iraq misadventure would do much broader damage to the conservative cause, and to the Republican Party. First, the war in Iraq truncated the Bush compassionate-conservative agenda and distracted attention from the considerable

Barry Goldwater's 1964 campaign gave Ronald Reagan a national stage for his emerging conservative message; here he speaks for Goldwater's campaign at the International Hotel in Los Angeles. COURTESY OF THE REAGAN PRESIDENTIAL LIBRARY

Ronald Reagan opened his 1980 general-election campaign with a speech extolling the virtues of immigration from New Jersey's Liberty State Park, with the Statue of Liberty in the background, on September 1, 1980. COURTESY OF THE REAGAN PRESIDENTIAL LIBRARY

President Ronald Reagan speaking at an ecumenical prayer breakfast at the Reunion Arena in Dallas in August 1984. Four Augusts earlier, Reagan's appearance at an evangelical gathering in the same arena marked the marriage of the conservative and evangelical movements. COURTESY OF THE REAGAN PRESIDENTIAL LIBRARY

The changing of the guard: Now–former president Ronald Reagan and Nancy Reagan are escorted away from the Capitol by the newly sworn-in president, George H. W. Bush, and Barbara Bush, January 20, 1989.

The bookends of a forty-year conservative story: President Ronald Reagan talking with Donald Trump and Ivana Trump at a state dinner for King Fahd of Saudi Arabia in the White House, 1985.

A young Grover Norquist meets his hero, President Ronald Reagan. Norquist was part of a small army of Reagan followers who created a conservative infrastructure in Washington. WHITE HOUSE PHOTO COURTESY OF GROVER NORQUIST

President George H. W. Bush, with General Norman Schwarzkopf, visits troops in Saudi Arabia in November 1990 before launching the first Gulf War. COURTESY OF THE GEORGE H. W. BUSH PRESIDENTIAL LIBRARY

President George H. W. Bush pitches horseshoes at Camp David with Soviet leader Mikhail Gorbachev in 1990. The end of the Cold War made the world safer but robbed the conservative movement of some of the glue that held it together. COURTESY OF THE GEORGE H. W. BUSH PRESIDENTIAL LIBRARY

Ross Perot, here at an October 1992 presidential debate with President George H. W. Bush and Democratic candidate Bill Clinton, carried populist messages into the political mainstream—and may have robbed Bush of a second term in doing so. COURTESY OF THE GEORGE H. W. BUSH PRESIDENTIAL LIBRARY

When support for free trade was mainstream and bipartisan: President Bill Clinton at the White House in 1993 with former presidents Jimmy Carter, George H. W. Bush, and Gerald Ford when all appeared at an event to back the North American Free Trade Agreement. COURTESY OF THE CLINTON PRESIDENTIAL LIBRARY

House Speaker Newt Gingrich and President Bill Clinton at either end of a conference table aboard a flight to Israel for the November 1995 funeral of slain prime minister Yitzhak Rabin. Gingrich's belief that he was treated badly on the trip helped produce a budget fight and a fateful government shutdown. COURTESY OF THE CLINTON PRESIDENTIAL LIBRARY

House Speaker Newt Gingrich listens as President Bill Clinton delivers his State of the Union address on January 27, 1998. By year's end, Gingrich would be leading the fight to impeach Clinton. COURTESY OF THE CLINTON PRESIDENTIAL LIBRARY

President George W. Bush at Ground Zero, the site of the 9/11 terror attack in New York, which changed the course of his presidency and the conservative movement. COURTESY OF THE GEORGE W. BUSH PRESIDENTIAL LIBRARY

President George W. Bush presides over a meeting with congressional leaders on the burgeoning financial crisis, September 25, 2008. At the far end of the table is then–Democratic presidential nominee Barack Obama, and at the near end is then–Republican presidential nominee John McCain, whose uncertain response at the meeting was seen as harmful to his campaign. PRESIDENTIAL MATERIALS DIVISION, NATIONAL ARCHIVES AND RECORDS ADMINISTRATION

President George W. Bush, after addressing the annual Conservative Political Action Conference in February 2008, alongside David Keene, chairman of the American Conservative Union. COURTESY OF THE GEORGE W. BUSH PRESIDENTIAL LIBRARY

Senator Ted Cruz with the giant painting of President Ronald Reagan that adorns a wall of his Senate office.
MELISSA GOLDEN/REDUX

Democratic president Barack Obama talks with House Republican whip Eric Cantor at the White House in November 2010, just after Republicans won control of the House. The two had a testy relationship. COURTESY OF THE BARACK OBAMA PRESIDENTIAL LIBRARY

Jenny Beth Martin, co-founder of the Tea Party Patriots, speaking at a rally on Capitol Hill in September 2015.
AP PHOTO/CAROLYN KASTER

Republican presidential nominee Donald Trump with his running mate, Governor Mike Pence, at the 2016 Republican National Convention in Cleveland.
AP PHOTO/MARK J. TERRILL

President Donald Trump shakes hands with radio personality Rush Limbaugh at the Turning Point USA Student Action Summit in West Palm Beach, Florida, in 2019. AP PHOTO/ANDREW HARNIK

achievements of his first term. "It drowned out everything else," Rove says simply. "The president has a gigantic megaphone, but there's only so much space in that megaphone for messaging, and so much of it was focused on the war."

In particular, the war got in the way of one Bush dream that would have been the fulfillment of generations of conservative yearning: He set out to reform the Social Security system. He wanted to allow Americans to put their retirement savings into private accounts instead of directing their retirement payroll deductions into the government-run system. The very idea sent liberals into paroxysms. They considered Social Security the crowning achievement of their party's patron saint, Franklin Roosevelt, and considered Bush's idea a step toward privatizing the crown jewel of government activism. For the same reason, conservatives loved the idea.

Yet, try as he might throughout 2005, Bush couldn't find the political equation to pass the changes. He might get a few votes from Democrats for tax cuts, but there wasn't much hope of that on a change to Social Security. Meanwhile, Republicans were simply scared. Voters of both parties loved Social Security, and seeming to mess with Grandma's retirement safety net was a tricky business in anybody's district or state. They also worried that diverting away from the government trillions of dollars in future tax payments would make the federal books look even worse than they already did. They also simply weren't convinced that Bush, his popularity slipping because of Iraq, had the political stroke any longer to sell the program. So they demurred. The principal domestic initiative of the second Bush term died and, along with it, so did a long-held conservative dream.

Meantime, the terror attacks and the subsequent fear of a repeat undercut the traditional conservative belief in both small government and the primacy of personal liberty. In the wake of the terror attacks, the Bush administration proposed, and Congress created, the Department of Homeland Security, a giant cabinet agency that drew together a whole smorgasbord of government agencies that were involved, in one way or another, with protecting Americans where they live.

To say the new DHS is sprawling is like saying Texas is large: It's true but insufficient. This new agency ultimately would be put in charge of, among other things, protecting the country's borders, enforcing its immigration and customs laws, guarding its computer networks, checking those coming and going in airports, protecting election systems, thwarting the flow of illegal drugs, and even responding to natural disasters. All these tasks were being performed somewhere in the government, but overseeing them all was such a large job that there was no building big enough to house the new cabinet agency. So the Bush administration cleared out a thirty-eight-acre former naval facility in Northwest Washington to house the department.

Similarly, the administration sought, and Congress passed, the Patriot Act, a sweeping law that granted the government broader use of surveillance and wiretapping, loosened restrictions on search warrants, and opened more financial records to government perusal. Just as the creation of a giant new federal agency cut against traditional conservative instincts, so too did the Patriot Act and its erosion of at least some civil liberties. But the country was on a war footing, and much as Franklin Roosevelt had to shift from social engineer to wartime commander in the 1940s, so too did Bush.

The 9/11 attacks eroded the conservative ideals of George W. Bush in another way: The fear of outsiders that naturally follows a terror attack had begun to feed a growing anti-immigrant sentiment. For Bush, the former governor of a border state who held a Reagan-like view about the value of immigration to America, this was a distressing development. It cut against not only his personal belief that the United States should welcome immigration, but also his political analysis that Republicans were doomed to failure unless they did more to appeal to Hispanic voters.

Anyone who wonders how deeply Bush held these views should look back at his political campaigns. In 1994, when Republican Pete

Wilson was running for governor of California on Proposition 187, the effort to cut off all social services to illegal immigrants, Bush was voicing opposition to it while running in Texas.

And in his campaign for the presidency in 2000, the theme of embracing Hispanic immigrants continued. "The first ad that we ever ran in the Bush campaign—it's kind of mind-boggling to think about now—was a Spanish-language ad that we ran in the Iowa caucus," says longtime consultant Stuart Stevens, a member of Bush's advertising team. "And we made a big deal about it. . . . How many Hispanics are there in the Republican caucus in Iowa? Maybe ten. But we felt it was so important to send this signal." Later, Stevens shot footage of Bush officially opening a new bridge between his home state of Texas and Mexico, with an eye toward using that in a subsequent campaign ad.

Throughout that campaign, Bush peppered his campaign appearances with small bursts of Spanish. He even spoke Spanish in a primary-season debate, declaring, "There are a lot of Hispanics who live in this state." It was pretty bad Spanish, actually, but it helped Bush make his broader point: "Our party must broaden our base. I've tried to use my compassionate conservatism message to do just that, in the state of Texas and across the country."

That didn't mean Bush was in favor of illegal immigration, of course, but it did mean he was in favor of immigration reform that would grant legal status to the millions of Hispanics who had already entered the country and established lives in the United States, while better securing the southern border and increasing the levels of temporary legal immigration. Such a package embodied both Bush's own deeply and genuinely held Christian belief in treating strangers with compassion and his equally deeply held belief that Republicans had to do something big to convey to Hispanic voters the message that they weren't seen by the GOP as some kind of enemy force.

Bush's initiative was in sync with the views of most thought leaders in the conservative movement. Robert Bartley, the editorial page editor of *The Wall Street Journal* and a longtime intellectual leader of conservative forces, argued passionately that America and the world benefited from allowing the free movement of men and goods across international borders. Just six months after Bush took office, Bartley wrote a remarkable piece for the *Journal* headlined "Open Nafta Borders? Why Not?"

In it, he threw his support behind a call by Mexican president Vicente Fox for a system of "open borders for not only goods and investment but also people" throughout Canada, the United States, and Mexico, the countries of the North American Free Trade Agreement. Bartley wrote:

> Immigration continues to refresh and nourish America; we would be better off with more of it. Indeed, during the immigration debate of 1984 we suggested an ultimate goal to guide passing policies—a constitutional amendment: "There shall be open borders." The naysayers who want to limit or abolish immigration look backward to a history they do not even understand. Each new immigrant group has been derided as backward, unclean, crime-ridden and so on; each has gone on to adopt the American dream of a free and independent people, and to win advancement economically, politically, socially.

Just five years later, a lot of the wind had gone out of the sails of those pushing such a rosy view of immigration. Bush set out in 2006 to pass an immigration overhaul that combined more border security with legal status for undocumented immigrants already here and greater legal immigration. He failed when the House, though under Republican leadership, refused to go along. It had passed a different bill, one that emphasized border security and didn't include a new guest-worker program or a path to citizenship for undocumented workers already here. Representative Dennis Hastert, the Republican Speaker of the House, declared, "Our number-one priority is to secure the border, and right now I haven't heard a lot of pressure to have a path to citizenship" for undocumented immigrants. The two bills were never reconciled; immigration reform died.

That was the clearest sign that President Bush was leading a party that had splintered on immigration. More than that, the fact that it was done in by Republican House members, who have a better sense of sentiment on the ground than do those in their loftier Senate seats, meant Republicans felt a shift at the grass roots. The Reagan and business-community arguments on immigration had lost their primacy. Crucially, it was a lesson that would be delivered several more times in the coming few years.

Wehner was, and is, puzzled by the shift. "It's not like there was a massacre at a mall by an undocumented worker that triggered it," he says. "I have long believed immigration was a proxy for other things going on, including the loss of cultural influence of whites, America becoming more culturally diverse, and the enormous economic and cultural changes we've experienced. Whatever the cause, I noticed around 2005, 2006, that the issue started gaining traction with talk radio, which was a canary in the coal mine."

At about the same time, the Bush administration confronted a crisis that certainly wasn't of its own making but that engendered questions of competence. Hurricane Katrina roared across the Louisiana and Mississippi coasts in the last week of August 2005. It was a horrible storm in every way, carrying a deadly combination of high winds, rain, and a giant storm surge. Significant parts of New Orleans and the Mississippi coast were left underwater. Katrina would prove to be one of the deadliest hurricanes in American history, responsible for 1,833 deaths. It was the most costly ever, responsible for an estimated $108 billion in damages.

The problem for the Bush administration wasn't simply the storm, but the fact that the costs associated with it would drive up federal spending, already rising rapidly because of the wars in Iraq and Afghanistan. More than that, the administration's response was widely panned as insufficient and ineffective. Politics, like life, often is unfair, and the Katrina controversies were in many ways unfair to the Bush team. Decisions made long before had left the city of New Orleans with a levee system insufficient for a storm this size, and the sheer magnitude of the disaster would have overwhelmed the federal crisis management system in any administration. But the optics were bad, and the administration made them worse by seeming to proclaim that the recovery effort was going just fine when, in fact, it was drowning under the waters of Katrina.

By the midterm election of 2006, Katrina was only part of the perfect storm Republicans faced: unpopular wars, rising deficits, the appearance of incompetence. Under the leadership of Representative Rahm Emanuel of Illinois, who had worked in the Clinton White House and now was in charge of his party's House campaign committee, Democrats reran the Clinton playbook, moving to the ideological center by recruiting a wave of moderate Democrats to run for the House in swing districts. The strategy worked. Democrats won the national vote in House races by a wide margin—42.3 million to 35.7 million for Republicans—they picked up thirty-one House seats to take back the majority, and Representative Nancy Pelosi became the first woman to be elected Speaker of the House.

Shortly thereafter, the real hammer fell, in the form of a world-class (and, in fact, worldwide) financial crisis. Banks and other financial organizations had been feasting on the low interest rates the Federal Reserve provided for years after the 9/11 crisis, offering cheap home mortgages with little or no regard to the ability of home buyers to actually pay off those mortgages when interest rates, inevitably, started going back up. A giant bubble had formed.

The bubble started losing air in the spring of 2007 when subprime lenders—financial institutions that had issued variable-rate mortgages to underqualified home buyers—began failing. On the surface, things still seemed tolerable; the Dow Jones Industrial Average hit an all-time high in early October. But then the bottom fell out.

The Federal Reserve had to guarantee the bad loans of the Bear Stearns investment bank to allow it to be sold, but then refused to do the same for Lehman Brothers, which, as a result, went bankrupt. The federal government took over entirely the two quasi-private institutions designed to keep the mortgage markets moving, Fannie Mae and Freddie Mac. Bush proposed, and Congress passed, an economic stimulus package in early 2008 and then, that October, a $700 billion bailout plan to rescue American banks. The financial industry was bleeding money, and the federal government was bleeding red ink trying to save it.

A conservative president now was overseeing that least conservative of trends: a swelling of government deficit spending. Between the time Bush took office and when he left, annual government outlays as a share of the gross domestic product grew from 17.7 percent to 24.4 percent. The federal budget went from a surplus to a deficit of $458 billion in fiscal 2008, and then upward further to $1.4 trillion in fiscal 2009.

The 2008 financial crisis shaped the coming presidential election. More than that, it served, as much as any other event, to feed the growing populist mood in a nation already trending in that direction. Average Americans were losing their homes because they couldn't keep up with the ballooning payments on their variable-rate mortgages, but the banks that had peddled those mortgages were being bailed out by a conservative Republican administration. In other words, the small guys were being hammered, and the big guys with clout in Washington weren't.

For Bush and other conservatives, the financial crisis simply topped off a bad stretch in their effort to keep the dreams and ideals of Ronald Reagan alive. The financial crisis seemed to confirm critics' charges that deregulation had made the economy more dangerous. Meantime, the conservative gospel of free trade as a tide that would lift all boats was looking suspect. For those paying close attention, the consequences of the decision to open up trade with China started showing up early. Between the beginning of 2001, the year China was admitted into the World Trade Organization, and the time Bush left office, the number of manufacturing jobs in the United States plunged, from just over 17 million to 12.5 million. Technology and a shifting economy had something to do with that, but China and its economic and trade policies were giant factors as well.

The conservative cause was hurt by all this—but so was the entire Washington establishment. It was hardly all Bush's fault. He was dealt an extraordinarily difficult hand to play after 9/11, and on most fronts his steps had the backing of at least the Republican establishment, if not most of the bipartisan Washington establishment. Still, if you're looking for a time when the gates swung open for a populist uprising led by Donald Trump, look at the second Bush term.

Bush himself sensed this, better than most others. By the close of his administration, he was privately warning those around him of the forces gathering steam outside Washington. "He had a troika, a trifecta, of concerns: isolationism, nativism, and protectionism," recalls Wehner. "And he sensed that they were coming earlier than I did, earlier than other people did. He sensed that in the mid- and late 2000s." It would take others in the conservative movement, the Republican Party, and the nation a while to figure out the same thing.

CHAPTER 10

Into the Wilderness

John McCain was an American original, a free spirit with a personal story you couldn't make up, and a career that prepared him to take on just about anything in American public life. He was the son and grandson of prominent U.S. Navy admirals, so he grew up comfortable around power and those who exercise it. His education at the U.S. Naval Academy gave him an appreciation for American institutions, as well as for those who, like him, sometimes rebelled against them. His experience as a pilot in the Vietnam War gave him a lifelong respect for all who served in the military, and his horrible suffering as a prisoner of war after his plane was shot down gave him a deep personal empathy for those in personal pain.

After the war, he hitched his political wagon to Ronald Reagan and moved to Arizona, the home state of Barry Goldwater, giving him a good feel for the two patron saints of the conservative movement. Once he was in Congress, his deep roots in the American military left him fascinated with national security and the struggle between world powers, both of which he became an expert on. While in the Senate, he survived a near-death political trauma when he acknowledged he had improperly intervened on behalf of a friendly savings-and-loan magnate, which turned him into a crusader against the influence of money in politics.

The one thing this fascinating life story didn't prepare him for was handling an economic crisis. Yet that was exactly what McCain confronted when he got the Republican presidential nomination in 2008.

McCain had been pursuing the presidency for years, being beaten down and popping back up with more vigor than a carnival Whac-A-Mole. He pursued the nomination in 2000, started well behind the pack, and was the decided underdog until he won the New Hampshire primary. Soon after that glorious triumph, he was left for dead on the political roadside after he lost the South Carolina primary to George W. Bush.

He came back in 2008. This time, having made a credible run in 2000, he started out as the front-runner. He was beloved by many in the party for his bulldog approach to politics and life, his willingness to speak inconvenient truths, his impeccable national security credentials. McCain spoke reverently of Ronald Reagan, a man he knew and whose Cold War record he deeply admired.

He was not, however, the conservative favorite. Not by a long shot.

McCain had multiple problems on his right. Though he generally embraced conservative positions on taxes, regulation, and government spending, he was openly hostile to religious conservatives, and they to him. McCain also had a temper, and occasionally an acerbic tongue, which on occasion only aggravated his problems with evangelicals. The hostility on the religious right, in turn, made other conservatives skeptical that McCain would pick the kinds of judges they wanted for federal courts. He also liked working with Democrats a bit too much for the taste of some in his party.

McCain's passion was his crusade to rid the political system of big-donor money, but that position also didn't cut much ice with conservatives, who had other priorities and who, after all, were happy that some of that big-business money was being put behind the low-tax and small-government candidates they loved. He also tried to carve out a path as someone more concerned about the environment than was your average Republican, which stoked worries in the business community. McCain certainly was loved by neoconservatives, because he staunchly defended the war in Iraq and the surge of more American troops that President Bush was using to turn around the mess there—but that position was growing more unpopular with middle-of-the-road voters.

Instead, many conservatives threw their love toward former Massachusetts governor Mitt Romney—an odd choice in some ways, given that Romney had, as governor, championed a plan that inserted the state government deeply into the business of providing healthcare. The plan was loved in Massachusetts but would come to be loathed by conservatives when it was seen later as the template for Barack Obama's program for reforming the federal healthcare system. Moreover, Romney was a Mormon, which made him suspect in the eyes of many evangelical Christians. Still, Romney was a reliable proponent of low taxes and deregulation, and his business background left conservatives believing he understood markets and the private sector better than McCain did.

So Romney was a problem for McCain. Soon, another problem of a completely different variety emerged: A populist undercurrent, which had been flowing at the feet of the Republican establishment, broke to the surface again, just as it had earlier with Pat Buchanan and Ross Perot.

This time it was being propelled by former Arkansas governor Mike Huckabee, who had been a preacher and Christian broadcaster before going into politics, and who approached politics with a down-home appeal tailor-made for the blue-collar voters taking up more and more space in the Republican tent.

As Huckabee understood, the Republican Party had changed, and in a way friendly to someone like him. As the Democratic Party moved left on social issues such as abortion, school prayer, and gay rights, blue-collar voters began drifting toward the Republican Party. At first they were "Reagan Democrats," and then, over time, they became simply "Republicans."

But the party and its traditional economic posture of scowling at government programs, trying to pare back spending more on Social Security and Medicare, cheering low tax rates (no matter the beneficiary), and promoting laissez-faire economic beliefs when it came to matters such as the minimum wage wasn't fully in tune with this new crowd growing within the party.

Some Republicans had been warning of a disconnect. One of the first was Tim Pawlenty, the boyish-looking governor of Minnesota, who himself was up from blue-collar roots (son of a truck driver father who once was laid off, his boyhood surrounded by the meatpacking plants of St. Paul). He warned as early as 2002 that Republicans were becoming the "Sam's Club party" rather than the country club party. In 2007, Pawlenty showed up at the CPAC conservative conference and gave a speech offering multiple conservative heresies, including government subsidies for health insurance and alternative energy and more government activism for the working class. In truth, many of Pawlenty's governing policies as Minnesota's governor actually followed the conventional conservative formula of lower taxes and less spending, but he at least understood, and was willing to declare, that a rethink was in order.

Huckabee brought a similar appeal to the new Republican working class into the presidential arena. Much of his support came from evangelical voters; as a former minister, he spoke their language and cut a comfortable profile for them. But he also developed a populist economic message. He didn't embrace the traditional conservative position on free trade. He said he wanted "fair trade" and was skeptical about NAFTA, which remained a crown jewel of economic policy for most Republicans. He railed against Wall Street and the advantages enjoyed by wealthy Americans, and wanted to use government power to help the working class, through, among other things, farm subsidies and federal assistance on healthcare. He denounced the Internal Revenue Service's power.

Much of that message would be reprised by Donald Trump eight years later. It certainly wasn't a conservative message; indeed, the *Wall Street Journal* editorial page, guardian of conservative economics, agreed with a critic who called Huckabee a spokesman for the "religious left." But it made some sense, given the demographic changes in the Republican Party. What made less sense, and what ultimately got Huckabee into trouble, was his support for what he called a "fair tax." It was a radical idea, under which the entire federal tax system—income taxes, corporate taxes, even Social Security and Medicare taxes—would be replaced with a kind of national sales tax of 23 percent on nearly all goods and services.

There were a lot of problems with the idea, but two stood out. First, the plan essentially told voters that everything they bought would instantly go up in price by almost a quarter. Second, while income taxes are usually progressive, because the rich pay a higher share of their income than do poorer people, sales taxes are regressive, because the poor pay the same percentage as do the rich. The Huckabee plan provided for a kind of pretax subsidy to lower-income Americans to restore progressivity, but that undercut the simplicity of the plan, which was supposed to be its beauty.

Still, Huckabee was carving out a nice populist perch for himself, to the detriment of McCain, who liked to think his outspoken-rebel profile and his crusade against corporate money in politics gave him a fair amount of populist appeal, too.

Just as telling, as a sign of where the party was heading, was the buzz saw McCain was heading toward on a more emotional topic: immigration. As a disciple of Ronald Reagan, and a representative of a border state with a substantial Hispanic population, McCain tended toward the traditional conservative view of immigration as a net good for the country's economy and a practice in keeping with its founding ideals. In that sense, he and George W. Bush were of like mind. And when the Bush effort to pass a comprehensive immigration-reform bill collapsed in 2006, McCain took a bold step: He teamed up with the Senate's marquee liberal figure, Democratic senator Ted Kennedy of Massachusetts, to try to pick up the pieces.

Together with another ten senators from both parties—the group became known as the Gang of Twelve—they revived an immigration bill they had put together a couple of years earlier. The new version was grandly called the Comprehensive Immigration Reform Act of 2007, and it was a noble attempt to please everybody. For those worried about the influx of illegal immigrants, it proposed a series of border-security steps, including long stretches of new fencing and thousands of new border agents. For those who thought it silly to think the millions of immigrants already living and working in the United States would ever be rounded up and sent back home, it proposed a path to legal status for such long-term undocumented workers. It also would grant legal status to the so-called Dreamers—young immigrants brought to the United States as children through no choice of their own.

For those who thought immigration should be based more on merit than family connections, it ended the practice of allowing immigrants to gain admission for their extended families, and established in its place a new points-based merit system that rewarded education, skills, and jobs experience. For businesses wanting more seasonal workers, it offered a new class of temporary visas.

McCain strongly believed immigration reform was not only the right move for the country but also an essential move to broaden the base of the Republican Party to include more Hispanics, and smart politics for him personally to boot. The idea that it was politically advantageous was the subject of heated debate in McCain world, though. Others around him sensed the party moving to a much harder line on immigration, and feared that the McCain-Kennedy legislation would be labeled by McCain foes as simply a bill giving "amnesty" to immigrants who came to the United States illegally. "Amnesty" would prove to be a poisonous word with Republican primary voters circa 2008. "Some insiders thought it was going to be a huge problem, and might cost him the nomination," recalls Charlie Black, a longtime friend and McCain adviser in that campaign. "But he was going to stand his ground."

At one contentious dinner McCain had with his top campaign aides at Charlie Palmer's Restaurant, a downtown Washington steak house frequented by lawmakers and politicos, one adviser argued that the immigration bill was a potentially fatal problem for the campaign, because it was being portrayed as rewarding eleven million immigrants who had come to the United States illegally.

First and foremost, the adviser argued, voters needed to hear that the border with Mexico would be secured, and that those here illegally would move to the back of the line of immigrants hoping to get into America. Only then could one talk about legal status for illegal residents. McCain exploded in anger: *You're wrong. We're going to pass this bill, and President Bush will sign it. It will be over by the summer of 2007. I will be seen as the guy who solved immigration, and we'll have cover in the primaries because the Republican president will have signed it.*

McCain was wrong, and the skeptics were right. The McCain-Kennedy immigration effort collapsed in the Senate in the summer of 2007. One of the deepest blows came when a Democratic senator, at the encouragement of organized labor, supported what the law's sponsors considered a poison pill amendment, which would have shortened the amount of time allowed for a guest-worker program. To the fury of McCain supporters, that senator was Democrat Barack Obama of Illinois, who was lining up to mount his own presidential run.

Still, the fatal blow was opposition from within the Republican Party. Nor was the collapse of McCain-Kennedy the only sign of the changing winds on immigration. Another senator who was seeking the Republican nomination, Sam Brownback of Kansas, set out on his long-shot quest preaching what he considered the Reagan gospel on immigration, talking about its value to the economy as well as its role in ensuring that America remained a beacon to those around the world seeking a better life. As a senator from Kansas, he initially set out to make nearby Iowa a focus of his campaign effort. Yet in an interview in late 2007, he told me he had simply stopped going to Iowa, because every appearance there was just producing another argument with voters about immigration.

All told, then, with the 2008 election still a year or so away, McCain found himself in a kind of no-man's-land, running short of money and lacking the broad base of support a front-runner should have. Some of his opponents thought he was on the verge of collapse and might have to quit. His campaign pollster, Bill McInturff, who had known McCain for years, never thought so. "If he has no money, he will campaign door-to-door in New Hampshire," McInturff told a post-election conference of campaign advisers. "He will never quit. He will not stop."

What McInturff understood was that McCain was a force of nature, dogged and irrepressible. He won his first election, to a seat in the House of Representatives from Arizona, by taking on three better-connected members of the Republican establishment, and he defeated them by spending months in the hot sun knocking on thousands of doors to introduce himself to voters.

Similarly, in 2000, McCain simply willed himself to victory in the New Hampshire primary by deciding to compensate for a lack of money by making himself accessible—all the time, every day—to voters and the media. It is almost impossible to explain to anyone who wasn't there what it was like to cover McCain's 2000 campaign. I wrote about it later:

> He banked his whole campaign on winning the New Hampshire primary, and set out to do so by canvassing the state, day after day, on a bus filled with aides and reporters and straight talk. In fact, it became known as the "Straight Talk Express," and his dozens of town-hall meetings were a cross between religious revivals and voter-therapy sessions.
>
> He slaughtered his party's sacred cows and picked up support from disgruntled voters along the way. He said the GOP's big-money donors not only owned Mr. Bush, but were destroying democracy in the process. He said an emerging federal budget surplus should be used not for tax cuts, but to pay down debt and bank money for Social Security. He attacked the religious right, directly and repeatedly. . . .
>
> He became a kind of Pied Piper in New Hampshire. It wasn't just reporters who followed him around. Voters did, too; some of them trailing him in their cars from one town hall to another just to be part of it.
>
> In the end, he did win New Hampshire. It wasn't enough,

because he went on to lose to Mr. Bush in South Carolina and ultimately in the race for the nomination.

He never lost that lust for engaging in the national political conversation. At one point in 2007, when he was getting ready for his final presidential campaign, I made a request to interview him. I got an odd reply: Meet him in his Senate office at 10:00 on a Sunday morning.

The Capitol was deserted on that Sunday morning, except for John McCain. I arrived at his office, he shook my hand enthusiastically, and he declared: "Come on, follow me. I'm going to get a haircut. We can talk along the way." We proceeded briskly through the hallways to the Senate barbershop, where one of the barbers, who also had become a McCain pal, had come in specifically to give him a Sunday morning trim. McCain talked all the way to the barbershop, all the way through his haircut, and all the way back to his office—where he also signed a copy of his latest book for my father, a Korean War veteran. Interview complete.

So McCain stayed in the race. He lost the Iowa caucuses to Huckabee, a sign of the power of a populist message. But McCain bounced back by winning New Hampshire, again, and then rolled on to the nomination. At that point, he had to make the most high-profile decision facing any presidential nominee: picking a running mate.

McCain loved his maverick reputation, so he wanted to do something in keeping with it. More than that, given the troubles of the Bush Republican presidency at that point, he was running behind Obama, the presumed Democratic nominee, so he felt the need to do something dramatic to shake up the dynamics of the race. His first impulse was the most McCainist step he could imagine: He wanted to pick a Democrat to be his Republican running mate.

Specifically, he wanted to nominate Senator Joe Lieberman of Connecticut, a conservative Democrat who had been his own party's vice presidential nominee eight years earlier. The two men were close friends. Lieberman shared McCain's hawkish views on foreign policy and national security, and he had long displayed a McCain-like streak of independence. McCain loved the idea.

McCain's campaign team didn't love it. For starters, they knew picking a Democrat who supported abortion rights would set off a rebellion among evangelical Christians, an important part of the Republican base and one that already viewed McCain with great suspicion. A winning Republican coalition simply had to have their support; their *enthusiastic* support would be even better. Lieberman guaranteed the opposite.

Moreover, the Lieberman idea simply wasn't practical politically. When the notion was laid on the table at a meeting of campaign advisers, McInturff raised his hand and asked simply, "Has anybody in this room actually read the rules of the Republican National Convention?" The problem, McInturff pointed out, was that those rules required only the majority of four state delegations to put a name into nomination to be considered as the party's vice presidential pick. The chances were extremely high that four state delegations would band together to do exactly that, in order to push an alternative to Lieberman—and that, in turn, would guarantee a damaging floor fight at the very time the party gathering was supposed to be helping McCain take off.

So McCain fell back on another controversial choice that proved more telling for the long-term direction of the party. He chose Governor Sarah Palin of Alaska.

Some conservatives, most notably the editors of *The Weekly Standard,* had encountered Palin on visits to Alaska and were pushing her, but otherwise she was virtually unknown. She had been governor of Alaska for less than two years. In that time she had shown herself, to those who had been paying attention, to be the same kind of American-original figure McCain was. She had gotten into snarling fights with big oil companies in a Big Oil state. She was a woman, of course, and an attractive one at that, which didn't hurt with the male-dominated crowd atop the Republican and conservative worlds. But she also was the kind of woman who drove snowmobiles and went hunting, who cheered at her son's hockey games, and who took on the Republican establishment in her own state.

McCain liked that maverick persona, but he liked her mostly because she was such an unconventional choice that she had the potential to change the currents that were running in Obama's favor. Some in the campaign argued passionately for a more conventional choice: a traditionally conservative, anti-abortion governor from a swing state in the Midwest, such as Minnesota's Tim Pawlenty. But McCain was a fighter pilot, with a fighter pilot's mentality. If the plane was in trouble—and his campaign was in trouble at that point—you didn't just ride the plane down to disaster. You tried something drastic to pull out of the dive. Palin was going to be his dramatic gesture.

At first, it seemed an inspired choice. Palin was engaging and interesting and quickly became the toast of the Republican convention, in St. Paul, Minnesota, where she was officially nominated. She won over the crowd, and a national TV audience, with her folksy acceptance speech, in which she played up her love of small-town life and her kids' sports activities: "You know, they say the difference between a hockey mom and a pit bull? Lipstick."

And as she hit the trail, Palin showed the ability to excite that new wing of the Republican Party, Pawlenty's Sam's Club wing. She was totally different from the buttoned-down white men the party usually offered as its representatives on the national stage, and had particular appeal to blue-collar and older voters. In short, she found what would later become the Trump current. "You know, she would show up to these high school football stadiums, and the place would be packed and people would go, 'Oh, my God,'" recalls Steve Bannon, Trump's sometime political guru.

In fact, it wasn't just high school football stadiums. At one notable rally at the Villages retirement community, outside Orlando, she drew a crowd that the fire marshal estimated at sixty thousand people. Some thought that was an overestimate, but in any case it was enormous. Her rallies offered other distinct precursors of

Trump rallies to come: She had wildly enthusiastic supporters; at one appearance in Pensacola, Florida, the maximum-volume cheering that erupted after Palin was introduced went on for more than two minutes. She had attendees decorated head to toe in campaign gear. Her crowd offered taunts at the journalists who accompanied her. She spoke a language well understood by average voters who felt estranged from political insiders.

But beyond the cheers, Palin turned into first a problem, and then a liability. Her lack of knowledge on even basic policy matters was almost complete. In one memorable interview with CBS News's Katie Couric, Palin couldn't name a newspaper or magazine she read to keep up with events; she cited Alaska's proximity to Russia ("They are right next to our state") as a foreign policy credential; and she couldn't say whether she thought human activity contributed to climate change.

Palin's woes weren't McCain's biggest problem, however. Instead, the crisis that probably delivered the final, fatal blow to his campaign was the financial meltdown of 2008. That also happens to have been the problem that best crystallized the new mood of the Republican Party—angry and distrustful of its own leadership or anyone else seen as part of the "elites."

The clouds had been gathering for the better part of a year before they turned into a full-fledged storm in September 2008. A blizzard of cheap mortgage loans had been given to underqualified home buyers, and then sold and resold as exotic financial products, all with lax oversight by federal regulators. Rising interest rates had popped the resulting giant financial bubble, leaving homeowners unable to repay loans they never should have gotten. Big banks were teetering. Washington's leaders tried to weave together a safety net, with the Fed cutting interest rates and Congress passing an economic stimulus bill in midsummer, but the bleeding continued.

With the stock market in a free fall, the Bush administration frantically put together a bailout package for the financial industry, called the Troubled Asset Relief Program, or TARP. The TARP program empowered the government to purchase toxic assets and other securities they couldn't otherwise sell, thereby injecting badly needed funds into the financial system. The White House legitimately feared that the financial sector could collapse, with cataclysmic consequences, if Congress didn't pass the legislation immediately.

Yet conservative Republicans in the House were balking. A government rescue of big private institutions simply didn't comport with either their conservative views or the populist sentiment they felt at the grass roots. Besides, the rebels on the right had no faith that either the Bush administration or the leaders of their own party were telling them the truth when they tried to explain how bad things really were. One Republican who was a top congressional staff member at the time describes the mood as a total breakdown of trust.

On the campaign trail, as I wrote at the time, McCain had been doing his best Teddy Roosevelt, man-of-the people routine, arguing against using government money to bail out financial titans. Then, amid the mounting fear, he made a stunning decision: He announced he would suspend his presidential campaign and return to Washington to consult on the crisis. There were multiple problems with that move, the first being that he hadn't conferred with the Bush administration about his decision. Treasury Secretary Hank Paulson, the man at the center of the story, learned of McCain's decision when an aide handed him a handwritten note during a congressional hearing. There were no high-level meetings planned at which McCain *could* consult with anyone. By taking such an extraordinary step, McCain was simply adding to the air of crisis.

McCain returned to Washington to discover that a bank rescue already was being hastily assembled, one that was doing the kind of taxpayer bailout he had been warning against, with no input from him. Worse, McCain really had little to add to that conversation. Still, the White House hastily convened a meeting of congressional leaders, mostly so McCain could look engaged, and asked his general-election rival, Barack Obama, to attend as well. McCain

was so ill-prepared for the meeting that he essentially had to borrow a staff member from House Minority Leader John Boehner to
accompany him and lend some technical expertise.

The result was almost farcical. Paulson recounted the scene in
his memoir:

Bush and Paulson opened the meeting by sketching out the dire
situation and pleading for fast action on the bailout plan before
things got even worse. Protocol then called for Bush to turn to
Democrat Nancy Pelosi, the Speaker of the House. But Pelosi immediately declared that Obama would speak for the Democrats, an
indication they had a plan to use the meeting to showcase their
presidential nominee and put him in the best possible light.

Obama walked through discussions that were under way on the
TARP legislation and some changes Democrats would like, but he
concluded by saying that a deal was almost in hand and Democrats
would do their part by delivering the necessary votes. He then suggested McCain speak.

It was a brilliant maneuver, because, in fact, Republicans didn't
think an agreement was almost in hand. Obama's presentation
seemed designed to make it appear that McCain was responsible if
he couldn't similarly promise to deliver the necessary Republican
votes. McCain promptly made his predicament worse by saying,
"I'll wait my turn," and letting other Republicans take the floor.
The import was clear: He had turned the political world upside
down by forcing a crisis meeting at which he had nothing to say.

Other Republicans jumped in to say that their members were, in
fact, looking for changes in the bailout to reduce the exposure of
taxpayers. Multiple overlapping conversations broke out, before
Obama again said, over the din, that he wanted to know what
McCain had to say. McCain glanced at a note card he had brought
in and made a few general points, then declared that he was confident there could be an agreement.

That simply set off a new round of arguments over who was
really looking out for taxpayers, alongside Democratic complaints
that the Republicans had no plan. "Frankly, I'd never seen anything

like it before in politics or business—or in my fraternity days at Dartmouth, for that matter," Paulson wrote. Finally, he recalled, the president stood up and said, "Well, I've clearly lost control of this meeting. It's over."

Neither the urgent attempt to craft a rescue nor McCain's political fortunes had been improved by the spectacle. Boehner and his deputy, Representative Roy Blunt, tried mightily to convince their troops to vote for TARP. Representative Paul Ryan, who had what everybody considered sterling conservative credentials and who himself was highly reluctant to support a big government bailout of anything, argued for it, to no avail. At one point, Vice President Dick Cheney, who had been a first-tier conservative in the House before many of its members were even out of college, was dispatched to a meeting of House Republicans in the Cannon House Office Building, to plead with them to support the bailout. Someone who was there describes the Cheney message as: *I know the politics are awful, but this is something we have to do.* And the response from many members was simply: *No, we don't.*

So when the TARP package came up for a vote in the House, the stage was set for a disaster—which is what happened. As the roll-call vote proceeded and it became clear that House Republicans weren't going to support a rescue package their own president called essential, the stock market began one of the most frightening slides ever seen. I recall watching on TV in my office, slack-jawed, as the Dow Jones tumbled during the vote. Representative Joe Crowley, a Democrat from New York, stood on a chair in the well of the House chamber, yelling out the numbers as the Dow fell. A third of Republicans voted against the measure, it was defeated, and the stock market closed down nearly 7 percent.

The Senate quickly came up with its own version of a bailout bill and promptly passed it. House members, having scared themselves and the country with their initial rejection, this time voted to pass the legislation, and Bush immediately signed it into law.

But to those involved, it's now clear that the stimulus package marked a corner turned. "Looking back on it, that should have been some indicator that, hello, there's something else at work out there," says Eric Cantor, who was at the time the third-ranking Republican in the House. The views of genuine financial experts, such as Federal Reserve chairman Ben Bernanke, were simply dismissed. "I think that was the first time where solutions to something really didn't matter," Cantor concludes.

More immediately, a lot of political and psychological damage had been done. McCain was showing that he was no expert on how to handle financial markets, and Palin, with virtually no experience in financial matters, was hardly a reassuring figure when McCain could have used one by his side.

The die was cast. McCain and Palin went on to lose the presidential vote to Barack Obama and his running mate, Joe Biden. Republicans had gone from full control in Washington to full loss of control. Conservatives were in anguish.

Looking back now, Senator Marco Rubio sees in that 2008 campaign multiple harbingers of things to come: "I personally bought a home in 2005, in late 2005, in Miami, which was one of the epicenters of the bubble, and found that within three years my home was worth less than what I paid for it. I don't think anyone, any American, had ever lived in an era in which your home declined," he says. "So you saw the outlines of what Trump was able to channel as early as 2008." Rubio also points to the Huckabee campaign that year: "Huckabee had a more populist appeal. . . . He was like a precursor."

All told, the country would pay the price for the financial crisis for years to come—and the political system would as well.

CHAPTER 11

The Tea Party Erupts

I f you were looking for somebody to inspire a political revolution, Rick Santelli is about the last person you'd pick.

Santelli has plenty of passion, that's for sure, but it isn't a passion for politics or parties or legislation. Santelli's passion is financial markets—particularly the exotic and sometimes arcane machinations that excite people at the Chicago Mercantile Exchange, where he sets up shop every day.

Santelli works there as a market analyst for CNBC, the financial news network, but that doesn't mean he's a TV guy at heart, either. He got his CNBC post because he used to be a trader himself at the Merc, as the exchange is known. He arrived at the exchange out of the University of Illinois at Urbana-Champaign with a business degree and became a trader and order filler for those buying and selling treasury bills, foreign currencies, gold, lumber, livestock—the goods and products that hum through the background of America's economy every day. He then worked his way up through a variety of financial services firms before jumping ship to report on the markets for CNBC. Santelli was and is a markets guy, and to talk to him for even a minute or two is to feel how much he loves being inside the American market system.

But on February 19, 2009, Santelli did, in fact, have politics on his mind. For more than a year, he had been watching with growing agitation as the government, under both the previous president, George W. Bush, and the new one, Barack Obama, moved to bail out people who had made bad financial bets. Government rescues offended the free-market sensibilities of Santelli and the traders he conversed with every day at the exchange. They shared a kind of midwestern, rugged-individual view of the economy, in which market forces, not some government bureaucrat or agency, decided who won and who lost.

So Santelli had watched with consternation as the Bush administration reacted to the unfolding financial crisis by offering a stimulus plan and rescues of financial institutions. The new Obama administration promptly followed with a much bigger economic stimulus plan designed to juice up the economy with government spending.

Now, in mid-February, the next government rescue was teed up. It was the Homeowner Affordability and Stability Plan, announced as a way to funnel billions of dollars in federal funds to mortgage companies as an incentive so those mortgage companies, in turn, would lower mortgage payments for homeowners who otherwise might default and lose their homes. For Santelli, that was just too much government misuse of taxpayer dollars in yet another bailout of people who should bear the consequences of their own decisions. When the hosts of CNBC's signature *Squawk Box* turned to him for his thoughts at 8:30 on the morning after the plan was announced, he erupted.

"This is America!" Santelli shouted from the floor of the Merc, with traders milling behind him. He turned to the traders. "How many of you people want to pay for your neighbor's mortgage that has an extra bathroom and can't pay their bills? Raise their hand." Boos rained down. Santelli turned back to the camera and shouted, "President Obama, are you listening?" Then he suggested that people who were similarly upset do more than just yell in frustration: "We're thinking of having a Chicago Tea Party in July. All you capitalists that want to show up at Lake Michigan, I'm going to start organizing."

Santelli recalls now, "I was already wound pretty tight about how the markets were getting ruined by these hurry-up-and-pass-anything legislative measures." Yet he says the performance was "random and spontaneous. . . . I didn't think there was any reaction. It was just another day in the woods for me." After his TV segment, he went outside to smoke a cigarette. When he came back, he realized he had ignited, well, something. "All of a sudden," he recalls, "people were running up to me. I had no idea what was going on."

What was going on was that "the rant," as it would come to be known, had gone viral. It became, Santelli says, the most viewed segment CNBC ever posted online. Ironically, those in the government who designed the programs that set off Santelli actually had set out in the belief that their plans would save the very markets he loved, as well as the regular folks he was speaking for. Yet the rant brought to the surface a belief, bubbling with increasing energy just beneath the surface, that the financial and political systems were set up to protect those who played fast and loose with other people's money, while leaving the average guys and gals to not just fend for themselves but pick up the tab with their tax dollars.

The Santelli suggestion that it was time for a new Tea Party in America rang true for lots of Americans. One of them was Jenny Beth Martin. Martin was a computer programmer in Georgia who had been intermittently involved in politics, including in Newt Gingrich's campaigns. She had left work in 2001 to undergo fertility treatments, after which she gave birth to twins. Her husband, meantime, had formed his own company. But the company went out of business in 2007, just as the financial world was starting to shake, and the couple filed for bankruptcy and lost their house in early 2008. They had actually turned down an offer for a government-guaranteed loan that might have allowed them to keep the house, and were doing odd jobs to keep afloat.

Then along came the Santelli rant about taxpayers not being forced to pay for other people to stay in houses with extra bathrooms that they couldn't afford. "And we were actually cleaning our neighbors' bathrooms and houses rather than paying for a house with more bathrooms than we could afford, so it just really spoke to me," Martin recalls. "And I said, 'Well, I have to have a Tea Party.'"

Martin was an early user of Twitter, and she learned that a group called Top Conservatives on Twitter, led by a Tennessee activist, Michael Patrick Leahy, was organizing a conference call to take up the Santelli challenge. Martin joined about twenty others on it, and they discussed how to strike while the rant was still hot and in people's minds. Many of those on the call had other political lines out on the Internet—Martin herself also was involved in an online group called Smart Girl Politics—and they began spreading the word. That early organizational push underscores an aspect of the Tea Party's rise that was truly revolutionary: its dependence on the Internet and social media to take off. The whole movement was created, in large measure, because a video of the Santelli rant went viral online, an early example of how a politically charged message could spread instantly. Martin, because she was in the computer industry, was already online savvy. So were other early Tea Party pioneers with whom she connected immediately. They were inspired by an online message, they organized through social media, and they in turn used social media to spread their message much further.

In sum, the Tea Party was the first political movement born on social media, and the first to show that anger was the special rocket fuel that could propel such a movement. It would not be the last.

About a week after that first conference call, Tea Parties designed to pick up where the Santelli rant had left off were held in forty-eight cities—from Santa Monica to St. Louis to Washington, D.C.—attracting some thirty thousand people in all. The Tea Party was launched. In truth, it wasn't then, and never really became, a real political party.

"Tea Party" described a movement rather than something with a structure or a clear agenda. Its pioneers all considered themselves conservatives, and many were affiliated with online conservative groups. Some of the women who were involved at the outset had gotten involved in politics out of anger at what they perceived as mistreatment of Sarah Palin when she was the Republican vice presidential nominee.

Mostly, though, those who launched the movement were reacting to rising government spending amid the economic distress of the times. "It was economics that were motivating us to be involved," Martin says. "We just saw the government was getting too big and doing things that were outside the scope of the government."

A lot of their anger was directed at Republicans as much as Democrats. Tea Partiers were furious at Bush for proposing the big rescue package for teetering banks, and at McCain for ultimately voting for it in the Senate. Martin recalls that some people she knew took MCCAIN/PALIN bumper stickers and cut off the MCCAIN part. She took the government bailout of big banks very personally, coming as it did on the heels of the failure of her husband's business. "We weren't blaming other people for the mistakes in his business," she says. "We had to accept responsibility for that, and be an adult about it. And yet, here's Washington, D.C., bailing out these massive corporations that they somehow deemed too big to fail." Such sentiments were populism in pure form.

Martin and three compatriots took one of the earliest steps to actually organize the Tea Party insurgents when they formed a group called Tea Party Patriots in early 2009. By April 15, 2009—the day tax returns were due to be sent in to Uncle Sam—the movement had grown so rapidly that it inspired more than eight hundred "Tax Day Tea Parties" around the country, which organizers estimated drew more than a million people to complain about what they considered government overreach.

Soon the Tea Party movement had another grievance, and this time the target was placed squarely on Democrats. President Barack Obama and Democratic leaders in Congress proposed an ambitious overhaul of the nation's healthcare system, in which government's role would be significantly increased. The Affordable Care Act—which, inevitably, became known to Republican critics as

Obamacare—actually melded some long-standing Republican ideas for injecting market forces into the healthcare industry with longtime Democratic dreams of expanding healthcare to the poor, all in one giant package.

Obamacare would set up government-run "exchanges," or on-line marketplaces, where consumers could shop more easily for healthcare; it would also create an "individual mandate" imposing a tax penalty on anyone who didn't acquire insurance. Those steps were designed to create a more robust market for consumers to buy insurance, and to instill a sense of personal responsibility so that everyone, particularly healthy younger people, felt compelled to be part of a system that works best when all have coverage. Both originally were conservative ideas. Beyond that, though, Obamacare called for a broad expansion of the government-funded Medicaid insurance program for the poor and imposed requirements for the kinds of coverage private insurers had to provide in their plans.

Put those all together and you had a health plan that conservatives, and Republicans generally, could hate, and that Tea Party activists could see as another unacceptable expansion of government reach.

For Republicans in Congress, Obamacare arrived just as their relations with Obama had started sinking fast. Both parties were at least partly to blame for the deterioration, which began as soon as Obama took office.

Immediately after Obama won, he and Democratic leaders in the House set out to rapidly pass a new economic stimulus plan, to pull the economy out of the ditch into which it had been driven by the near collapse of the financial sector. Initially, it appeared there might actually be a bipartisan approach. Just before he was sworn in, Obama traveled to Capitol Hill to meet with congressional leaders of both parties to talk about how to proceed. They gathered in a room just off the Senate floor, and Obama declared he wanted Republican input for the coming stimulus package.

Both sides knew the incoming president and his Democratic colleagues didn't really need Republican help. They had a majority in the House and a big majority in the Senate, so both sides knew they could proceed without Republican votes. Still, the invitation for Republican input had been put on the table. Republicans formed a series of working groups to decide on the proposals they would present. Shortly after Obama had been inaugurated, he and congressional leaders met again, in the White House's Roosevelt Room. This time, the discussion would be for real; the economy was reeling and a new president was in charge, and things were about to begin moving.

Eric Cantor, who was by then the second-ranking Republican in the House, showed up for the meeting with copies of a set of Republican proposals for the stimulus bill. As the meeting unfolded, he spoke up and asked Obama whether he could give a copy to everybody around the table. It was, he acknowledges now, "audacious"to try to take the lead in a meeting called by a president of the opposite party, and some of the Democrats appeared none too happy. But Obama told him to proceed, and Cantor passed around his proposals for a handful of conservative Republican ideas that he argued should be made part of the stimulus bill. They included tax incentives for businesses to make capital investments as an alternative to government spending programs, and a lower tax rate on small-business owners who classified their business income as personal income.

Republicans, knowing their minority status, believed they had purposely not put on their wish list some items that they knew Democrats would dismiss out of hand, such as a deep cut in capital gains taxes. Cantor was hoping to succeed in getting an item or two into the bill so he could tell Republican members back on the Hill he had gotten something for them. And Obama's initial reaction was encouraging. He gave the list a quick read and declared, "There's nothing crazy here."

But as the conversation unfolded, the ground for cooperation appeared to shrink. Cantor argued that business incentives were a more potent investment for economic growth than the tax refunds Democrats were proposing. Obama responded, "You know, elections have consequences." Democrats had won the election, he indicated, and they would move in the direction they preferred.

Days later, when Pelosi and Representative Dave Obey of Wisconsin, the chairman of the powerful Appropriations Committee, released their version of the stimulus bill, Republicans saw in it none of the provisions they had requested. Instead, they believed the Democrats had simply cherry-picked some items Republicans had supported in the past and argued that their inclusion was enough to make the proposal bipartisan. House Republican leader John Boehner got Republicans to withhold all their votes. The stimulus passed anyway, entirely with Democratic votes, and the die was cast. Republicans began to consider themselves not just the minority party, but the opposition party. Privately, they began saying that their top priority now was to see to it that the Obama presidency failed and ended after one term—remarks that got back to the White House and created deep anger and mistrust there. Many Democrats simply stopped believing Republicans would make any good-faith efforts to work together.

When Obamacare rolled around, the dynamic stayed in place. Again, there were conversations between the Obama administration and House Republicans about finding common ground. Again, they went nowhere. Early in the process, an Obama healthcare expert, Nancy-Ann DeParle, visited Cantor's office for a small meeting and said she hoped Republicans could cooperate on health reform. One of the key things she and other Democrats were seeking, though, was something Cantor simply didn't think Republicans could buy: providing consumers with a so-called public option when they picked health insurance plans on the new online markets the administration envisioned creating. That is to say, one of the options consumers should have, the Democratic architects argued, was the chance to simply buy into the government-run Medicare or Medicaid programs as an alternative to private insurance. In the Democratic view, that would guarantee more competition in the insurance marketplace and produce pressure on private insurers to keep costs as low as possible, to match what the government provided.

For House Republicans, that was simply out of step with their conservative beliefs. In their view, a public option put the same people who regulated the healthcare system—government officials—in direct competition with the industry they regulated. It was, as they saw it, a profound conflict of interest, and unfair to the private sector. Cantor told DeParle he didn't think there was any way his members could support it. Republicans had other problems with the Democrats' plan. In particular, they adamantly opposed the individual mandate that required people to acquire health insurance as a way to spread costs and risks across the whole population, or to pay a tax penalty if they failed to do so. That was particularly galling to Democrats because the individual mandate originally was a conservative idea, designed to compel people to take personal responsibility for their own healthcare decisions.

The chances of any bipartisanship on healthcare slid further as the new and fired-up foot soldiers of the Tea Party revolution began going after the Obama plan. During the August recess of 2009, Tea Party activists went on a kind of citizens' rampage, pouring into town hall meetings being held by members back in their home states and districts and railing against Obamacare.

Republicans in the House, in particular, both admired and feared the passion the Tea Party had unleashed. There was little chance they were going to risk having its fire turned on them by cooperating with Obama on healthcare. Democrats were equally incensed; they felt their health plan actually honored the power of the marketplace. Moreover, Democrats had steered clear of the more extreme solution a lot of liberals wanted, which was an entirely government-run health system. There was no consensus.

Obamacare passed the House on a Saturday night in November, with only a single Republican member supporting it. Senate Democrats then used the muscle of their filibuster-proof sixty-seat majority to pass their own version. To please conservative Democrats, the public option was stripped out of the Senate version. Under normal procedures, what followed would have been a House-Senate conference committee to work out differences between the two versions. But Massachusetts senator Ted Kennedy had died and been replaced. He was the undisputed Democratic champion of healthcare reform, so it was ironic that his death cost Democrats their crucial sixtieth vote. That was the net effect when a Republican, Scott Brown, won a special election to take Kennedy's place in the Senate.

That meant Democrats now couldn't afford to convene a conference committee to work out a compromise version, because that new version would inevitably be blocked by a Republican filibuster when it came up in the Senate. So the House simply passed the Senate's version, and agreed to make some changes in it through the back door in a later budget bill.

A giant change in the nation's health system—something that touches every American—had just been completed, but in a messy, partisan, and unsatisfying fashion. There was no consensus; instead, what the country got was what it would be feeling a lot more of in the years just ahead: pure partisan anger.

Republicans then proceeded to ride that anger to a stunning series of victories in the 2010 midterm elections. As the election drew near, the *Wall Street Journal*/NBC News poll found that Tea Party supporters made up 35 percent of likely voters—and 84 percent of those Tea Party supporters planned to vote Republican. With that wind at their back, a whole series of Tea Party Republicans who would go on to become big figures in the party were sent to Washington, including Senators Marco Rubio of Florida, Rand Paul of Kentucky, and Mike Lee of Utah and Representatives Mike Pompeo of Kansas and Mick Mulvaney of South Carolina.

Most important, Republicans picked up sixty-three seats and took control of the House away from the Democrats. The Tea Party had given both the conservative movement and the Republican Party a charge of new energy just when both really needed one, after the disappointments of the second Bush term and Obama's victory.

The Tea Party revolt did something more problematic at the same time: It made the conservative movement and the Republican Party more angry and more populist, more interested in fighting and less interested in accepting the Reagan principle that getting 80 percent of what you want is better than going off a cliff in pursuit of 100 percent. With the Republican successes in the 2010 election, John Boehner now was Speaker, and Eric Cantor was the majority leader. Both were, by any previous definition, genuine conservatives. Yet, as they soon discovered, they weren't in charge— not of their own House caucus, and not of the Republican Party.

A significant chunk of the House Republican caucus now consisted of members who pledged allegiance to conservative principles but who were simply skeptics of the powers that be. By some counts, well more than a hundred House Republicans had won their elections with significant Tea Party backing. Representative Michele Bachmann of Minnesota, who actually preceded the Tea Party wave by two years but shared the group's cantankerous approach, soon organized a Tea Party Caucus within the House.

As a general rule, Tea Party activists despised Obama; they considered his views to be far to the left of theirs and, perhaps as important, believed he looked down upon and belittled people like them. They felt his 2008 campaign comment that many working-class Americans were "bitter" and would "cling to guns or religion or antipathy toward people who aren't like them" was pointed directly at them. Tea Party lawmakers disliked Obama with a similar passion, and they were nearly as furious at their own leaders in the House when they saw those leaders trying to do deals with Obama. The Tea Party had helped Republicans gain power, and then stood in the way of Republican leaders who tried to govern once in power.

"It was like blind motivation," Cantor says. "Just to say no, without any visibility into what's next. It's really almost an irresponsible position." That attitude led, over the next couple of years, to a series of crises: a debt-ceiling crisis, a "fiscal cliff" crisis, and, ultimately, a government shutdown.

The scenario began to unfold when the federal government was about to hit its legally mandated debt ceiling in mid-2011. The debt ceiling is something of a Washington artifice, a legal limit on the amount of money the government can borrow. Because the government budget usually is in deficit, the U.S. Treasury keeps selling bonds routinely, meaning it eventually hits the debt ceiling. In a kind of ritual Kabuki dance, Congress would then wring its hands over the accumulated debt before voting to raise the ceiling, allowing life to move on.

The new Republican majority in the House, fired up by the Tea Party, wanted to change that game. They set out to use the need to raise the debt ceiling as a way to force big cuts in government spending. Without the cuts, Republicans wouldn't support a debt-ceiling increase. Without a higher debt ceiling, the Treasury couldn't pay its bills, including the interest payments due on existing debt. The U.S. government would go into default. In short, the new Republican majority in the House wanted to create a crisis, so they voted down a bill to simply raise the debt limit, as had been the practice.

Boehner and Cantor didn't disagree with the strategy; they, too, wanted to use the debt lever to extract spending cuts to reduce the deficit. But the Tea Party crowd wanted to go well beyond that. They were demanding a big cut in spending, a legal cap on future spending—*and* a constitutional amendment mandating a balanced budget. Some House members openly suggested they saw no reason to raise the debt ceiling at all, a position that would have required brutal spending cuts to keep the government functioning.

For their part, Democrats were prepared to accept some spending cuts to reduce the deficit, but they wanted a bigger chunk of tax increases to do the deficit-cutting job. Boehner and Obama met on the White House patio in shirtsleeves to negotiate a compromise. In fact, they were secretly negotiating a "grand bargain" in which Boehner would accept $800 billion in tax increases in return for

$1.2 trillion in spending cuts, including curbs in the Democrats' cherished Social Security, Medicare, and Medicaid entitlement programs. The debt ceiling would be raised, but both sides would get something they wanted.

The deal fell apart, though, when Obama decided he needed to get more in tax increases to sell the deal to congressional Democrats and it became apparent Boehner was going to have big problems convincing the Tea Party Caucus to accept the tax increases he had already agreed to. In a crisis atmosphere, and with the financial markets quaking, the two parties agreed to a budget deal that kicked a lot of the tough decisions down the road but raised the debt ceiling. More than sixty House Republicans defied their leaders and voted no. Public approval of the new House majority began to slide.

And that deal just set up an even more perilous moment a year later, by creating the so-called fiscal cliff. The budget deal, somewhat unrealistically, mandated billions of dollars in automatic spending cuts at the end of 2013 unless Congress had agreed by then on a big, long-term plan to cut the deficit—which, of course, lawmakers didn't do because of the deep divides between the parties. At precisely the same time, the big Bush-era tax cuts, which were built to go away automatically after a decade, were set to expire. So the country would be getting, automatically and simultaneously, $136 billion in federal spending cuts and $532 billion in federal tax increases—a combination that Fed chairman Ben Bernanke famously warned amounted to a "fiscal cliff" that, if driven over, would send the economy into the deep ravine below. It was the kind of disaster only Washington could devise, and only Washington could fix.

Some House conservatives were happy to go off the cliff. They didn't like the idea of letting the Bush tax cuts expire, of course, but they did like the idea of forcing big, automatic spending cuts. Above all, they disliked the idea of negotiating with Obama and the Democrats on some deal that envisioned anything less than a full extension of all the Bush tax cuts. But Democrats were in charge of the

Senate and weren't going to simply vote to continue a set of tax cuts they never embraced in the first place.

The obvious compromise—and the one Boehner doggedly pursued—was to save as many of the Bush tax cuts as possible and get some spending cuts. He worked out one that preserved most of the Bush tax cuts, except on the wealthiest Americans, and got at least some spending cuts.

That was a compromise House conservatives weren't going to buy. In their mind, a vote that eliminated any of the Bush tax cuts was effectively a vote for a tax increase. It didn't matter that even Grover Norquist, the Republican Party's chief watchman against anything that even sniffed of higher taxes, said such a vote shouldn't be considered a vote for a tax increase. The Tea Party Caucus view was: *Preserve all the Bush tax cuts—or nothing*. Even Cantor adopted that position. Congress careened through Christmas and New Year's without a deal, and with another crisis atmosphere forming, before agreeing to a plan just after New Year's Day in 2013. In the end, 151 Republicans voted against the compromise.

The frustrations that grew out of that fight merely fueled the desire within the Tea Party movement and among its congressional allies to seek what they hoped would be victory in an even more important battle: a fight to kill off Obamacare. The tool for doing this was going to be the bluntest of all. The insurgent strategy was to simply strike out of the federal budget any and all money needed to implement the new health plan, and to then shut down the government by refusing to pass funding bills unless Democrats went along.

Many Republican leaders thought the strategy was doomed to fail. Democrats were simply not going to agree to strangle their proudest domestic achievement of recent years, and Republicans didn't have the votes in the Senate to force them to do so. Worse, they saw the effort as a suicide pact. If the government did shut down, the shutdown would be blamed on Republicans, and there would be a deep price to pay with the broader voting public.

The crusade went forward anyway. Heritage Action, the

new political-action arm of the Heritage Foundation think tank, began pressuring Republican lawmakers to get behind the effort. ForAmerica, a Tea Party–inspired political organization, began running ads calling congressional leaders, including Senate Republican leader Mitch McConnell, "chickens" because they wouldn't get behind the defunding effort. The Tea Party Patriots distributed a "tool kit" to activists, telling them how to agitate to kill Obamacare funding.

ForAmerica leader Brent Bozell, a longtime conservative activist, teamed up with Jenny Beth Martin of the Tea Party Patriots to tour the country, turning up the Obamacare pressure not just on Democrats but on Republicans who were deemed insufficiently devoted to killing the healthcare program.

"We stopped in Eric Cantor's district," in Richmond, Virginia, Martin recalls, "and there were hundreds of people outside of his office where we stopped. And they went on to have a town hall that night that was essentially an empty-chair town hall, because Eric Cantor did not show up. And they were angry." Martin thinks she saw a glimpse of the future that night: "I'd been all over the country at that point and saw something in that district. That was much different than anywhere else in the country."

Egged on by two conservatives in the Senate, Ted Cruz and Mike Lee, the House rebels battled on. And the pressure worked, to the extent that it compelled the House to pass a series of spending bills that included cuts to Obamacare funding. The Democratic Senate simply lobbed them back with Obamacare funding intact. Ultimately, the clock ran out and most government agencies shut down on October 1, 2013, because they hadn't been funded. Obamacare was alive, but the rest of the government was in a coma. Pelosi called it the "Tea Party Shutdown."

The government stayed in that coma for more than two weeks, during which public pressure to reopen the government grew—and it fell largely on Republicans. They lapsed into intense internal feuding and finger-pointing. The House, with its powerful Tea Party contingent, couldn't agree on any compromise that might pass the Senate and earn Obama's signature. Finally, in mid-October, the Senate passed a budget that continued Obamacare funding, and the House had no choice but to accept it.

In retrospect, Cantor isn't sure the Tea Party movement, while it labeled itself a conservative uprising, actually was about conservative principles at all. The rhetoric of the movement was about fiscal sanity and limited government, he notes, yet many of its adherents subsequently did a 180-degree turn on fiscal matters when they threw their support behind President Donald Trump as his administration allowed the federal budget deficit to soar, reaching $1 trillion annually. "The conservative movement was co-opted in a way, because the goalpost kept moving."

He thinks the insurgency may have been rooted as much in cultural anxiety among working-class Americans as in economic anxiety. "There was at some point a conflagration, if you will, of cultural change . . . you know, increasing diversity in the classroom, people speaking different languages." And did the fact that Barack Obama was the first African American president feed that cultural anxiety? "I would hate to think that that was what did it, but I have to believe there is a certain segment of population that that didn't sit well with," Cantor says. "I mean, as a Jew, I know that it didn't sit well with a certain segment of population that I was in office."

In fact, the Tea Party would later be accused of being essentially a racist movement, both because much of its vitriol was directed at Obama and because various right-wing xenophobic and racist activists latched on to the movement. Yet there's really no sign that its founders and leaders, or most of its supporters, were motivated by racism.

They were, however, propelled by emotion. "There was a wave, there was energy, there was excitement," Cantor says. "There was anger. . . . It became very powerful, very galvanizing and unifying for Republicans to be angry at what was going on and to be angry at President Obama."

In a watershed moment, Cantor himself would become a victim of that anger. In 2014, a virtually unknown and severely underfunded challenger, a college professor named Dave Brat, ran against Cantor in the Republican primary in his district. It should have been no contest: a nonentity against a nationally known and powerful leader. But Cantor took a lot of heat from Tea Party activists who thought he hadn't done enough to kill off Obamacare. Then a second front was opened against Cantor: Anti-immigration forces began accusing him of being soft on illegal immigration, mostly because he favored legislation that would have provided a legal status to the Dreamers, the young immigrants brought to the United States as children.

In fact, Cantor began getting hit from both sides on immigration as the primary season went on. On one day in May 2014, groups favoring immigration reform held a rally in his district, blaming Cantor for failing to bring a comprehensive immigration-reform bill to the House floor. Meanwhile, anti-immigration activists gathered to loudly protest his position on the Dreamers, saying it was a sign he was in favor of "amnesty" for those who broke immigration laws.

Most analysts dismissed the protests as just so much political noise that would go away after Cantor easily won reelection. That didn't happen. In a stunning upset, Brat defeated Cantor. The second-ranking House Republican had fallen to a Tea Party revolt.

Cantor says now that Democrats crossing over to vote against him out of spite were the force that did him in. Yet he also acknowledges that he was a target of the growing anti-establishment, anti-elite sentiment within his own party. "By definition, if you're the leader, and there's this anger out there, I'm responsible for everything," he says.

Steve Bannon points to the Cantor loss as a sign of what was to come: "When Cantor falls? That shows you that anything's possible. That's when you know there's a real revolt going on."

CHAPTER 12

Trump Storms In

Nothing—no trend, no event, no milestone—so clearly marked the Republican Party's turn from Reagan conservativism to Trump nationalism as the searing internal debate over immigration that exploded immediately after the 2012 presidential election. Immigration brought the party and the conservative movement to a fork in the road. Down one path lay the course the party establishment wanted to follow. Down the other lay what we can call, for lack of a better term, the Steve Bannon/Ann Coulter/Donald Trump choice.

In 2012, with a populist tide rising, Republicans did an odd thing. They chose perhaps the least populist man in America, Mitt Romney, as their nominee to try to beat President Barack Obama. Romney was an establishment guy through and through: Son of a onetime auto-company CEO who became governor of Michigan. Privileged upbringing. Product of Stanford University, Brigham Young University (in keeping with his Mormon faith), Harvard Law, Harvard Business School. He was a management consultant, then ran a private-equity company and became very wealthy himself before being elected governor of Massachusetts.

At the time, though, Romney was an entirely logical choice, for a variety of sound reasons. First of all, it was Romney's turn to be the nominee, and the Republicans still tended to pick the big-name candidate whose turn had arrived. That person usually was somebody who had run before and done respectably well, because experience then still mattered a lot to Republicans, and Romney had run a good, respectable race for president in 2008.

In that race, Romney had erased some of the conservative doubts about his style, as well as his record as the Massachusetts governor who had enacted a big government-run health program. He had successfully portrayed his version of healthcare reform as one that inserted market discipline more than big-government intrusion into the system. His views on taxes, the economy, and regulation were all standard-issue conservative material. Before becoming governor, he had run a respectable though ultimately unsuccessful campaign against Senator Ted Kennedy, bête noire of all conservatives, so that was a plus for him, too. His background as a successful businessman made lots of Republicans comfortable.

On top of that, Romney was a decent, polite, articulate man who embarrassed no one. He had a lovely wife, Ann, who was fighting a heroic battle against multiple sclerosis with great dignity. With his full head of dark hair, with just a trace of silver in it, his square jaw, his deep baritone voice, he looked and sounded the part of a president in every way.

At its outset, the 2012 Republican primary seemed to have one candidate for each available ideological and strategic lane. Former Pennsylvania senator Rick Santorum ran as a traditional religious and fiscal conservative. Texas governor Rick Perry was the small-government champion from outside the Washington establishment. Representative Ron Paul was the libertarian. Representative Michele Bachmann ran as a Tea Party favorite. Herman Cain was an African American, a former businessman, and a low-tax crusader.

Conservatives initially expected Arkansas governor Mike Huckabee to present the strongest challenge to Romney, given that he was an evangelical favorite with a genuine populist touch that worked well enough to help him win the Iowa caucuses in 2008. But Huckabee chose not to run, and Santorum took over Huckabee's space by winning Iowa this time. But eventually, the strongest challenge to Romney came from Newt Gingrich, who was trying to revive his electoral career by running as a little bit of everything: an original Reagan conservative, tax cutter, relentless scourge of liberals, and spokesman for the average man. Above all, Gingrich ran as the slayer of all sacred cows and enemy of the prevailing system and its political correctness.

After desultory showings in Iowa and New Hampshire, Gingrich made his charge in the crucial next state up, South Carolina. And his manner in doing so was prescient. He did it by attacking the press, showing just how much mileage a Republican politician could gain by doing so.

I had a front-row seat to this. We at *The Wall Street Journal,* along with Fox News, hosted the first of two Republican debates in the run-up to the South Carolina primary, and I served as one of the moderators. The first half of the debate proceeded in a fairly orderly fashion. I had asked Paul about his desire to cut the defense budget, which brought a bristling response from him in which he criticized the premise of my question, producing in turn another round of applause and hoots from the audience at my expense. But all that was within the normal range for such affairs.

Then Fox's Juan Williams spoke up to ask Gingrich a question. Williams, who is African American, asked Gingrich about a recent comment he had made: "Speaker Gingrich, you recently said black Americans should demand jobs, not food stamps. You also said poor kids lack a strong work ethic and proposed having them work as janitors in their schools. Can't you see that this is viewed, at a minimum, as insulting to all Americans, but particularly to black Americans?"

Gingrich responded not by backing away from his remark but by doubling down on it and going after Williams for implying he had said something racist: "Well, first of all, Juan, the fact is that more people have been put on food stamps by Barack Obama than any president in American history. Now, I know, among the politically correct, you're not supposed to use facts that are uncomfortable." He went on to argue, "So here's my point. I believe every American of every background has been endowed by their creator with the right to pursue happiness. And if that makes liberals unhappy, I'm going to continue to find ways to help poor people learn how to get a job, learn how to get a better job, and learn someday to own the job." The audience booed Williams first, and then cheered Gingrich wildly heading into a commercial break.

Gingrich had just revived his campaign, using Williams, the press, and liberals all as punching bags. During the commercial break that followed the volley, Gingrich walked over to those of us at the moderators' table and chatted with us convivially, as if to say there should be no hard feelings about the exchange. But he knew the tactic had worked, and he used it again in the next debate, this time going after CNN's John King even more harshly. After that, he won the South Carolina primary over Romney. Chances are good that Donald Trump was watching, and taking mental notes.

It wasn't enough to push Gingrich over the top, though. He followed South Carolina with a strong second-place finish in Florida but then began running out of money. He faded, and Santorum was the alternative to Romney who proved to have the greatest staying power. Gingrich, in retrospect, would see his 2012 campaign as a precursor to Trump's—albeit without the same reservoir of cash. "The thing that Trump had that I did not have was the sheer weight of money," Gingrich says. "I have zero doubt that if I had been able to match Romney financially, we would have beaten him."

In the end, Romney outslugged Santorum to get the nomination, then made another move to protect his conservative flank. He chose as his running mate Representative Paul Ryan. Those who were on the inside of the Romney campaign thought ideology had little to do with the choice of Ryan. Romney had been taken with the Wisconsin congressman's smarts and style since they first met at a meeting on Capitol Hill years earlier—"It was love at first sight," a Romney aide told me later—and always considered him his top choice. In any case, Ryan's credentials on the right were impeccable, and he was more than willing to argue for cutting taxes and taking steps to curb the rising costs of Medicare and Social Security. That attitude also helped ease conservative anxieties about Romney.

The other person who was driving conservatives deeper into Romney's arms was President Obama, whose election-year actions deepened antipathy toward him on the right. Obama came out in favor of gay marriage—an issue on which he had equivocated previously—and issued an executive order protecting the Dreamers from deportation. His administration infuriated the Tea Party movement when the Internal Revenue Service subjected Tea Party organizations to unusual scrutiny and delays when they sought the same kind of tax-exempt status enjoyed by similar groups.

As Obama moved to the left on immigration, Romney tried to stay on the right. He opposed legislation to put Dreamers on a path to citizenship, arguing that they had no right to move to the front of the immigration line. Most famously, he said at one debate that his answer to ridding the country of illegal immigrants would be "self-deportation"—that is, he suggested a plan under which un-documented workers would be unable to find work legally and would simply pull up stakes and head back to their country of ori-gin. "If people don't get work here, they're going to self-deport to a place where they *can* get work," he said. Giving "amnesty" to those already here would only encourage new waves of illegal im-migration, he said.

Romney was trying to pull off a tough balancing act. He sensed the populist anger at the surge of illegal immigration over the pre-vious two decades, and he was getting grief on the right over a story disclosing that a company he had hired to take care of the lawn at one of his houses employed undocumented workers. But he also wanted to sound reasonable to Hispanic voters wary of signs of in-sensitivity to those with roots south of the border. He never en-tirely pleased either side, though many in his campaign and the party worried that the tough immigration rhetoric might lose him more support than it gained him. As the election drew to a close, Kevin Madden, Romney's top communications aide, was asked by a reporter what factors he thought would be most important if Romney were to lose. Madden's reply: "Immigration."

It also didn't help that, with weeks to go in the race, a videotape surfaced of Romney saying at a fundraiser that 47 percent of voters would support Obama "no matter what," because they pay no income taxes and "believe that they are entitled to healthcare, to food, to housing, to you-name-it." The quote smacked of a rich guy looking down on half the country's citizens, and played directly into the stereotype of Romney as out of touch with average Americans.

Still, the race was close. In the final weeks, Romney was drawing big and enthusiastic crowds, and *Wall Street Journal*/NBC News polling showed Obama and Romney nearly neck and neck nationally. In the end, though, Obama voters showed up in greater strength than Romney voters, and late-deciding voters broke slightly more for Obama. The president won reelection by a 332–206 margin in the Electoral College.

Republicans and conservatives, caught up in their own scorn for Obama, thought the late-breakers would go Romney's way, and they were somewhere between crestfallen and furious at the outcome. The idea that Obama had narrowly but consistently bested Romney in a whole series of swing states—Virginia, Florida, Iowa, Ohio, Colorado, Nevada, Pennsylvania—led to not just anger but serious doubts about whether the Reagan conservative message that had carried the party for thirty-two years had simply run its course.

In response, Republican National Committee chairman Reince Priebus did something unusual: He ordered a post-election "autopsy" to figure out what had gone wrong. The autopsy—technically called the Growth & Opportunity Project—was written by a committee of five party operatives but was the cumulative result of focus groups, interviews, conference calls, and surveys of Republicans all around the country. A lot of the ninety-seven-page report dealt with ways the Republicans needed to improve on the mechanics of campaigning, but the most important pieces had to do with the messages Republicans were sending to voters. The upshot of that part of the document was simple and direct: The conservative message was out of date; the Republican Party was seen by far too many people as the party of old white guys; and, above all, Republicans had to present a much friendlier face to Hispanics.

"At our core, Republicans have comfortably remained the Party of Reagan without figuring out what comes next," it said. "Ronald Reagan is a Republican hero and role model who was first elected 33 years ago—meaning no one under the age of 51 today was old enough to vote for Reagan when he first ran for President."

The document sounded a few populist notes: "We have to blow the whistle at corporate malfeasance and attack corporate welfare. We should speak out when a company liquidates itself and its executives receive bonuses but rank-and-file workers are left unemployed." Notably, the word "trade" was not mentioned.

Most important, though, the document went on to sound a very Reaganesque note on immigration. "If Hispanic Americans perceive that a GOP nominee or candidate does not want them in the United States (i.e. self-deportation), they will not pay attention to our next sentence. It does not matter what we say about education, jobs or the economy; if Hispanics think we do not want them here, they will close their ears to our policies. . . . We are not a policy committee, but among the steps Republicans take in the Hispanic community and beyond, we must embrace and champion comprehensive immigration reform." More than that, the document called for the Republican Party "to carefully craft a tone that takes into consideration the unique perspective of the Hispanic community. Message development is critical to Hispanic voters."

That was definitely not the message Steve Bannon took away from 2012.

Bannon had moved into his own as a kind of professional provocateur. He was a Navy veteran, former investment banker, maker of political films, and chief of the right-wing Breitbart News organization, which was emerging as the ladle that stirred the bubbling cauldron of populist and nationalist causes. He was allied with no particular political figure to carry those causes into the national debate, though he had already had one brief encounter with Donald Trump. When Trump briefly considered entering the 2012 presidential race, he talked periodically with political activist David Bossie about the idea. Bossie and Bannon were friends, having worked together on some controversial conservative documentary films, and at one point Bossie told Bannon that Trump was considering running for president. "Of what country?" Bannon recalls replying. Still, Bannon agreed to accompany Bossie to a session in New York to meet Trump in Trump Tower and talk through the possibilities.

Once in New York, Bossie gave Trump an overview of the traditional Reaganesque Republican political message, and then turned to Bannon, who proceeded to argue that the times required a much more populist message, invoking Pat Buchanan, Ross Perot, and even William Jennings Bryan in doing so. "That's the populist message," Bannon said. Trump replied, "That's what I am: a popularist." *No,* Bannon corrected, *it's "populist."* On the train back home to Washington, though, Bannon concluded, "He's actually right. He's not a populist. He'll be a popularist, because it's all about him." That, however, was the end of the Bannon-Trump dalliance that cycle, for Trump decided against running.

Which was why, after the 2012 election, Bannon was trying to find a populist candidate to shake up the Republican Party. So in January 2013, he recalls, he convened a dinner at the Capitol Hill townhouse he uses as a kind of combination home/office/command center. There he hosted Senator Jeff Sessions, a Republican from Alabama, and a former Sessions aide, Stephen Miller, who was just off the distinctly unsuccessful Michele Bachmann presidential campaign. (Bannon had made a movie about Bachmann and gotten to know Miller along the way.) The one thing the three shared was a particularly hard-line view of immigration, followed by deep skepticism about the virtues of free trade.

"We plot out the 2016 campaign," Bannon recalls. "And what we say is that we're going to take immigration from like the number three or four issue . . . to number one. And trade from number one hundred to number two, because they're two sides of the same coin. Mass illegal immigration and so much legal immigration is just to suppress workers' wages. Massive illegal immigration is to suppress low-skilled, working-class Hispanics and blacks and whites by the Chamber of Commerce. And then legal immigration is just to suppress tech workers. And trade is the same thing: It's just competition from foreign workers, except overseas. We'll make that number one and two.

"I tried to talk Sessions into running," Bannon continues. "And I tell him, 'You're not going to be president of the United States, okay? In fact, you're not going to be the nominee. But you're going to be the vehicle that we get the stuff out with.'" After a long conversation, Bannon says, Sessions said it was unlikely he would run. But, he added, the guy to carry the message would show up, somehow.

A kind of civil war over immigration was breaking out. Many Republicans agreed with the diagnosis from the official autopsy: The party had a problem with Hispanic voters—71 percent of whom had voted for Obama—and needed to do something about it. Doug Heye, a top aide to Eric Cantor, recalls that Cantor planted himself in his office shortly after the election and called dozens of his colleagues to get their takes on what they had learned in the campaign. "Overwhelmingly," Heye says, "the feedback was that we had an immigration and Hispanic problem."

And the solution, many thought, was to get behind a new immigration-reform plan that provided some legal status to undocumented immigrants already living and working productively in the United States, along with provisions to finally succeed where the Reagan-era reform had failed in effectively securing the southern border.

Senator Marco Rubio of Florida promptly stepped up to fulfill that desire. He combined with seven other senators from both parties—who became known as the Gang of Eight—to propose a new immigration measure that amounted to a sweeping overhaul of the immigration system. The bill would have spent $3 billion on border security and beefed up the ability of employers to electronically check that prospective employees were in the country legally. Most of the eleven million illegal aliens already in the country would be able to apply for legal status and, eventually, citizenship, provided the steps to secure the border were under way. The so-called young Dreamer immigrants could get legal status more quickly.

The bill embodied what most considered at the time a bipartisan consensus on how to solve the immigration puzzle. Rubio knew that the path to citizenship would spell trouble on the populist right, so he set out to head off that problem first. Along with New York Democrat Chuck Schumer, the other leading champion of the legislation, he traveled secretly to New York to have dinner with Rupert Murdoch and Roger Ailes, the leaders of Fox News, in hopes of convincing them to have their conservative commentators swing behind the effort, or at least give it a chance to succeed. Rubio also went on Rush Limbaugh's show in January 2013 to convince him and his listeners of the wisdom of the effort—and he seemed to succeed. At the end of their conversation, Limbaugh declared, "You have a difficult job ahead of you, because you are meeting everybody honestly, forthrightly, halfway, you're seeking compromise." Limbaugh wished him luck. Similarly, Fox News's Sean Hannity had nice things to say about the effort.

It didn't last. Ann Coulter, who had her own faithful following on the right, tore into the immigration effort in her columns, social media posts, and TV appearances. She declared that the plan to give citizenship to illegal aliens amounted to "amnesty," a word that became a cudgel used to bludgeon those who backed the Gang of Eight. Never a practitioner of understatement, Coulter wrote a column declaring that the reform plan would be the "end of America."

Tea Party activists began beating the drums in similar fashion. Hannity soon turned against the effort, calling Republicans who supported it "suckers." And by June, the influential Limbaugh was hosting Ted Cruz, who was leading the Senate opposition to Rubio's bill; Limbaugh noted that Republican political consultants were pushing the immigration plan as good politics and declared, "The fact they believe this is frightening to me. Where does this stop, Senator?" In fact, if there was any doubt how deep the Republican schism ran, one needn't have looked any further than the opposing positions taken by Rubio and Cruz, both sons of Cuban immigrants, nearly identical in age, both from large states in the South with large Hispanic populations.

As the nasty fight in the Senate played out, the Republican caucus in the House, heavily populated as it was with Tea Party supporters, was rapidly deciding it wanted nothing to do with immigration reform, regardless of what the party's post-election analysis said. "It always seemed clear that passing the Senate bill was going to be an uphill slog, at best, but more likely just impossible," says Heye. "Our conference did not want that bill and really didn't want to move anything on immigration." The Gang of Eight bill passed the Senate but was simply ignored in the House.

Donald Trump was watching it all with great interest. He had begun nibbling around the edges of presidential politics. He did so on the Republican side, though that actually wasn't a foregone conclusion. He was barely a Republican. When *The Wall Street Journal* checked into his party registration over the years, it found he was registered as a Republican in 1987, switched to the Independence Party in 1999, became a Democrat in 2001, returned to the Republican Party in 2009, gave up his party affiliation in 2011, and came back to the Republicans in 2012. Since 1999, he had given more money to Democrats than to Republicans.

On the surface, the two men who stand at either end of this story, Ronald Reagan and Donald Trump, have little in common. Reagan grew up a midwesterner of modest means with an alcoholic father. Trump is a privileged New Yorker whose wealthy father gave him his launch in life. One went to little Eureka College, the other to the University of Pennsylvania, an Ivy League school.

Reagan was usually upbeat, optimistic, and welcoming. Trump is often slashing and insulting. Most important, Reagan had a core set of deeply held convictions he brought to the White House, and measured nearly all his decisions against the standards of those basic beliefs. Trump has no fixed ideology; each decision seems based on what he thinks will work, and work for *him,* at the time.

Trump's transactional style may be best explained by the way he clawed his way to prominence in the cutthroat world of New York real estate in the 1970s. Donald Trump entered that decade lacking fame, connections, a business foothold in Manhattan, or a place in its social hierarchy. By the time the decade ended, he had all of those, using many of the same stratagems that later would drive his political career.

When the decade began, Donald Trump was a recent graduate of the Wharton business school at the University of Pennsylvania and the very junior business partner of his father, Fred, a successful Queens-based builder of unglamorous apartment buildings. Young Donald was put in charge of managing fourteen thousand apartments in New York's outer boroughs. He could drive a Cadillac to and from work, but the work itself wasn't glamorous: overseeing rent collection, trash collection, maintenance. Nor was the Trump clientele especially glamorous; at one point, Donald was so distressed over his tenants' practice of tossing trash out their windows that he established a program to educate them on the use of incinerators.

What Trump really wanted to do was move across the river to the bright lights of Manhattan. So, while still working for his father in Queens, he got himself an unexceptional apartment in Manhattan, commuted to work, and began plotting ways to get into Manhattan real estate.

When the Penn Central Railroad went into bankruptcy, putting up for grabs some swaths of property the railroad had owned, Trump portrayed himself to the New York media as a major New York builder, which he wasn't really yet, to help land a claim on some of the property. He then used his father's influence with the administration of New York City mayor Abe Beame, as well as some financial backing from his father, to win the right to redevelop the Commodore Hotel, near Grand Central Station, his first big foothold in Manhattan real estate.

That deal established Trump and helped him secure in short order the option for a more prized piece of Manhattan real estate: the building housing the upscale Bonwit Teller department store, in Midtown. That block of Fifth Avenue, between Fifty-sixth and Fifty-seventh Streets, was to become the site of the signature Trump real estate project, Trump Tower, a gleaming glass tower of upscale shops, offices, and high-end condos. Trump used connections and loopholes to get around zoning laws that otherwise would have compelled him to lower the height of his planned building, and by the end of the decade construction on the showcase was under way.

Throughout, the young Donald Trump learned that a certain political flexibility, along with sheer ambition, manipulation of his media image, and a bit of artful conniving, all were helpful in the task. Those skills would again prove helpful as Trump morphed later into a reality TV star.

That Trump experience is far removed from Reagan's early years in the small-town Midwest, or even in radio and movies. Yet for all their differences, Reagan and Trump had a similar understanding of their political base. They both understood that their support lay out beyond Washington and the elites, and that the secret to their political success came in appealing to people who didn't consider themselves part of the political system. Both were former Democrats who considered themselves more observers of than part of the political establishment around them. And, crucially, each had a keen understanding of the theatrical element of politics, something the former actor and the former reality TV star both learned while in the entertainment world. Neither talked in a political vernacular, but rather in language directed to those sitting around the proverbial kitchen table. By reaching working-class Americans, both succeeded in winning over nontraditional Republican voters.

If Trump wasn't necessarily considered a true Republican, he certainly wasn't considered a reliable conservative. Nonetheless, he chose his appearance at the Conservative Political Action Conference in 2011 to make one of his first public declarations that he was thinking of running for president. First he earned boos from the audience by declaring that Representative Ron Paul, the longtime darling of libertarians, was a nice guy who couldn't be elected. Then Trump flirted with the crowd on behalf of himself: "And I can tell you this: If I run and if I win, this country will be respected again." That brought a big cheer.

He also grew into a kind of high-profile rabble-rouser, mostly by going after Barack Obama. Trump became the most prominent peddler of the bogus theory that Obama had been born in Kenya, home country of his father, rather than in the United States, and therefore wasn't even eligible to serve as the country's leader. He offered no proof, of course, because there was none to offer, but probably was as responsible as anyone for compelling a highly annoyed Obama to publicly release his birth certificate showing he was born in Hawaii. Obama in turn mocked Trump when he was seated in the audience as Obama spoke at the annual White House Correspondents' Association dinner in 2011. We at the *Journal* were seated not far away from Trump as he endured Obama's mockery, followed by mockery from comedian Seth Meyers. Trump grinned slightly and rocked back and forth, but as the jokes at his expense rolled out, his jaw grew visibly tighter. He was officially a part of the national political dialogue, and insisted later he actually enjoyed it.

After toying with the idea of running in 2012, Trump had declined and instead endorsed Romney at a strange joint appearance in Las Vegas. After Romney's loss, though, the idea of running was never far from Trump's mind. Within days, he had filed for a trademark for what he already knew would be his signature phrase, "Make America Great Again."

He appeared at CPAC in 2013, 2014, and 2015, using the annual meeting of conservatives less because he identified with attendees in ideological terms and more so that he could test-drive his message that he was an outsider eager to bash the establishment and the news media. He attacked China, charged that foreign countries were stealing American jobs, and tried out his attacks on immigration: "With immigration, you'd better be smart and you'd better be tough and they're taking your jobs," he declared at CPAC in 2014. He went on to declare that, unlike Paul Ryan and other conservatives, he had no interest in cutting Medicare, Medicaid, and Social Security. Trump was, in short, honing his campaign message right under the noses of the political establishment. So he probably knew all along he would run in 2016, even if, as he later admitted, his family wasn't wild about the idea, and others simply didn't take him seriously.

From the beginning, the Trump campaign was different, strange. He announced his candidacy with a melodramatic ride down the escalator in his own Trump Tower building, which seemed as much advertising opportunity as political event. As the camera shots for the announcement were being set up, Corey Lewandowski, Trump's first campaign manager, realized that the camera that would capture Trump and his wife, Melania, riding down the escalator would have a sign in the background reading CURRENCY EXCHANGE, which hung from a shop in the Trump Tower lobby. "And I said, 'Sir, I'm going to put a Trump sign over this,'" Lewandowski recalls. "He said, 'No, Corey. I love that. Leave that up there.' Okay, now who in their right mind says leave the currency exchange?" For Trump, a currency exchange sign said something about wealth and financial acumen that he wanted to play up.

Trump had a prepared text for his speech, which was fairly conventional, but it bore only a passing resemblance to the remarks Trump actually delivered, which almost mocked traditional political convention. His text called for him to say, "When was the last time we beat . . . Mexico at the border?" No more than that. What Trump actually said was "When do we beat Mexico at the border? They're laughing at us, at our stupidity. . . . They're sending people that have lots of problems, and they're bringing those problems with us. They're bringing drugs. They're bringing crime. They're rapists. And some, I assume, are good people." His critics were agog, particularly given that the remarks came from a candidate in a party that had been in agony about its support among Hispanics in the last presidential race. Trump appeared not to care in the least.

Trump was walking into what most analysts considered the strongest Republican primary field in decades, full of accomplished politicians and well-credentialed conservatives. The candidates included former Florida governor Jeb Bush, a brother and son to presidents, who seemed to have access to more campaign contributions than he could possibly need; four highly regarded senators, Marco Rubio, Lindsey Graham, Ted Cruz, and Rand Paul; four governors with national standing, Scott Walker, John Kasich, Chris Christie, and the recently retired Rick Perry; two former presidential contenders with strong standing among evangelicals, Rick Santorum and Mike Huckabee; and, literally, a former brain surgeon, Ben Carson.

Stacked up against those candidates, Trump was considered almost a joke. But a funny thing happened. He shot to the top of the polls almost instantly. In a *Wall Street Journal*/NBC News poll taken just before he announced in June 2015, he had the support of a mere 1 percent of Republican voters. By July he was atop the field, with 19 percent. By September he remained in the lead, with 21 percent. By October, his support was 32 percent.

Most Republican Party leaders and journalists were in denial, assuming Trump was a fluke. But the party was in a rebellious mood, far more rebellious than most realized. In fact, those early polls may have misstated Trump's support, because they tended to miss some nontraditional working-class voters who didn't normally vote but were prepared to move into Republican primaries to vote for Trump.

If there was any doubt that Trump's own performance was going to be nonconforming, it was erased at the outset of the first Republican primary debate when Fox News anchor Bret Baier asked the assembled Republican candidates whether any of them would decline to pledge to support whoever ultimately won the Republican presidential nomination. Trump's hand was the only one that went up. It was a finger in the eye of the establishment, but it was more than that: Trump knew that he could force the party to bend to him if he kept alive the possibility that he would bolt and run as an independent candidate, which would have split the Republican vote and dealt the party a grievous blow.

Conservatives were particularly apoplectic, because Trump had no particular regard for the positions they considered important, and his style made a mockery of the upright, morally correct, and intellectually vigorous style that conservatives liked to think their movement represented.

For one thing, he had no time for traditional conservative concerns about fiscal discipline. At one point, when candidate Trump was visiting Washington, Representative Paul Ryan, the very personification of conservative tax-and-deficit views, invited him to a briefing on runaway spending on entitlement programs—Social Security, Medicare, and Medicaid—and why Republicans needed a plan to deal with them. Trump and Lewandowski dutifully came to the meeting, on the fourth floor of Republican National Committee headquarters on Capitol Hill, where they were met by Ryan, Representative Kevin McCarthy, the second-ranking House Republican, and national party chairman Reince Priebus. Ryan began to run through his presentation on why entitlement programs needed to be reformed.

After listening for a while, Lewandowski recalls, Trump spoke up: "Hey, Paul, you and Romney tried this, you tried to take away healthcare for seniors. And you guys lost the election because of it. Let me get through the election before we start talking about entitlement reform." As he and Lewandowski left the building, Trump turned to his campaign manager and declared, "Can you believe this guy? No wonder why they lost."

Besides his own money, Trump had virtually no campaign funds. For a long while, he also had virtually no campaign apparatus, beyond a private airplane and a few aides. On an early trip up to New York to visit the Trump high command, I found the campaign headquarters to consist of a largely unfinished floor of Trump

Tower, furnished with borrowed and mismatched desks and chairs, with electrical wires dangling from the ceiling and uncovered heating and cooling pipes. Lewandowski, the campaign chief, sat behind a desk that looked as if it had recently arrived from a furniture rental company. I had seen House campaigns that appeared more professional.

Trump's preferred mode of communication was the 140-character burst on Twitter, a medium no previous candidate had relied upon. Many of his tweets were insults aimed at other Republicans, totally stripped of the typical political decorum. Trump, who had avoided the draft during the Vietnam War by having a doctor say he suffered from bone spurs, said he didn't respect John McCain, a legitimate war hero who endured years of torture by Vietnamese captors, because he had allowed his plane to be shot down. He often adopted the demeanor of a schoolyard bully, mocking Jeb Bush by calling him "low energy," and Rubio by calling him "Little Marco."

But something was happening. Trump lost the caucuses in Iowa, where evangelical voters are strong and where a candidate must do the kind of retail, small-group, living-room politicking Trump eschews. But then he went on a tear, winning New Hampshire, South Carolina, and Nevada in rapid succession. By the time he won seven of eleven states on Super Tuesday, there was no denying he was the favorite to win the nomination.

Trump had discovered that voters loved seeing the political establishment attacked in crude terms. He also discovered something about the news media. He could insult the press all he wanted—at one rally in Florida in early 2016, he called journalists "the most dishonest people on earth . . . disgusting, dishonest human beings"—and cable news channels would eat it up, give him hours of free coverage, and ask for more. They simply loved the shock value he provided. Just after Super Tuesday, while other candidates were busy doing actual campaign events in the upcoming states, CNN and other cable networks infuriated the rival campaigns by showing an empty podium for half an hour while awaiting Trump's arrival, with analysts pontificating on what Trump might say when he did show up. Though the cable universe would turn on Trump later, it did as much as any force in the country to bring about his presidency.

His opponents, as well as the Republican establishment, became increasingly desperate to stop him, because they foresaw a Trump nomination as not just an ideological disaster but the precursor to a landslide defeat at the hands of Democrat Hillary Clinton. Cruz became the last line of defense for conventional conservatives, and he tried to fortify his position by cutting a deal with Rubio. Using a fellow senator, Utah's Mike Lee, as a go-between, Cruz attempted to offer Rubio a deal just before the primary in Rubio's home state of Florida in mid-March: If Rubio would drop out and throw his support to Cruz, then Cruz, if he got the nomination, would make Rubio his running mate.

"I was never interested in it," Rubio recalls. "My view of it was, we had just run a very long campaign, and it just didn't work out. . . . I couldn't imagine being part of any sort of agreement or arrangement. I just wasn't in the mood for it, to be frank, and I just don't think those things work." Rubio stayed in, lost the Florida primary to Trump, and ceased to be a viable alternative.

Cruz hung on to win a series of caucuses, where his strength as the choice of party mainstream figures counted for more than it did in a primary, but it wasn't enough. By the time Trump won all five primaries on the last Tuesday in April, it was over, barring some revolt at the party's nominating convention. The rise of Trump in the 2016 primaries was telling the party a lot, and also revealing a lot about how the Republican Party was being transformed—and, specifically, transformed into a party propelled as never before by white men without college degrees. Data from the *Wall Street Journal/ NBC News* poll tell the tale. In 2010, 40 percent of self-identified Republicans were college-educated white Americans. By 2016, that share had fallen to 33 percent. Over the same period, the share of white Republicans without a college degree rose from 50 percent to 59 percent. The difference makers in the party now were blue-collar workers, mostly men, many with little or no college education.

There were plenty of college-educated Americans unhappy with the political system who signed on, too. All told, Trump's blunt, insult-driven style turned on his fans just as much as it turned off party regulars.

As Trump cruised toward the Republican nominating convention in Cleveland, longtime friends and allies were falling out with one another over the question of whether to support or shun him. One, religious conservative leader Tony Perkins, came to the Cleveland convention and declared in a speech, "I will be voting for Donald Trump in November, and I will urge my fellow Americans to do the same." He explained his position in large measure by saying Trump would appoint conservative judges to the federal courts. Another deeply religious conservative, former George W. Bush political adviser Pete Wehner, went the opposite direction, writing an op-ed for *The New York Times* entitled "Why I Will Never Vote for Donald Trump."

Senator Jeff Flake of Arizona and Senator Ben Sasse of Nebraska both decided it would be better to stay home than to come to the convention. Sasse's spokesman told the newspaper *The Hill* he would rather "take his kids to watch some dumpster fires across the state" than be there. House Speaker Paul Ryan, who stood as not only the nominal leader of Republicans in Congress but an intellectual leader of the conservative movement, had such a bad relationship with Trump that there had been uncertainty whether he would take on the usual job of serving as chairman of the convention. Ultimately, Ryan did endorse Trump—but that, in turn, prompted conservative columnist George Will to publicly bolt from the party. Will says he changed his registration the day after Paul Ryan's endorsement.

Trump still faced a big decision in picking a running mate, an interesting exercise in a party where many of the main figures, including many he faced in the primaries, loathed their own candidate. A committee of three—Lewandowski; Paul Manafort, who had replaced him as chief of the campaign; and A. B. Culvahouse, a top figure in Republican legal circles and former White House counsel—reduced the field of possibilities to three: Chris Christie, Newt Gingrich, and Indiana governor Mike Pence. As much as the Trump campaign prided itself on its outsider, anti-establishment image, the three knew at that point they needed to build at least some bridges to traditional Republican constituencies. With that in mind, they zeroed in on Pence. "Mike Pence was the social conservative," Lewandowski says. "He checked the box as being one of the D.C. crowd," having served six terms in the House. He had then gotten experience as an executive by serving as governor. "And you know, and Trump has said it very publicly, Mike comes out of central casting." Which is to say, with his prim and proper appearance, Pence looked the part of a vice president.

Trump and Pence formed an odd couple if ever there was one: the thrice-married New York socialite who ran casinos and carried a long history of ogling women and bragging of sexual conquests, sharing a ticket with the ultra-devout governor of Indiana. But the combination helped bring along religious conservatives, even if others on the right kept their distance, and that proved crucial to Trump.

Despite the reassuring presence of Pence, the Republican and conservative establishments, to put it bluntly, began freaking out at the idea that Trump was their standard-bearer. Party regulars felt a bit like longtime residents of a comfortable beach community who suddenly realized the hurricane offshore actually might be headed straight for them. At one point, Ward Baker, the executive director of the National Republican Senatorial Committee—the party organization designed to help elect Republicans to the Senate—sent a memo to candidates with advice on how to view Trump. "Trump has risen because voters see him as authentic, independent, direct, firm—*and believe he can't be bought*." It went on to advise candidates thusly: "Trump is a Misguided Missile. Let's face facts. Trump says what's on his mind and that's a problem. Our candidates will have to spend full time defending him or condemning him if that continues. And, that's a place we never, ever want to be."

But that was exactly the place where the party ended up. The questions came fast and furious throughout the summer and fall. *Do you defend or condemn Trump when he says, falsely, that "thousands and thousands" of terrorist sympathizers in New Jersey cheered when America was attacked on September 11, 2001? When he proclaimed, over and over again, that he would force Mexico to pay for a border wall hundreds of miles long, when there was no realistic prospect that would happen? When he said that one of his Republican opponents, Ben Carson (someone he would later appoint to a cabinet post), had a "pathological temper" and compared him to a child molester?* The list went on and on, and was topped off only a month before the election when there emerged a tape of Trump telling a television personality, Billy Bush, that he once tried to have sex with a married woman, and would forcibly kiss women and "grab 'em by the pussy"—comments that were made in 2005 while he was married to Melania Trump.

After the mess that tape produced, most of the establishment bailed out on Trump, and party donors scrambled to focus on saving Republicans' hold on the House and Senate, lest Trump take the whole lot down with him. The groping tape also, and obviously, produced a dilemma for the evangelical conservatives, who couldn't avoid seeing a man who, to put it mildly, didn't share their values. Miraculously, after wavering, most decided to hang in with Trump, largely because they trusted him to appoint conservative, anti-abortion judges.

For other conservatives, though, the dilemma ran deeper. They worried about the consequences if Trump proved to be not an aberration but rather a game changer. "His nomination would pose a profound threat to the Republican Party and conservatism, in ways that Hillary Clinton never could," Pete Wehner wrote during the primary season. "For while Mrs. Clinton could inflict a defeat on the Republican Party, she could not redefine it. But Mr. Trump, if he were the Republican nominee, would."

The opposite case was made, forcefully, in a widely noted piece in September by a pseudonymous conservative author in the *Claremont Review of Books*. The piece was entitled "The Flight 93 Election," a reference to the plane that terrorists seized during the

9/11 terror attacks, until a group of passengers rushed the cockpit to take back the aircraft and crash it into a field in Pennsylvania so it couldn't be used as a weapon to strike the Capitol or the White House. The thesis of the piece was that liberals, including Hillary Clinton, posed such a grave threat to the nation and its culture that conservatives had no choice but to submerge their misgivings and support Trump, lest those on the left steer the nation into an even bigger disaster. The choice was to "charge the cockpit or you die. You may die anyway." The author, later revealed to be Michael Anton, who became a Trump White House aide, acknowledged, "To ordinary conservative ears, this sounds histrionic."

Party leaders also worried at the way the Trump campaign radiated chaos, with management shifting from Lewandowski to Paul Manafort and finally, after the party convention, to the combination of Steve Bannon and pollster Kellyanne Conway. Ironically, though, the key, campaign-saving decision was made by the very party establishment Trump constantly attacked.

Republican National Committee chairman Reince Priebus decided to swallow his misgivings and turn the keys to the party's entire infrastructure over to the Trump campaign, giving him the campaign apparatus he hadn't fully built for himself: voter data, communications, ground workers. It was like a campaign-in-a-box gift to the Trump team, and it may have been the single most important decision made during the campaign's stretch run. In that decision, the party became officially wedded to Trump, and party figures who earlier wanted nothing to do with him became, in effect, leaders of his campaign. The RNC leaders' unspoken calculation was that Trump wasn't likely to win anyway, but by supporting him in this way, they couldn't be blamed later for his loss.

In retrospect, it's clear that Trump was the recipient of good fortune in being able to run against Hillary Clinton, a highly intelligent and abundantly qualified Democrat who also happened to be perhaps the only person in her party who engendered as much intensely negative feeling within the electorate as did Trump.

The difference was that Trump also engendered intensively passionate feelings from his supporters, which became clear in the stretch run as the nominee drew big, raucous crowds to his rallies. Establishment Republicans were steering clear, which seemed to bother neither Trump nor his supporters. Indeed, at a late October rally in Wisconsin, Paul Ryan's home state, Trump's supporters began chanting, "Ryan sucks," attacking the man who nominally stood alongside Trump atop the Republican Party because he wasn't making an appearance with the nominee.

Though they were dismissed or discounted by the political pros, the crowds and their passion were a sign that something was happening. Moreover, Bannon convinced Trump to stay focused on his big three messages: *I'll stop illegal immigration and reduce legal immigration; I'll hammer China on trade; I'll stop pointless wars.* In many ways, each of those positions was at least in part a repudiation of actions conservative presidents of his own party had taken earlier. Trump didn't mind that, and, as wildly undisciplined as he seems, he actually was incredibly disciplined in staying on that message day after day, rally after rally. By the end, "we were on fire," Bannon says.

Still, even most people in Trump world didn't think he would win. In a phone call on the eve of the election, some leaders of the Trump campaign's system for gathering data on voters put his chances of winning at 15 percent. Bannon insists he believed Trump would win by carrying the industrial Upper Midwest, but he also recalls getting a phone call from a prominent Republican Trump supporter the weekend before the election trying to set up an appointment the week after the election, when he assumed Trump and Bannon would have nothing else to do.

On Election Night, the story was told in Florida. Things were going according to plan until it became clear in the state's conservative and more downscale Panhandle—Trump country—that his voters had shown up big, while Clinton voters were showing up in more or less the predicted numbers elsewhere in the state. That shifted the picture in Florida in dramatic fashion. When CNN's John King called Florida for Trump, I walked out of my office and into the *Journal*'s Washington newsroom and told our reporters to start getting the "Trump wins" story ready. If that was the pattern in Florida, there was every reason to think it would be the case in Pennsylvania and Michigan.

As it was. And, as it turned out, in Wisconsin as well. Trump lost the popular vote but won the Electoral College because he turned out white middle-class voters in big numbers, while key would-be Hillary Clinton supporters either stayed home or cast their votes for third-party candidates out of disgust.

The impossible had happened. The shock in Washington was near total, and the mood among conservatives was funereal. Trump was, of course, giddy, pretending he'd seen it coming all along. Whether Trump had changed the Republican Party or a changed Republican Party had produced Trump seemed suddenly immaterial. The fact is that Trump had sensed something in the country others hadn't. His message actually was very similar to the one Pat Buchanan had crafted three decades earlier—indeed, Republican pollster Bill McInturff referred to Trump as "Pat Buchanan with his own airplane"—but Trump had arrived with the message at precisely the right time, with precisely the tone to fit the angry times.

Trump set about the job of trying to staff and run a government, unlikely as that seemed. As he prepared to leave New York for Washington, a few of us from *The Wall Street Journal* trooped into his personal office at Trump Tower for a transition-season interview. Trump in private and in person is quite different from the Trump of public performance. He is charming and solicitous. He still dominates any conversation and can veer off on tangents much as he does in public presentations, but he often pauses to ask his visitors for their opinions.

The president-elect sat at his giant desk, with the majestic view of the New York skyline and Central Park in the background, two cellphones at his fingertips. On that day, as on so many, the worlds of celebrity, business, and politics were intertwined for him. We had been preceded into his office by Steve Harvey, the game-show host, Eric Schmidt, the former head of Google, and Senator Roy

Blunt of Missouri, head of the inauguration that was about to unfold.

Trump was still on message, unreeling his views, utterly un-
changed by the fact that he now was speaking as the next president
of the most powerful nation on earth. He wanted a good relationship with China, he said—he had just gotten a "beautiful card"
from President Xi Jinping—but China had treated the United
States very badly. Restrictions on Muslim immigrants would go up
instantly. He wasn't trying to micromanage American businesses,
but he would shame them into keeping their plants in the United
States.

And the Washington establishment was a failure. "Our country
has been run by people who truly didn't know what they were
doing," he said. "It's sort of like sometimes you have an employee
and every year you give them an increase, and you pay them more
and more and more and more. And then after fifteen years you say,
'Man, I'm paying this person three times what they're supposed to
be making.' And you have to cut them."

Thus did the notice go out: The establishments of both parties
—and of the conservative movement that had enjoyed such power
for almost forty years—had just been told by the new boss, borrowing the catchphrase of the reality TV show he once hosted, "You're
fired."

CHAPTER 13

Shock Waves

David Bossie is a burly, plainspoken conservative warrior, a blue-collar political operative who works on the hard-right edge of the Republican world by day while serving as a volunteer firefighter in his off time.

He cut his political teeth by serving as an investigator in the House of Representatives examining Bill and Hillary Clinton during the 1990s, after which he became a kind of permanent thorn in the Clintons' side. He served as president of Citizens United, an organization that tried to spread the conservative gospel by producing documentary books, videos, and documentary films—including, most famously, one sharply critical of Hillary Clinton, ahead of the 2008 Democratic primaries. Citizens United used its attempts to publicize that film as a tool to seek and then win a Supreme Court decision knocking down a federal ban on independent expenditures by corporations and unions on behalf of political candidates just before elections.

That case opened the gates for a flood of new expenditures by outside groups explicitly advocating the election or defeat of candidates—a development that horrified liberals and campaign-finance-reform groups, drew a personal condemnation from President Barack Obama during a State of the Union address, and thrilled conservatives.

Bossie also became an early booster of the Tea Party movement and personally helped organize some of its first rallies. Beyond that, he was noteworthy among conservatives because he had spent several years trying to convince Donald Trump to run for president, at the same time that many other conservatives either overlooked him or were aghast at the idea.

Bossie had met Trump through Steve Wynn, a casino magnate who was a supporter of Citizens United. Bossie had been, to say the least, underwhelmed by the Republican Party's recent nominees—George W. Bush, John McCain, and Mitt Romney—which was why he was attracted to Trump. He saw in Trump somebody who, while certainly not a conventional conservative, shared his desire to bust up the political establishment and was willing to go on the attack to do it. So after Trump's decision not to run in 2012, Bossie, starting in 2014, began making the case for running in 2016.

When Trump jumped into the race, Bossie didn't officially join his campaign but rather served as a kind of outside adviser and sounding board. Then the Trump campaign fell into chaos in the late summer of 2016, with the firing of its second campaign chief, Paul Manafort, who was replaced by Steve Bannon, Bossie's friend and sometime partner in political action. Bannon recruited Bossie to formally join the campaign as deputy campaign manager.

Thus did Bossie walk into an office in Trump Tower in August 2016 to begin working officially for the candidacy he had so long promoted. As it happened, he moved into an office that had been occupied by Manafort's deputy. Bossie sat down at the desk there, opened the drawers to see what he had inherited, and found at the bottom of one drawer a thick book: the plan that Mitt Romney had ordered prepared in 2012 to plot how he would set up his administration had he won the election that year. Bossie chuckled and threw the plan back in the drawer. At that stage, three months before the election, Trump was well behind Hillary Clinton in the polls, and virtually nobody thought the Trump team would be needing a plan on what to do after winning the election.

On the day after the election, Bossie walked back into his office and pulled out the Romney transition plan. It was useful, because there really was no Trump master plan on what to do next. There had been transition planning done in advance by a small team led by New Jersey governor Chris Christie, but its work was literally thrown out—the result, some in Trump world thought, of a feud between Christie and Trump son-in-law Jared Kushner. That feud had its roots in the work Christie had done years earlier as a federal prosecutor pursuing Kushner's father. So now the old Romney planning book served as a starting point.

Surprising as it was, though, Trump's election was decidedly not a fluke. Trump represented a new version of the Republican Party, one that was more Main Street than Wall Street. The foot soldiers in this new Republican Party, who had shown up in larger numbers than expected on Election Day 2016, and in the key places, shared Trump's disdain for anything that smacked of "the establishment."

Trump's view of the establishment was formed in part by his own life experience in the New York City environs. He was seen by some of the social and financial elites in Manhattan as a nouveau riche intruder from Queens. In the same way, Trump Republicans felt they were looked down upon and ridiculed by arrogant cultural liberals and the well-educated denizens of the new-tech economy. They, too, believed they had been overlooked, ridiculed, and taken advantage of by the elites.

Among other things, many of these new Trump stalwarts had limited appetites for traditional conservative principles. They didn't want to hear that the government programs on which they and their families relied—Medicare, Medicaid, Social Security, disability payments—had to be cut in order to chase some ideologue's dream of a balanced budget. They had been hearing from conservative Republicans for two generations that they would benefit from trade agreements, but they didn't see much evidence of that in the precincts where they resided. Conservative thinkers saw immigrants as a boon to an economy that thrived on the free movement of goods and people, while many of these new Republicans saw them as interlopers who took jobs, drove down wages, and diluted their view of what America should be.

Above all, they wanted to be citizens of America, not citizens of the world.

Donald Trump told them they were right about all these things—and he began to govern accordingly. Concern about deficits? That went out the window as Trump budgets drove the federal deficit toward $1 trillion annually. Limited powers of the chief executive? In his first week alone, Trump issued executive orders declaring, on his own authority, that the United States would withdraw from the Trans-Pacific Partnership trade agreement in Asia, build a wall along the southern border with Mexico, take federal funds away from so-called sanctuary cities that provide safe haven to undocumented aliens, suspend a refugee program, and temporarily ban entry to the United States from a series of Muslim-majority countries.

Trump was the same sort of exotic hybrid that Ross Perot had been: a billionaire populist whose antipathy toward the establishment around him made his fans admire his wealth without holding it against him. He had an instinctive understanding of the new Republican Party that escaped many others.

This meant Trump simply didn't have the same sympathy toward traditional big-business positions in favor of immigration (a good source of labor and highly skilled workers) and trade (the best way for a mature economy such as America's to continue growing). The shift became obvious during the presidential campaign, when the U.S. Chamber of Commerce, the traditional bastion of big-business sentiment and sensibility and normally a reliable ally of Republicans, attacked candidate Trump and was, in turn, attacked by him. At one point, Chamber president Thomas Donohue called out Trump by name, saying he "has very little idea about what trade really is."

When candidate Trump became President Trump, he didn't forget. Early on, aides sent out the word: No Chamber of Commerce officials would be hired for the administration (an edict that in fact didn't last). In hopes of smoothing over relations, a White House aide invited the Chamber to send a representative to a meeting Trump was holding with business representatives to discuss his agenda.

There was too much presidential antipathy toward Donohue to invite him to personally represent the Chamber, so Thomas Collamore, the group's longtime executive vice president, drew the assignment instead. Collamore knew he might be heading into hostile territory, so he sought to make his presence low-key. At the outset of the meeting, with a contingent of White House reporters and network cameras in the room to catch a few minutes of the session, the business representatives each, in turn, identified themselves and their organizations. Collamore dutifully did so.

Then Trump shooed away the press and turned to Collamore. "Hey, Chamber guy," he said. "What's the problem with you guys?" Trump complained that the Chamber hadn't been "nice to me" during the campaign and expressed annoyance that it wasn't with him on trade issues. Collamore recalls that he did his best to calm the waters, replying, "Well, Mr. President, the Chamber has a long history of not getting directly involved in presidential campaigns. But we had an awful lot to do with making sure you had a Republican majority in the Senate and House to work with."

Trump persisted, protesting again that the Chamber hadn't been good to him on trade and wondering why that was. Collamore demurred, saying that Trump might find that, overall, he and the Chamber would have a lot more on which they agreed than disagreed. Trump replied: *Well, I'm not very happy about it all. But you can go back and tell your boss we're going to turn the page and work together.*

In fact, the Chamber, like a lot of other groups and individuals, began to build bridges to Trump, despite misgivings about his new approach to Republican governance. When the president made his first appointment to the Supreme Court, Donohue decided the Chamber would break its own precedent and publicly endorse the nominee—and include senators' votes on his nomination on the scorecard the business group keeps on key votes, for determining whether to support a lawmaker at election time.

At another point, the Chamber gave Vice President Mike Pence a book its staff had spent six months preparing, detailing a raft of federal regulations it advocated eliminating. Pence received the tome gratefully. Some of the Chamber suggestions soon made it into the list of regulations the administration was eliminating, either by executive order or in conjunction with the Republican-controlled Congress.

Moreover, many business leaders, chagrined as they might be about Trump's anti-free-trade rhetoric, quietly agreed with him that China had become a mercantilist threat taking advantage of the international trade system to hurt American companies and stealing American companies' intellectual property. Many Democrats also agreed with Trump that China's behavior was out of bounds, though the extent of that agreement often was lost in the constant partisan sniping that surrounded the Trump administration. At one point, Democratic Senate leader Chuck Schumer, who otherwise engaged in an almost constant war of words with his fellow New Yorker, stepped back to send a tweet to President Trump telling him to "hang tough on China . . . Don't back down."

Early in Trump's first year in office, a few *Wall Street Journal* colleagues and I walked into the Oval Office for an interview with Trump that came to be dominated by the trade confrontation with China that was just taking shape. Almost all other presidential interviews in which I've been involved took place in a relatively informal atmosphere, on the chairs and sofas that form a kind of semicircle in front of the fireplace in the Oval Office. Trump has a different style. He sat behind the massive Resolute Desk, a nineteenth-century gift from the British government. Built from the timbers of a British ship, the HMS *Resolute,* it has been deployed as the desk of presidents on and off for more than a century.

From the Resolute Desk, Trump could see his interviewers arrayed in chairs around the desk, and at one point he punched a button on his desk to summon a White House steward to bring his favorite beverage—Diet Coke—for him and his guests. At another point in the interview, when the conversation turned to alleged Chinese manipulation of its currency to gain unfair advantage in international trade, the president had an aide summon Treasury Secretary Steven Mnuchin, who came hustling in from the Treasury Department, next door.

Trump said he had told his Chinese counterpart, President Xi Jinping, of his views on Chinese behavior when they met at Trump's Florida golf resort in the early days of his presidency: "I said you have the Chinese taking advantage of the United States for many years—many, many years, long before the Obama administration. I told him, 'We've built China with the money you've taken out of the United States. We have rebuilt China, and we can't build our own roads.'" That state of affairs, Trump declared, was going to change, with or without an agreement with the Chinese.

But then he offered a fascinating insight into the Trump vision of how international dealmaking should work. He'd cut a deal more favorable to China on trade if the Chinese helped the United States rid its next-door neighbor, North Korea, of nuclear weapons. He said he'd told Xi that the prevailing trade deficits were unacceptable, then added, "'But you want to make a great deal? Solve the problem in North Korea.' That's worth having deficits. And that's worth having not as good a trade deal as I would normally be able to make."

In other words, everything was negotiable.

With that in mind, the business world basically struck an implicit bargain with Trump. Business leaders and the financial markets calculated that they would get from the president the two things they wanted most dearly—tax cuts and deregulation—without suffering the third result they feared, which was an all-out trade war. They counted on Trump to get tough with China without letting things get out of hand. And through most of the Trump first term, the business world was satisfied with the bargain. They got a big tax cut and deregulation, on the one hand; on the other, while Trump walked repeatedly up to the brink of an all-out trade war with China, he also regularly stepped back from the red line.

Yet businesses also got as part of the bargain something less pleasant, which they should have seen coming. Whereas traditional conservatives instinctively dislike the idea of government intervention in the marketplace, Trump intervened incessantly. Economic sanctions and denying access to financial markets became his tools of choice in penalizing foreign countries that crossed him. He publicly rebuked companies and pressured them to make business decisions to his liking. He attacked General Motors for its plans to build a factory in Mexico and urged motorcycle buyers to boycott Harley-Davidson if it built a plant overseas.

Oddly, this willingness to attack big corporations sometimes put Trump on the same side as Democratic liberals and their crusades against big businesses. Pharmaceutical companies were a regular target of Trump's, for example, just as they were regularly in the sights of Democrats. When Democratic House Speaker Nancy Pelosi introduced a bill designed to lower drug prices, which many conservatives thought amounted to an attempt to impose price controls, Trump tweeted out his pleasure. He also took on the hospital and health insurance industries in a populist fashion when his administration ordered them to disclose for the first time the rates they secretly negotiated with each other, allowing patients a new look at some of the forces driving up health costs.

At one point, in the midst of his trade fights with China, he tweeted that he "hereby ordered" American companies to look for places other than China to do business and, in the same tweet, commanded Amazon, FedEx, and UPS to simply refuse to deliver shipments of opioid drugs from China. His imposition of tariffs on China cost American companies and consumers billions of dollars in higher costs for Chinese products, while the retaliatory tariffs China imposed cost American farmers billions of dollars. And when farmers—Trump loyalists for the most part—felt the pain, Trump maneuvered for government aid to be sent to them. Thus, his policies changed the marketplace, and then tried to use government funds to make up for that change. It's hard to imagine a scenario less in keeping with classic conservative economic beliefs.

Of course, leaders are rarely pure in putting their beliefs into action. Even Ronald Reagan imposed tariffs on a broad range of Japanese goods, in what his administration described as an attempt to jolt the Japanese into adopting fairer trade practices. But Trump proved to be far more profligate in his use of government powers, generally showing less fealty to the "invisible hand" of the market-place than to the visible hand of presidential pressure.

Sometimes Trump's actions seemed detached from any political philosophy whatsoever, driven instead by instinct or down paths paved by personal relationships. At one point in the midst of his trade fight with China, Trump's administration had banned U.S. companies from exporting electronic components to Chinese phone maker ZTE, which had been accused by American officials both of using its phones to help the Chinese government spy on Americans and of defying American economic sanctions by selling to Iran and North Korea. American components were so important to ZTE that the ban threatened to put ZTE out of business.

While the controversy was roiling, Trump hosted a group of Republican lawmakers at a meeting in the White House and star-tled them by declaring that he was going to find a way to lift the ZTE ban. He had been asked to do so as a "personal" favor by Chi-nese president Xi Jinping, Trump explained, and he wanted to lend a hand to his Chinese counterpart.

As that suggests, even on the core issue of trade with China, Trump was never quite as dogmatic as his rhetoric made it appear, and the bottom line could simply be moved. For example, a signifi-cant shift in China trade strategy came in mid-October 2019, when the president abandoned his long-standing position that all the trade disputes with China had to be resolved in one comprehensive pack-age rather than piece by piece. Trump's advisers worried increas-ingly that the all-or-nothing approach would inevitably lead to an increase in the tariff wars and potentially push down the economy by year's end, when an increase in the existing tariffs and the addition of new ones were to hit. The president's big three advisers on trade strategy—trade representative Robert Lighthizer, National Economic Council head Larry Kudlow, and Treasury Secretary Steven Mnuchin—all were hoping to head off new tariffs.

So Kudlow arranged for a group of Trump-friendly economic thinkers to gather for an Oval Office meeting with the president, at which the experts warned that a new round of tariffs could harm an otherwise good economy. Trump, of course, knew that a sliding economy at the end of 2019 spelled trouble for his 2020 reelection bid. Meantime, Trump's in-house advisers began gently suggesting a shift to a phased approach. Thus, the ground was laid when Chinese negotiators arrived in Washington for a new round of talks. Mnuchin hosted them at a dinner at which he floated the idea of working through the trade issues in stages. Suppose, he suggested, the Chinese agreed to buy a lot of American agricultural goods and made some moves to help Americans protect their intellectual property while operating in China in return for a pullback on American tariffs. Could that work? The Chinese seemed agreeable. Finally, in the Oval Office the next day, Trump was presented with the idea of such an agreement as a first step, and he said he could live with it—even though the outcome would fall well short of the sweeping deal he had once sought.

By the end of 2019, the Trump team and China had negotiated a "Phase One" trade agreement that dealt with some, though hardly all, of the American complaints about China's trade practices. The deal called for China to resume and then increase purchases of American agricultural products in return for a hiatus on more tariffs on Chinese imports. The deal didn't address the more systemic and intractable American complaints about the unfair subsidies and aid China provides its own companies, issues that were left for later negotiations. Trump didn't have the comprehensive solution that he sought, but a temporary truce was enough to please the financial markets.

As that suggests, trying to predict Trump's gut-level calls can be a risky proposition. At another point in mid-2019, the country's three biggest airlines—United, Delta, and American—sought his help in a running feud they had been conducting with the national airlines of Qatar and the United Arab Emirates. The American air carriers had long argued that the Persian Gulf airlines engaged in unfair competition, because they received giant subsidies from their governments that allowed them to undercut American carriers, which amounted to unfair practices that were taking away American jobs and profits.

The Persian Gulf airlines, in a kind of truce, had agreed earlier not to open any new air routes from their countries to the United States. But the U.S. airlines were incensed that Qatar Airways appeared to have found a clever way around that promise. The Qatar airline had acquired 49 percent of a small Italian airline, rebranded it Air Italy, and begun offering nonstop flights from Milan to U.S. destinations—a move that effectively allowed Qatar Airways to book customers from the Persian Gulf to new destinations in the United States via Milan.

Surely, the airlines' executives thought, an America-first, nationalist president would want to help. So the carriers asked for a meeting to plead with Trump for help in forcing Qatar Airways to stop the practice. The airlines' chief executives were duly invited to meet with Trump.

A few days before the CEOs walked in, though, they were startled to learn that the White House had invited another guest to the Oval Office discussion: Akbar al Baker, the Qatar Airways chief executive and, in the American executives' eyes, the real villain in this drama. Al Baker, it turned out, was a longtime Trump social friend. Trump and his wife, Melania, had attended a Qatar Airways gala at New York's Lincoln Center in 2007 to mark the airline's inaugural flights to New York's John F. Kennedy Airport. Pictures from that night show the smiling Trump couple standing alongside al Baker and his wife, Samara. They continued to move in similar social circles.

So when the airline executives walked into the meeting, the

president introduced al Baker as his friend. And the meeting went downhill from there.

When Trump was told that the Delta Airlines chief executive, Ed Bastian, wasn't attending because he had a personal commitment, the president flew into a rage at what he considered a snub. Then, according to those briefed on the meeting, when the discussion turned to the American air carriers' complaint, al Baker walked over to the president's desk and handed him a piece of paper that listed the number of Boeing airliners each of the airlines was planning to buy. It showed that Qatar Airways had just made a purchase of new Boeing airliners, while Delta had switched to Europe's Airbus for its newest generation of planes. That also sent Trump into a fury.

Of course, there were more substantive reasons to oppose the big American airlines' pleas for help. Several top Trump aides thought the Middle Eastern airlines were providing American fliers with good service and low prices and shouldn't be stopped from doing so. Frederick Smith, the chief executive of FedEx, the air cargo giant, also attended the meeting and sided against the American airlines, knowing that starting a fight would disrupt the good working relationship his company had with Qatar and other Persian Gulf states. In the end, a meeting that the airline executives thought would produce some help from a president who had sided with American companies on other trade fronts yielded next to nothing for them. The airline executives were told, essentially, to file a complaint with the Transportation Department—which wasn't even represented at the meeting.

Trump's departure from his party's prevailing national security principles was equally jarring. Neoconservative internationalists had enjoyed great sway with Republican decision-makers since Reagan's day, but Trump simply didn't buy into the neocons' inclination to try to advance American interests by intervening abroad. In fact, Trump seemed to think that their instincts had gotten American interests exactly backward. The basic problem with prevailing national security policy was that it had America overextended around the globe, especially militarily, Trump believed.

One senior official who worked closely with Trump came to believe that his aversion to international engagements was the result of his "coming of age" in the 1970s, when the Vietnam War racked the country. Trump came away from that period, this official believes, with his own personal version of the Vietnam Syndrome—an aversion to military engagements abroad. Trump believed Vietnam not only had harmed the country's military but had produced stagflation—a period of stagnant economic growth and inflation that affected him personally as he was starting out his career as a New York real estate developer. Moreover, Trump's personal instincts were reinforced by a kind of isolationist wing within the Republican Party, led by Senator Rand Paul of Kentucky and the influential Koch brothers, David and Charles, the wealthy political donors who were more libertarian than conservative.

Trump's distaste for what he called "foreign wars" was so well known within his circle of advisers that it created a problem early in his administration: There needed to be a decision about the extent and future of America's military presence in Afghanistan. Top aides, knowing the subject would raise Trump's ire, were simply reluctant to bring it up. But General H. R. McMaster, the president's national security adviser, decided it was his responsibility to walk into the buzz saw by putting the question on the table. McMaster knew a lot about Afghanistan—more than anyone else around the president. He had served in Kabul, Afghanistan's capital, as a top military planner from 2010 to 2012. Beyond that, he had been a combat commander in Iraq and had overseen Pentagon planning for a comprehensive strategy in the greater Middle East.

By the time McMaster arrived in the White House, the United States was trapped in a cycle of military deployments that no longer seemed tied to a discernible plan to bring an end to the Afghan conflict. But simply pulling the plug on Afghanistan hardly seemed the answer to the quandary. So McMaster arranged a series of sessions with Trump and his top national security aides to give the president some options.

Once those conversations began, Trump's attitude was reflected in the questions he raised, one official recalls: *Why do we care? Why does it cost so much? Why can't others do it?* Beyond his obvious skepticism about the virtues of remaining engaged in Afghanistan, his deeply ingrained distrust of the establishment around him came to the fore as well. Trump thought the military leaders he heard from, including McMaster, had botched the military mission in Afghanistan, leading to a decade and a half of low-level warfare, so he made clear that he didn't trust them. He compelled McMaster to arrange a White House lunch with four enlisted servicemen who had served in Afghanistan. They brought to the table the typical grunt's cynicism about what the higher-ups were doing, thereby reinforcing Trump's own cynicism.

Most advisers thought it important to remain engaged in the country from which Islamic militants planned the 9/11 terror strikes, so they mounted counterarguments. One was to convince Trump that America's commitments abroad, while important, actually were smaller than he realized. In fact, when Trump took office, American military deployments were at their lowest level in sixty years.

The debate came to a head—or at least it was supposed to—at a meeting between Trump and his top national security aides at the White House in July 2017. The president's top national security officials—McMaster, Defense Secretary Jim Mattis, Secretary of State Rex Tillerson—went in hoping to convince Trump not only to abandon his idea of pulling out of Afghanistan but to actually add a few thousand troops. The trade-off was that those troops would be allowed to become more aggressive in going after the Taliban militants who were threatening Afghanistan's legitimate government. Meanwhile, under this approach, the United States also would put new pressure on neighboring Pakistan to stop throwing a lifeline to the Taliban.

As the conversation unfolded, Trump fumed again at his options, but he didn't say no.

The issue lingered until the end of that summer, when there finally was a climactic meeting at the Camp David presidential retreat. Trump was still resisting staying in Afghanistan. His advisers pushed back, though, by appealing to Trump's basic, black-and-white instincts about winning and losing: If he left Afghanistan, that could give Islamic State militants a base from which to launch new attacks on the United States. But he could win if he added some American troops, gave those troops more leeway to engage the Taliban, and launched a peace process with the Taliban on a parallel track.

Mattis finally turned the tide by convincing Trump that he wouldn't be simply blessing more of the same, but embarking on an entirely new approach. Trump bought the idea, though grudgingly, and gave a speech to the nation essentially saying he was going against his instincts and staying in Afghanistan. Thousands more troops would go in.

Still, the push and pull between Trump's nationalist/populist instincts and the Republican foreign policy establishment didn't abate. Rather, it emerged as the clearest divide between Trump and the majority of Republicans.

In fact, the drama was replayed over and over again in decisions about other spheres of the world. When Turkish president Recep Tayyip Erdoğan visited the White House just weeks after the Afghanistan decision, he sat down for a meeting in the Roosevelt Room with Trump and his national security team and launched into a long complaint that the United States had begun to send arms to a Kurdish military group next door in Syria. The Kurds had emerged as America's most reliable partners in fighting the Islamic State, or ISIS, in Iraq and Syria. They were the forces most willing to step in and do the kind of fighting Trump didn't want American forces undertaking.

Erdoğan, by contrast, considered the Kurds the real terrorists, because their brethren just across the border in Turkey had long mounted an insurgency against the Turkish regime, and he said so, bluntly. Trump listened patiently for a while—surprisingly patiently, in fact—and then responded by suggesting maybe the United States should avoid the problem by simply leaving the region. Trump asked: *Why am I in your neighborhood anyway? Why don't you take on ISIS? It's your problem, not mine.*

Trump's comments were startling. Was the president of the United States really threatening to abandon the fight in Syria, where American forces had worked so hard to eliminate the ISIS caliphate, widely seen as a threat to the whole region? Was he just going to turn the whole thing over to a foreign strongman of dubious reliability?

To the relief of the other Americans around the table, Erdoğan backed down. *No,* he said, *you should stay involved in Syria.* He didn't want Trump to go that far.

Yet two years later, in late 2019, Trump would do exactly what he suggested in that meeting. When Erdoğan told the president in a phone call that he wanted to send his troops across the border into Syria to clean out Kurdish fighters, Trump said he would move the relatively few American troops left in Syria out of the way. Not only would Kurds who had stood by America's side be left to fend for themselves, but the move would give Trump the opportunity he had been looking for to simply get most American troops out of Syria altogether. Proclaiming he wanted to finish off the cycle of "endless wars" in the Middle East, Trump ordered most American forces withdrawn from northern Syria and moved into Iraq. Instead of relying on the United States, the Kurds shifted their alliances toward Russia, Syria, and Iran, who were willing to stay engaged in Syria.

The reaction to Trump's Syria move showed that he was indeed leading a new kind of foreign policy—but also that there remained plenty of dissenters within the conservative movement and the Republican Party. Senator Lindsey Graham of South Carolina, normally a staunch Trump ally, spoke out on Twitter in strong disagreement: "American isolationism: Did not work before WWII. Did not work before 9/11. Will not work now. When it comes to fighting ISIS it's a bad idea to outsource American national security to Russia, Iran and Turkey. To believe otherwise is very dangerous."

Fellow Republican senator Rand Paul of Kentucky, though, expressed precisely the opposite view in supporting Trump. He took to Twitter to praise Trump as "the first President in my lifetime to understand what is our national interest and what is not. He is stopping the endless wars and we will be stronger as a result. The Cheney/Graham Neocon War Caucus has cost us too much fighting endless wars."

Trump's disdain for traditional military commitments extended to the most basic of them all: the North Atlantic Treaty Organization, the Western alliance credited with successfully protecting the West's political and economic systems throughout the Cold War. "He sees no point to NATO," one former top Trump adviser says bluntly. In fact, Trump came far closer to simply withdrawing America from this crown jewel of alliances than was generally known. At a summit meeting with other NATO leaders in Brussels in the summer of 2018, Trump was so critical of what he considered the alliance's unfair reliance on American military, and even of the amount of money NATO had spent on a new headquarters building, that his fellow leaders convened a special closed session to discuss his grievances. National Security Adviser John Bolton accompanied Trump to the meeting, which turned tense and testy. At one point, Bolton called White House Chief of Staff John Kelly, a retired four-star Marine general, who had intended to skip the meeting to deal with other business, and told him: *You'd better get over here. We're about to withdraw from NATO.* Kelly hustled to Trump's side and found that the president was, in fact, considering simply declaring America was out. According to one former adviser, Kelly quickly talked Trump off that ledge, in part by convincing him he would be crucified by the political establishment and the press if he took such a step. Still, Trump aides remained worried that he still might pull the plug on NATO at some point.

Few episodes better illustrated the divides Donald Trump opened within the Republican Party. Overall, his approach immensely pleased his supporters, who shared his view that America had been taken advantage of in the global marketplace, that it had lost more than its share of young soldiers in the effort to keep the world safe from bad actors, and that the masters of the economy deserved a little pushing around. Bannon liked to point out that core Trump supporters—the families of those soldiers who put their lives at risk in the Middle East, and those white working-class voters who felt endangered by immigrants in their communities and trade deals that ushered factories abroad—were in sync with the president they had helped elect.

Moreover, there was simply no disputing that the economy was doing well under Trump. It had already been embarked on a long period of steady growth under Obama—something Trump never admitted—but the trend continued and stretched out into the longest economic expansion in American history. The stock market was pleased. It took off shortly after Trump was elected and, except for a brief period at the end of 2018 when a combination of interest rate increases by the Federal Reserve Board and a bout of worries over whether the trade argument with China might spin out of control, it stayed high. It fell back to earth only when worries over a coronavirus outbreak sent shudders through the economy in early 2020. That rosy economic picture had a lot to do with Trump's consistently strong support among Republicans. In early 2019, a *Wall Street Journal*/NBC News poll found that 88 percent of Republican voters approved of the job Trump was doing, a higher level of support than Ronald Reagan had enjoyed within the party at the same point in his administration.

Yet the deep, passionate splits over Syria, trade, and immigration showed that a big question mark continued to hang over conservatives: Had Donald Trump transformed the Republican Party and the conservative movement permanently? Or was he an aberration whose influence and views would fade away when he left the scene?

CHAPTER 14

What Just Happened?

The Reagan conservative movement—and it really was Ronald
Reagan's movement, built around his personality and his personal success—transformed American politics.

It reshaped the Republican Party, sapped power away from the
Democrats, moved the country to the right, and changed the national debate. Reagan inspired the construction of an entire new
infrastructure of conservative institutions in Washington and
around the country, and he empowered a generation of young, aspiring politicians and policymakers. For twenty of the thirty-six
years after Reagan was elected, someone pledging loyalty to his
precepts occupied the Oval Office. From there, they filled the
American judiciary with a generation's worth of conservative
judges. Waving the conservative banner, Republicans won control
of the White House and the Senate in 1980, reclaimed control of
the House in 1994 after a four-decade drought, and then did so
again in 2010.

Beneath the surface, though, the conservative movement had
started to run dry as the new millennium dawned. So what happened? What brought about the decline of Reagan conservatism?

"We're victims of our own success," argues Karl Rove, who was
the chief political strategist for President George W. Bush. "We
said, 'If you put us in power, we will bring down the Soviet Union,'

and it happened. 'Give us the reins and we will have a country that is far more prosperous.' And we were far more prosperous. And after 9/11, 'We will keep you safe. There will be no more attacks on the home.' And it happened.

"And that was a period where we really needed to be engaging and rethinking how we take our conservative principles and apply them to the new circumstances the country is facing."

Yet a lot of other forces were at work to slowly undermine the conservative movement and open the door to Trump populism. As it grew in size and strength, the conservative movement had taken on followers who all called themselves conservatives but actually carried widely varying agendas. Some conservatives (classic libertarians) were for keeping government out of the bedroom, while others (in the religious right) wanted to ban gay marriage. Some valued personal liberty above national security, others the reverse.

George Will, the conservative columnist who was as close to Reagan as any journalist, concludes that the rise of Trump shows that the conservative movement simply wasn't as broad as imagined, in part because it had come to include a lot of people who mouthed conservative principles they didn't, down deep, really believe. "There are a lot fewer conservatives of my sort in the country than I and others thought," he says. "A number of people got tired of pretending to believe it, and they didn't" really embrace conservative principles.

Along the way, the glue that had held all the conservative pieces together—the crusade against Communism—had dried up with the decline and then the fall of the Soviet Union, and with China's turn toward a kind of central-command capitalism. As a result, the pieces didn't stick together so well. After that, the disastrous war in Iraq, started and prosecuted by a Republican president, thoroughly undercut the credibility of the party's neoconservative wing of national security thinkers who were the cheerleaders for the conflict.

Perhaps most important, a socioeconomic change was sweeping over the Republican Party, one that most of its leaders either missed or underestimated. Millions of middle-class and blue-collar workers switched to the Republican Party over time, not for economic reasons but for cultural ones. Many simply couldn't abide Democratic positions on issues as diverse as abortion, gay rights, prayer in schools, and gun control; the parties' economic views were secondary for these voters. The Tea Party wave in 2010 accelerated these trends, wiping out Democratic lawmakers in rural and working-class districts across the Midwest and the Southeast and completing the transformation of those areas into Republican strongholds.

Meantime, the rise of the high-tech industry and the information economy sent money, jobs, educated Americans, and economic power migrating toward parts of the country that are Democratic bastions—the West and East Coasts, and urban centers. Those areas already leaned Democratic, and simply became more so.

One consequence of these changes is that the Republican Party has moved more downscale over time, while the Democratic Party has moved more upscale. Between the elections of 2008 and 2018, economic output from congressional districts represented by Republicans remained essentially flat, while the economic output in districts represented by Democrats rose 37 percent on average. Over the same period, median household income jumped nearly 17 percent in Democratic districts while falling 3 percent in Republican ones.

Today, Democrats represent the areas of the nation with the highest levels of college graduates, as well as the largest clusters of jobs in technology and finance. Republicans, meanwhile, represent the districts with the largest clusters of manufacturing, agriculture, and mining jobs. When congressional districts are measured in terms of concentration of residents with bachelor's degrees, the top seventeen districts all are represented by Democrats. Plenty of well-to-do and well-educated Americans remained where they had always been in the Republican Party, of course, loyal still to its traditional economic and cultural values. Yet the demographic mix of the GOP had changed around them.

Trump ultimately won the 2016 presidential election over Democrat Hillary Clinton because of his ability to turn out working-class and middle-class Americans in Michigan, Wisconsin, Pennsylvania, and Ohio. "Those were all Reagan voters," says Steve Bannon, Trump's onetime political guru and a driving force behind the new populism. "Some of these people hadn't voted since Reagan's second term. These are hardcore Reagan Democrats and working-class Americans." That alignment made it possible for Trump to win the presidency in the Electoral College even as Clinton took the popular vote by some three million.

These Republican foot soldiers didn't think the increasingly globalized economy was working for them. In fact, they thought they were directly harmed by it. Traditional conservatives missed the rise of anti-globalization sentiment at the base of their own party, "and they missed it in a big way," says Bannon.

Yuval Levin, though personally and stylistically different from Bannon in almost every way, agrees. Levin became interested in the conservative movement as a high school student in New Jersey, inspired in some measure by reading a George Will book, *Statecraft as Soulcraft*. As a high schooler, he worked in the local office of a Republican member of Congress, decided he wanted to go to college in Washington, and enrolled in American University, in the nation's capital. Eventually he found his way into Republican staff jobs in Congress and ended up on the staff of Newt Gingrich. After Gingrich's abrupt departure from Congress, Levin returned to school to get a Ph.D. at the University of Chicago, worked in the George W. Bush White House, and ended up in the think-tank world.

He is a conservative intellectual who is contemplative and speaks quietly and carefully. After years of toiling in the conservative and Republican vineyards, he now is convinced that conservatives lost their way on economic policy over the years, allowing their thinking to become simply libertarian—that is, convinced that a hands-off government policy was the right answer in almost every case.

That trend, he says, made conservatives miss the fact that their policies generally weren't appealing to working-class voters who needed help, and specifically were undercutting conservatives' social goals of promoting strong families. "What became clear over time was the sense that middle- and working-class families were not part of the coalition, and that was a real political problem," he says. So Levin now is trying to craft policies that steer conservative tax plans to help families by providing tax benefits that specifically make it easier to raise children and send them to college, and to provide healthcare for them along the way.

Economic inequality—the gap between those at the upper end of the income and wealth scales and those in the middle and at the bottom end—has grown steadily since Ronald Reagan took office. Critics see tax cuts and more open international trade as being at least partly responsible, because they gave new economic advantages to those in the top tiers.

The limits of conservative economic ideology were laid bare by the financial crisis that began in 2007. The federal government's rescue of big financial institutions seemed to many voters a sign that the free markets conservatives talked about endlessly weren't free at all but rather were rigged to benefit the rich and powerful. The magic of markets was supposed to bring rigor and discipline to the economic life of the nation and create a system in which the strong would survive because they deserved to, and the weak would be weeded out because they needed to be. When a conservative administration chose to bail out one big financial house, Bear Stearns, and then let another, Lehman Brothers, go under, the government seemed to be picking winners and losers—a very un-conservative idea.

Perhaps most important, conservatives missed a deep cultural anxiety that had taken hold at the grass roots of the new Republican Party amid these socioeconomic changes. A growing number of new-wave Republicans were less worried about free-market economic philosophy or international power struggles than about their feeling that they were being shut out of the country in which they grew up. The number of undocumented aliens—illegal aliens in the vernacular—more than doubled in the 1990s to an estimated 8.6 million, and then grew further to 12 million by 2007, undermining the traditional conservative message on immigration. Many in the heartland felt that immigrants and the Spanish language were becoming too prominent in their communities, that society's religious bonds were being frayed, that they were being forced to accept gay marriages and transgender rights whether they liked it or not—and, in fact, they didn't like it.

By 2016, conservatives were united more by what they were against—progressives and liberals—than what they were for. The door to a populist uprising had been swung open, and Donald Trump walked through it.

CHAPTER 15

What Now?

On a midsummer's day in 2019, a group of political thinkers and activists gathered at the Ritz-Carlton, a luxury hotel situated in Washington's West End, on the boundary between downtown's stuffy law and lobbyists' offices and the chic trendiness of Georgetown. Their audacious goal: Redefine what it means to be a conservative.

Specifically, the topic of the conference was "National Conservatism," and its underlying premise was that conservatives should embrace, rather than recoil from, the nationalist and populist themes coursing through American politics. Nowhere in the summary of the conference's goals did the name Trump appear, but the connection was obvious and inevitable. This was a gathering meant to find a formula for squaring the conservative movement of Ronald Reagan with Donald Trump's "Make America Great Again" view of the world.

Yoram Hazony, an Israeli-born political thinker and the driving force behind the conference, best summarized the arguments in an address early in the conference. Hazony, with his neat hair and wire-rimmed glasses, looks more like a junior high math teacher than a political rabble-rouser, but his looks belied the passion and even anger he brought to the task.

He started by establishing his own roots in, and fealty to, the

Reagan Revolution. "As a high schooler, I played Ronald Reagan in a mock debate," he said. "In college, I founded a Reaganite magazine."

In the years since Reagan's presidency, he argued, the conservative movement had gone seriously astray: "Something went terribly wrong with American conservatism after the fall of the Berlin Wall in November 1989. . . . In the 1990s, the conservative movement was drunk with the feeling of power as a result of the victory over Communism, and people who are drunk with power lose touch of reality."

Conservatives, he argued, bought in to the "nonsense" that a new world order was possible after the fall of Communism, that economic considerations prevailed over all else, and that America could thrive as a kind of borderless state in the middle of a global economy in which national identity didn't matter. American conservatism had, in fact, become libertarianism, in which the only thing that mattered was individual freedom. Hazony viewed that instinct as being at odds with the true vision of conservatism articulated by British philosopher Edmund Burke, who saw conservatism as properly rooted in customs, tradition, and, above all else, religion.

So, Hazony argued, true conservatives should embrace nationalism and its fealty to traditional cultural values, as well as its skepticism about immigration. "The real political world is one of competing tribes and nations," he said. "It's the real existence of tribes and nations that generates political phenomena such as national borders, independent national governments, national traditions, national cohesion, and national dissolution."

The "elites" trained in American universities had become "completely blind" to the traditional views of the broader public, he argued. "It doesn't make a darn bit of difference what the economic arguments are," he said. "If the country is fraying so badly, the cohesion is so shocked, that adding more immigrants is going to literally tear the country to pieces, stop. . . . Have some common sense."

As he marched through his arguments, Hazony arrived at what sounded like a clarion call to, in the words that had propelled Trump into the White House, make America great again: "America has been in the business now for three generations of uprooting every traditional concept that has made this country recognizable. Within two generations people can't tell the difference between a man and a woman. They can't tell the difference between a foreigner and a citizen. They can't tell the difference between this side of the border and the other side of the border. They can't tell the difference between paying back your debts and simply borrowing forever."

The split over nationalism neatly framed the identity crisis into which conservatives had fallen. What Hazony was calling a return to the true roots of conservatism others saw as an invitation to xenophobia, racism, and divisive tribalism. In their eyes, that amounted to a rejection of the kind of conservatism Reagan preached, which embodied a belief in free trade, the virtues of immigration, and a strong American leadership role beyond America's borders.

"There are those of us who really do believe in a conservative attitude towards government as well as policies," says Eric Cantor. "I don't think right now the movement is being helped by what's going on. I mean, essentially, you have nationalists in charge of the government. You've got socialists wanting to take over, and you've got the old Republicans and the old Democrats trying to figure out how they're going to reemerge."

The man who stood in the middle of this debate was, of course, President Trump. Conservative writer Robert Tracinski perhaps best summarized the argument that the embrace of Donald Trump actually represented not the embrace of old principles but the abandonment of all principles. Writing for *The Bulwark,* a new online site populated by anti-Trump conservative writers and thinkers, Tracinski said,

> The big thing we've discovered over the past four years is the number of people for whom the actual content of ideas and policy is largely irrelevant, compared to the pure tribal satisfac-

tion of venting their hatred for the "elites" and the "mainstream media." The source of Donald Trump's bizarre allure among conservatives is the constant, unrelenting intensity with which he allows them to indulge in this—a form of tribal hatred that is all the purer precisely because it has been freed from any pretense of having to be loyal to abstract principles.

Over time, conservatives split, roughly speaking, into three camps when it came to Trump.

First are the Trump true believers, people such as David Bossie of Citizens United, who believe Trump really is a logical descendant of Reagan and an embodiment of what conservatives need to be to respond to the changes in the country in the years since Reagan rode into the sunset.

"Everybody had their own reasons for being nervous about a Trump candidacy, a Trump presidency," Bossie says. "But he has turned out to be, for the conservative movement, everything that we have been looking for since Ronald Reagan. If you look at deregulation, you look at tax cuts, you look at the economy, the economic boom, you look at a guy who walks up and hugs the American flag—that is the imagery people have with Ronald Reagan in their mind."

Into this category fall numerous evangelical leaders, who decided that Trump's record in appointing conservative judges and in supporting the anti-abortion cause was more than sufficient to justify their support for him, despite his personal life and his casual relationship with organized religion. So do anti-immigration forces and officials such as White House adviser Peter Navarro, who had long shared Trump's views that China was fleecing America through bad trade arrangements and relentless theft of the intellectual property of American companies. For them, Trump is a refreshing voice of candor on issues where they had strong feelings long before he showed up on the political radar screen.

Second are the straddlers. These people have misgivings about Trump, sometimes deep misgivings, but either decided that he had put his finger on some important challenges facing America, or felt they needed to bend to Trump in order to accomplish things they considered important in a government in which he holds such a preeminent position. The alternative was ineffectiveness.

In this category fall many, if not most, elected Republican officials in Washington, including Senate Majority Leader Mitch McConnell.

Senator Ted Cruz explains that his decision to swing behind Trump in late 2016 was the result of a fairly hardheaded calculation that, whatever Trump's flaws, the policies he promised simply would be better for the country than the policies of Hillary Clinton and Democrats on the left would have been. "When one candidate is promising to do bad things, and the other is promising to do good things, as a rational voter I support the one who's promising to do good things," Cruz said over dinner one night in a restaurant not far from the Capitol. "Now, Trump both says and does many things that I wouldn't say or do. And, you know, we talked about Reagan, about language that was unifying and uplifting. That's not a descriptor many would attach to him. Do I wish he would rein in his tone and rhetoric? Yes. Frankly, I wish a lot of people in the political arena would rein in their tone and rhetoric. This has become an angry and divided town."

Larry Kudlow also found his way to Trump's side. Kudlow was, in his own words, a member of the "Reagan Cub Scouts"—that is, a group of young and eager conservatives who signed on with the Gipper as aides in the 1980s. Kudlow worked in the Reagan White House and had a hand in crafting budget and tax policies, then became an investment banker, a policy advocate, and a journalist with a high profile as an analyst on the CNBC network making supply-side economic arguments.

That TV profile led directly to Kudlow's being hired by Trump to run his National Economic Council in 2018. It was an odd choice in many ways, because Kudlow, by his own cheerful admission, disagreed with Trump on trade, and specifically opposed the use of tariffs as a trade tool. (Supply-side conservatives such as Kudlow, after all, think of tariffs as merely indirect taxes on American consumers.) Yet Kudlow says he saw in Trump a belief in some core Reagan economic values, which was sufficient for him to enter the president's inner sanctum. "I'm still a supply-side tax cutter and a supply-side deregulator, which were huge Reagan themes," Kudlow says. "And so is Trump."

Others who didn't naturally fit into the Trump camp but served in his administration anyway, including Kudlow's predecessor at the National Economic Council, Gary Cohn, and onetime defense secretary Jim Mattis, eventually decided they couldn't stay in Trump's orbit.

Third are the Never Trumpers, who tend to be repelled by Trump and who also reject the idea that he embodies conservative principles. Into this category fall, for example, former Bush aide Pete Wehner, *Weekly Standard* founder Bill Kristol, longtime Republican campaign impresario Mike Murphy, and conservative columnist George Will. They view Trumpism as essentially an abandonment of principles.

Murphy told me bluntly, "There's no doubt that Trump has blown up what used to be the ideological core of the party." Will explains his concerns about the Trump version of the Republican Party this way: "It's a populist party, and whatever populism is, conservativism isn't. Populism is the belief that the passions of the people should be aroused and transformed into public policy by a strong leader of the sort who might say, 'Only I can fix it.' Conservativism, Madisonian conservativism, says passions are *the* political problem."

Trump himself fumes at such Republicans (and former Republicans) who refuse to bend to him or defend him. At one point in late 2019, he referred to the Never Trumpers collectively as "human scum."

That, in turn, prompted Paul Rosenzweig, a former Bush administration official and alumnus of conservative bastions such as the Heritage Foundation and the Federalist Society, to respond with an essay on *The Atlantic* magazine's website proclaiming that he would wear the "human scum" tag as "a badge of honor. . . . I'm a proud 'Never Trumper Republican.'" He went on: "What makes me human scum? Evidently, a belief in enduring American ideals, like the rule of law and the value of a free press. A belief in a system of governance that enshrines the principle of checks and balances in our Constitution—a system in which Congress and the judiciary serve as limits on authoritarian executive overreach."

Such complaints from the right served only to feed Democrats' hatred of Trump, which at times in his first term seemed all-consuming. Trump's populism and nationalism both enraged and energized the Democratic left, where activists equated Trumpism with racism and xenophobia. Moreover, they barely considered Trump a legitimate president, because he had lost the popular vote to Hillary Clinton. From the time Trump was elected, many Democrats were convinced he had colluded with the equally nationalist Russian government of Vladimir Putin to get covert help in the 2016 election, and they not-so-secretly hoped an investigation into Russia's role by special counsel Robert Mueller would provide the smoking gun they needed to impeach Trump and drive him from office.

Mueller didn't provide that smoking gun. Almost immediately, though, Democrats thought they spotted a different one, in the revelation that Trump had pressured the newly elected president of Ukraine to investigate the activities of former vice president Joe Biden and his son Hunter in that country. The elder Biden had been in charge of Ukraine policy during a crucial period of the Obama presidency, at the same time his son sat on the board of a Ukrainian energy company. Trump always thought Ukrainian leaders opposed his election in the first place, and now he was pressuring a new Ukrainian leader, President Volodymyr Zelensky, to "do us a favor," as Trump put it in a phone call, by investigating whether Joe Biden, a top political rival, could be found to have aided corruption.

Democrats launched a formal impeachment inquiry into whether Trump has abused his presidential power by pressuring a foreign country to do him a political favor. Democrats opened a series of intense hearings to explore the charges and, on one level, hit pay dirt. Public polls showed that a majority of Americans believed the argument House Democrats advanced, which is that Trump improperly withheld congressionally appropriated military aid from Ukraine, and also refused to give Zelensky a symbolically important White House meeting, until he provided the help Trump sought. Emboldened by such signs of public support, House Democrats voted in December 2019 to impeach Trump on two counts: abuse of power and obstruction of Congress by refusing to allow his aides to cooperate in the investigation. He became just the third president in American history to be impeached.

Yet the impeachment process, like so many other controversies, served not to shift opinions so much as prompt people to dig in deeper in their views of Trump. The vote to impeach the president in the House was almost entirely on party lines: All Republicans voted against impeachment, and all Democrats, save for two, voted for it. And one of the dissenting Democrats promptly switched parties to become a Republican after taking Trump's side.

The articles of impeachment moved to the Senate for a trial, where emotional arguments for and against Trump produced a similarly partisan outcome. All Democratic senators voted to convict Trump. All Republicans, save for one—former Republican presidential nominee Mitt Romney, now a senator from Utah—voted to acquit him.

Impeachment became a microcosm of the effect Trump was having on the whole political system. The dwindling band of Never Trump Republicans saw the Ukraine affair as proof of what they had always described as the dangers of their party hitching its wagons to him. Democrats were intent on trying to push Trump out of office less than a year before he would have to face voters again anyway, seemingly oblivious to the very real risk that such a crusade might simply further energize already fervent Trump voters.

Above all, and odd as it seemed, impeachment served only to tighten the bonds between Trump and the Washington Republican establishment that once despised him. As I wrote as the Senate acquittal of Trump drew near: "Contrary to some expectations, impeachment drove Republican leaders even further into the embrace of a president they once viewed skeptically. By uniting so decisively behind Mr. Trump, Republicans find their fortunes locked with his. . . . For his part, Mr. Trump found himself dependent on a Republican establishment he once scorned, and ultimately became proud of its solid backing. If there was doubt before that the Republican party has become Mr. Trump's party, it has largely evaporated during the impeachment fight."

There was no better barometer of this establishment embrace of Trump than Senator Lindsey Graham of South Carolina. When campaigning against Trump in 2016, Graham said: "I think he's crazy. I think he's unfit for office. And I'm a Republican and he's not. He's not a conservative Republican. He's an opportunist." By the time of impeachment, Graham had become Trump's golfing partner, and his most outspoken Senate defender. Graham declared that he had made up his mind about Trump's innocence before the impeachment trial even began, declared he saw no reason to hear from any witnesses, and mocked the Democrats' case daily.

To some extent, Trump benefited from Democratic overreach, and what appeared to his supporters to be Democrats' irrational, almost unhinged, hatred of him. Yet some of the party's swing behind Trump also arose from simple fear. No Republican in Congress wanted to incur his wrath by appearing to waver in their defense of him.

Any hint of wavering angered the president. Senator Lamar Alexander, a universally respected Republican veteran about to retire from the Senate, did Trump a big favor by speaking out against calling witnesses to testify in the Senate trial, a move that would have extended the trial and opened the door to potential bad surprises for the president. In announcing his decision, Alexander said what many Republicans thought, which was that Trump's behavior toward Ukraine was wrong but not an impeachable offense. Alexander's statement did as much as anything to enable Senate Republicans to bring the trial to a speedy conclusion in Trump's favor. Yet rather than express gratitude, Trump was soon privately complaining in phone calls to his supporters that Alexander had criticized him in public. Beyond his treatment of Alexander, the president, predictably enough, heaped public scorn on Romney as well, going so far as to suggest in public that Romney, a devout Mormon, was lying in saying he had let his religious faith guide him in his decision to vote against Trump.

Trump's enhanced control of the Republican Party, and his success at turning its Washington leaders into his soldiers, was illustrated at a strange celebratory gathering the president called in the White House East Room the day after his acquittal. The room was filled with Republicans from the House and the Senate who had stood by the president, and he spent more than an hour alternating between praising them, one by one, and offering withering, and at one point profane, criticisms of Democrats.

Yet equally important for Trump was the way support for him among his core voters surged during impeachment. He understood his supporters, they understood him, and they reacted to impeachment in the same way. Amid the impeachment debate, one reader emailed me that he was prepared to crawl on his hands and knees across broken glass to vote for Trump, and would walk through fire to do so as well if given the chance. And, he added, he had friends who felt even more strongly. More telling were the signs that some Trump doubters also reacted adversely to the Democratic impeachment efforts. Trump's job approval rose in the venerable Gallup poll, and *Wall Street Journal*/NBC News polling indicated that his approval among independent voters ticked up.

Yet the debate about Trump personally, important and consuming as it is, glides past two deeper questions: What is going on in America that made the rise of Trump possible—perhaps even inevitable? And where do conservatives and Republicans go from here?

Christopher DeMuth, one of the deans of Washington's conservative thinkers and himself a speaker at the National Conservatism

Conference, thinks much of today's ferment can be traced to conservatives and Republicans losing touch with economic anxieties around the country, and offering what became pat but unsatisfactory answers. "Washington consensus conservatism was much too smug on these matters, and much too detached from a lot of pain and suffering that was going on in the country," he says. "It had these kind of smug, formulaic answers that really weren't up to it."

That realization, DeMuth says, has led a lot of conservatives to rethink their adherence to small-government policies and open their minds to a bigger role for government in attacking economic problems. Increasingly, he says, some conservatives have an attitude of "This thing about conservatives not wanting to use government power? We've got big problems out there, and damn it, we're going to use government power to fix it."

One such new-wave conservative is Oren Cass, who has created an organization, American Compass, dedicated to redefining conservatism, especially economic conservatism. Cass does not think of Trump as a good vessel to deliver a new, improved twenty-first-century conservative vision. "No, definitely not," he says. "I see myself as engaged in the project of post-Trumpism."

In that post-Trump era, Cass argues, conservatives have to move beyond their tendency to instinctively fall back on the view that market forces and a light government hand automatically offer the best answers. "What we call conservative economic policy isn't actually small-c conservative in its orientation," he says. "It's libertarian economic policy."

In fact, he argues, the prevailing conservative economic policies of recent decades actually sowed the seeds for some significant problems, which the movement failed to see taking shape. "Whether you want to talk about concrete economic outcomes, the hollowing out of manufacturing and the industrial economy, rising inequality, the increasing reliance on the college degree, even as we completely failed to move people to college degrees—on all those dimensions, the eighties and nineties were really, if you had your finger on the pulse, exactly when we should have been noticing those things and reacting to them."

So now Cass is advocating something conservatives a generation ago would have considered an apostasy: industrial policy. Cass argues that, contrary to what most conservative economists argue, free markets don't allocate resources well across all sectors of an economy. Specifically, markets leave some important sectors without sufficient investment. One of those sectors is manufacturing, and manufacturing is especially important for both the economy's overall health and the well-being of American society.

"Manufacturing provides particularly well-paying, stable employment—especially for men with less formal education," he said in remarks at the National Conservatism Conference. "Manufacturing also tends to deliver faster productivity growth, because its processes are susceptible to technological advances that complement labor and increase output."

Thus, Cass argues, government should have policies that actively favor the expansion of manufacturing. Specifically, he advocates funding more research that can help manufacturing companies; giving engineering majors in colleges more government aid than, say, English majors; putting a "bias" in the tax code to help manufacturers; reducing, to nearly zero if necessary, the number of visas given to Chinese citizens until China changes policies that harm American companies; and requiring American-made components in key products.

"In the real world as we find it, America has no choice but to adopt an industrial policy, and we will be better for it," Cass said.

Even George Will, a staunch free trader who disagrees with Cass on the idea of industrial policy, acknowledges that "the winds of globalization have casualties, and the Republicans did not address it." He adds, "Republicans were rightly committed to protect free trade, but somewhat careless about the casualties. So along comes Trump and says, 'You've been saying for forty years you're for free trade, and you aren't anymore.' And they said, 'Okay, we're not.'"

Important as economics might have been in opening the way for Trump, alienation and a deep cultural divide in the country appear to have been even bigger forces.

Matt Schlapp, chairman of the American Conservative Union and a former White House official under President George W. Bush, says liberals' condescending attitude toward social conservatives provided fuel to the fire that burst out in the form of the Trump presidential campaign. "They've been told that they're hateful, and they're shamed," Schlapp says. "And so when you quiet them, it's eventually going to come out in another way, as it did going into 2016."

Pete Wehner agrees that anger helped draw Republicans into Trump's orbit: "What was it about Trump that pulled them in? It can't have been philosophy. It can't have been policy agenda. And the answer, I think, is that he embodied a certain kind of style—resentments, grievances. There had been building an anger on the American right, and certain pathologies were developing." Trump appeared to disaffected Americans, Republican and independent alike, as a kind of "wrecking ball" prepared to lay waste not just to Democrats and liberals but to Republicans who were seen as part of the despised elites, Wehner says.

When asked what fed and spread that anger, Eric Cantor reaches into his pocket and pulls out his smartphone, by way of saying that the power and prevalence of social media have played a powerful role. A presidential Twitter feed that stokes existing grievances and resentments, the ability of online communication to place people in information stovepipes with like-minded voters, and echo chambers where their preconceived emotions are stoked by others who share them—all have fed an angry debate.

Senator Marco Rubio tried to address some of the unhappiness with traditional conservative prescriptions in his own 2016 campaign, but he found his message drowned out by Trump's megaphone and all the controversies he generated. Now he thinks the anger at the economic status quo and the political establishment is a sign that America has reached a kind of crossroads.

"If you look at human history, when these sentiments are not addressed, people throughout history always tend to go in one of two directions," he says. "Socialism—let the government take over everything and make things right—or ethnic nationalism, which is *Bad things are happening to me and it's someone else's fault. And they happen to be from another country or another skin color.* Neither one of those ends up in a good place. And both are actually a fundamental challenge to the very concept of America, what makes us unique and special."

Cruz argues that conservatives have to decouple their efforts from any "cult of personality." When asked about the future of the conservative movement and his party after Donald Trump, Cruz offers this formula: "If we are about the inherent dignity and worth of every human being as a creation of God, if we are about the Constitution, serving, as Jefferson put it, as chains to bind the mischief of government, if we are about empowering small businesses to grow and create jobs and raise wages, if we're about protecting individual liberty, whether it's speech or religion or life, then we will be on firm footing. If we are instead simply about personality, we would have lost our way. And I hope that that is not the direction of the day."

Acknowledgments

This book, to say nothing of my career, would have been impossible without the support of *The Wall Street Journal*. I started at the *Journal*'s Dallas bureau as a college intern, and have been in its embrace ever since. Today and for years previously, I have been lucky to work alongside wonderful friends and colleagues in the *Journal*'s Washington bureau, all of whom have contributed to this book, whether they know it or not.

I am particularly indebted to two friends who have served, in succession, as the *Journal*'s editor in chief, Gerry Baker and Matt Murray. We share a wonderment at the passing political scene, and they both encouraged this project.

A big thank-you goes to my agent, Rafe Sagalyn, who provided sage counsel throughout the creation and completion of this book. I am also grateful to two gifted editors at Random House. Roger Scholl was the first to envision a deep look at the conservative movement, arguing that it was the most important force of recent political history. Later, the highly capable and impressive Derek Reed took up the editing reins and guided it home.

I am also grateful to the many fascinating political players I met along the way who agreed to sit down and tell their stories. Special thanks to Gene Gibbons, who covered the Reagan and Bush presidencies with me. He read the manuscript, offered thoughts, and fixed a few goofs.

But most of all I have to thank my partner in all things, my wife, Barbara Rosewicz. She is a gifted reporter, writer, and editor in her own right. Every step of this journey, from Kansas to Washington to Cairo and back, we took together. I can't imagine doing any of it without her at my side. This is all yours as much as mine.

Notes

A great deal of the basic information in this book springs from my own personal experience in covering the events chronicled here. However, to fill in the many blanks, to add crucial details, and to put events in perspective and historical context, I interviewed some four dozen people who were direct participants in the four-decade arc of this story, almost all of them on the record. Unless otherwise noted, the quotes in this book come from my conversations with those people. I am deeply grateful to all of them for their generosity in taking the time to relive the fascinating times recounted here. Many of these interviewees are longtime acquaintances and sources, and their recollections were invaluable. Beyond those interviews, here are other sources of information.

Preface

ix **He was ardent** Monica Langley, "Ted Cruz, Invoking Reagan, Angers GOP Colleagues, but Wins Fans Elsewhere," *Wall Street Journal,* April 18, 2015, p. A1, https://www.wsj.com/articles/ted-cruz-invoking-reagan-angers-gop -colleagues-but-wins-fans-elsewhere-1397874857.

xi **In fact, most conservatives** "Ronald Reagan's Remarks at Liberty State Park, Jersey City, New Jersey, on September 1, 1980," Ronald Reagan Library, Simi Valley, Calif., https://www.reaganlibrary.gov/9-1-80.

Chapter 1: The Rise of the Reagan Revolution

3 **There was little doubt** The best guide to presidential job approval ratings over time is the Gallup Organization's "Presidential Job Approval Center," which can be found online at https://news.gallup.com/interactives/185273 /presidential-job-approval-center.aspx.

5 **"In a nation that was proud"** Jimmy Carter, "Energy and the National

Goals—A Crisis of Confidence," July 15, 1979, video, 4:16, American Rhetoric (website), https://www.americanrhetoric.com/speeches/jimmycartercrisis ofconfidence.htm.

7 **The year's events** A treasure trove of economic statistics and their changes over time is the Federal Reserve Bank of St. Louis's Economic Data site: https://fred.stlouisfed.org.

9 **He decried the nation's** Ronald Reagan, "A Time for Choosing," October 27, 1984, video, 4:03, American Rhetoric, https://www.americanrhetoric .com/speeches/ronaldreaganatimeforchoosing.htm.

11 **Reagan seemed to address** "Transcript of Reagan's Remarks to the Convention," *New York Times,* August 20, 1976, https://www.nytimes.com/1976 /08/20/archives/transcript-of-reagans-remarks-to-the-convention.html.

12 **By the spring of 1979** Washington Whispers, *U.S. News & World Report,* April 2, 1979.

13 **Then Reagan began** "Ronald Reagan's Announcement for Presidential Candidacy," November 13, 1979, Ronald Reagan Presidential Library, https://www.reaganlibrary.gov/11-13-79.

21 **Reagan then rose to speak** Ronald Reagan, "National Affairs Campaign Address on Religious Liberty," August 22, 1980, video, 25:57, American Rhetoric, https://www.americanrhetoric.com/speeches/ronaldreaganreligious liberty.htm.

Chapter 2: Storming the Gates

24 **Lou Cannon, a reporter** Lou Cannon, *President Reagan: The Role of a Lifetime* (New York: Public Affairs, 1991), p. 18. This book and Cannon's earlier Reagan biography, entitled simply *Reagan* (New York: G.P. Putnam's Sons, 1982), are the most complete and authoritative works on Ronald Reagan's life and presidency.

25 **To the surprise of some** Barry M. Goldwater, *Conscience of a Conservative* (Blacksburg, Va.: Wilder Publications, 2014; first published 1964), p. 11.

30 **At times, and despite** "Defense 1981: Overview," *CQ Almanac 1981* (Washington, D.C.: Congressional Quarterly, 1981).

30 **The centerpiece** "Historical Highest Marginal Income Tax Rates," Tax Policy Center, 2018, https://www.taxpolicycenter.org/statistics/historical -highest-marginal-income-tax-rates.

31 **So Reagan went before** Public Papers of the Presidents of the United States: Ronald Reagan, 1981 (Washington, D.C.: U.S. Government Printing Office, 1982–1991), p. 108.

32 **Moreover, even if cutting taxes** "Consumer Price Index, 1913–," Federal Reserve Bank of Minneapolis, https://www.minneapolisfed.org/about-us /monetary-policy/inflation-calculator/consumer-price-index-1913-.

32 **The prime interest rate had reached** "United States Prime Rate," www .fedprimerate.com.

32 **The risks in Reagan's strategy** Laurence I. Barrett, *Gambling with History* (Garden City, N.Y.: Doubleday, 1983).

37 **Hyperbole is common** "Federal Tax Policy Memo," vol. 5, no. 7. (September 1, 1981), Tax Foundation.

Chapter 3: Growing Roots

44 **Meanwhile, Delaware governor Pete du Pont** Newt Gingrich, *Lessons Learned the Hard Way* (New York: HarperCollins, 1998), p. 106.

Chapter 4: The Gipper

49 **To some in the capital** Lou Cannon, *President Reagan: The Role of a Lifetime* (New York: Public Affairs, 1991), p. 229.

52 **The letter found** The exchange of letters can be found in the online collection of papers at the Reagan Presidential Library website.

53 **Then, a miraculous turnaround** "Real Gross Domestic Product," Federal Reserve Bank of St. Louis, https://fred.stlouisfed.org/graph/?g=eUmi.

57 **In the end, what did the Reagan presidency** "Historical Tables," Office of Management and Budget, White House.

57 **If the goal** "Real Gross Domestic Product," Federal Reserve Bank of St. Louis, https://fred.stlouisfed.org/graph/?g=eUmi.

57 **Yet there also were** Thomas Piketty, Emmanuel Saez, and Gabriel Zucman, "Distributional National Accounts: Methods and Estimates for the United States," National Bureau of Economic Research, December 2016.

58 **Domestically, the most significant** "Judgeship Appointments by President," United States Courts (website), https://www.uscourts.gov/judges -judgeships/authorized-judgeships/judgeship-appointments-president.

59 **That belief was enshrined** "At Its 25th Anniversary, IRCA's Legacy Lives On," Migration Policy Institute, 2011, https://www.migrationpolicy.org /article/its-25th-anniversary-ircas-legacy-lives.

60 **Legislative maneuvering aside** Ronald Reagan, "Farewell Address to the Nation," January 11, 1989, Ronald Reagan Presidential Foundation and Institute, https://www.reaganfoundation.org/ronald-reagan/reagan-quotes -speeches/farewell-address-to-the-nation-2.

Chapter 5: Turning Over the Reins

65 **Fitzwater, a Kansas native** Gerald M. Boyd, "Man in the News; A New Chief Spokesman for the President: Max Marlin Fitzwater," *New York Times,* January 13, 1987, https://www.nytimes.com/1987/01/13/us/man-in-the-news -a-new-chief-spokesman-for-the-president-max-marlin-fitzwater.html.

73 **And it didn't** "Desert Shield and Desert Storm," Strategic Studies Institute, U.S. Army War College, March 1991.

73 **Their view on Iraq** Gerald F. Seib, "U.S. Dilemma: How to Hammer Iraq in a Battle Without Smashing It, Emboldening Iran, Syria," *Wall Street Journal,* December 26, 1990.

76 **Even worse for Bush** "Real Gross Domestic Product," Federal Reserve Bank of St. Louis, https://fred.stlouisfed.org/series/A191RL1Q225SBEA.

76 **The unemployment rate, a more politically sensitive** "Unemployment Rate," Federal Reserve Bank of St. Louis, https://fred.stlouisfed.org/series/UNRATE.

Chapter 6: Newt Steps In

81 **Sure enough, though** Elon Green, "Early Press Mentions of the Candidates," *The Awl,* December 7, 2011, https://www.theawl.com/2011/12/early-press-mentions-of-the-republican-candidates.

87 **So he came up with** "Newt Gingrich Transcript," Conversations with Bill Kristol (website), November 21, 2014, https://conversationswithbillkristol.org/transcript/newt-gingrich-transcript.

88 **Ironically, Gingrich was** Gerald F. Seib, "Three Reasons Gingrich Will—and Won't—Fly," *Wall Street Journal,* December 6, 2011, https://www.wsj.com/articles/SB10001424052970204083204577079753685773894.

94 **The contract was identified** Lou Cannon, *President Reagan: The Role of a Lifetime* (New York: Public Affairs, 1991), p. 756.

95 **"Before there was"** Lee Edwards, *The Conservative Revolution* (New York: Free Press, 1999), p. 293.

Chapter 7: The Best of Times, the Worst of Times

98 **Both men knew** David Rogers and Gerald F. Seib, "Different Drum: GOP, Despite Slips, Manages to Change Government's Course," *Wall Street Journal,* April 7, 1995, p. A1.

99 **The battle between** Bill Clinton, *My Life* (New York: Alfred A. Knopf, 2004), p. 631.

101 **In a typical broadcast** "The Rush Limbaugh Show," WABC-Radio, February 18, 1994, available at C-SPAN, https://www.c-span.org/video/?54681-1/rush-limbaugh-radio-talk-show.

103 **Ailes hailed from** A detailed and authoritative account of the founding of Fox News and Ailes's role in it is found in a lengthy piece media reporter Ken Auletta wrote for the May 19, 2003, edition of *The New Yorker*: "Vox Fox: How Roger Ailes and Fox News Are Changing Cable News."

104 **On January 30, 1996** In 2006 Fox News aired a tenth-anniversary special, in which Murdoch, Ailes, and others talked about the launch of the channel.

111 **Most striking of all** "Bill Clinton—Key Events," Miller Center, University of Virginia, https://millercenter.org/president/bill-clinton/key-events.

112 **"We cannot tolerate"** "1996 Democratic Party Platform," American Presi-

dency Project, University of California–Santa Barbara, https://www
.presidency.ucsb.edu/documents/1996-democratic-party-platform.

113 **"Regardless of how"** Gerald F. Seib, "Full Circle: Foray into Politics Brings
Patriot Party Back to Ross Perot," *Wall Street Journal,* May 29, 1996, p. 1.

115 **But beneath the surface** *CQ Almanac 1997* (Washington, D.C.: Congressional Quarterly, 1997), pp. 1-6–1-10.

116 **Gingrich survived** Newt Gingrich, *Lessons Learned the Hard Way* (New York:
HarperCollins, 1998).

116 **Clinton, meanwhile, was headed** Susan Schmidt, Peter Baker, and Toni
Loci, "Clinton Accused of Urging Aide to Lie," *Washington Post,* January 21,
1998, p. A1, https://www.washingtonpost.com/wp-srv/politics/special
/clinton/stories/clinton012198.htm.

117 **The results were seen** Clinton, *My Life,* p. 826.

Chapter 8: Conservatives Ride Again

121 **"Are you insane?"** "Breitbart VS Madden Uncut Video," video, 2:19, uploaded by Tania Gail, February 20, 2010, https://www.youtube.com/watch
?v=TDyxYRsh1wc.

122 **When former vice president** "Dick Cheney Heckled, Called 'War Criminal' at CPAC," video, 1:56, uploaded by u/bobored, February 10, 2011,
https://www.reddit.com/r/politics/comments/fj2y6/dick_cheney_heckled
_called_war_criminal_at_cpac.

122 **The young conservatives** Erin Gloria Ryan, "Former CPAC Head Lisa De
Pasquale on Love, Inclusion, and Barf," *Jezebel,* March 3, 2015, https://jezebel
.com/former-cpac-head-lisa-de-pasquale-on-love-inclusion-a-1688984820.

123 **So when Bush spoke** "CPAC: A Detailed History of the First 30 Years,"
American Conservative Union, https://conservative.org/article/cpac-detailed
-history-first-30-years. "CPAC Over 30 Years: Conservatives Have Come a
Long Way," *Human Events,* February 3, 2003, https://humanevents.com/2003
/02/03/cpac-over-30-yearsbrconservatives-have-come-a-long-way/.

123 **The love affair** Andy Barr, "Bush a Four-Letter Word at CPAC," *Politico,*
February 28, 2009, https://www.politico.com/story/2009/02/bush-a-four
-letter-word-at-cpac-019433.

129 **As a result, millions of dollars** Spencer MacColl, "Capital Rivals: Koch
Brothers vs. George Soros," Center for Responsive Politics, September 21,
2010, https://www.opensecrets.org/news/2010/09/opensecrets-battle-koch
-brothers.

130 **These offices were charged** George W. Bush, "Faith Based Initiative Executive Orders Signing Address," January 29, 2001, video, 8:49, American Rhetoric, https://americanrhetoric.com/speeches/gwbushfaithbasedinitiatives.htm.

130 **The second item** "No Child Left Behind" act, George W. Bush White
House Archives, https://georgewbush-whitehouse.archives.gov/news/reports
/no-child-left-behind.html#11.

132 **On top of that** Gerald F. Seib, "The Right Stuff: Conservative Pals Step Up for Bush," *Wall Street Journal,* April 25, 2001, p. A22, https://www.wsj.com /articles/SB988143054922868802.

133 **But none of that** "Remarks by the President in Tax Cut Bill Signing Ceremony," June 7, 2001, George W. Bush White House Archives, https://george wbush-whitehouse.archives.gov/news/releases/2001/06/20010607.html.

134 **In reality, as the years** United States Trade Representative, "2017 Report to Congress on China's WTO Compliance," January 2018.

Chapter 9: The High Price of Terror

139 **The neoconservatives then** William J. Burns, *The Back Channel* (New York: Random House, 2019), p. 161.

141 **Cheney gave speeches** Burns, *The Back Channel,* p. 172.

141 **As the shock waves** "President Bush's Eulogy at the Funeral Service for President Reagan," George W. Bush White House Archives, https:// georgewbush-whitehouse.archives.gov/news/releases/2004/06/20040611-2 .html.

145 **Throughout that campaign** "George W. Bush Speaks Spanish," December 6, 1999, video, 0:45, C-SPAN, https://www.c-span.org/video/?c4547274/user -clip-george-bush-speaks-spanish.

146 **In it, he threw his support** Robert L. Bartley, "Open Nafta Borders? Why Not," *Wall Street Journal,* July 2, 2001, https://www.wsj.com/articles/SB9940 28904620983237.

146 **Just five years later** Carl Hulse, "House Adds Hearings on Immigration," *New York Times,* June 21, 2006, https://www.nytimes.com/2006/06/21 /washington/21immig.html.

147 **At about the same time** "Extremely Powerful Hurricane Katrina Leaves a Historic Mark on the Northern Gulf Coast," National Weather Service, August 2005, https://www.weather.gov/mob/katrina.

149 **A conservative president** "Office of Management and Budget Historical Tables," https://www.whitehouse.gov/omb/historical-tables.

149 **For Bush and other conservatives** "Employment, Hours and Earnings from the Current Employment Statistics Survey," Bureau of Labor Statistics, https://www.bls.gov/help/one_screen/ce.htm.

Chapter 10: Into the Wilderness

154 **Some Republicans had been** Matthew Continetti, "Tooting the Horn of Pawlenty," *Washington Examiner,* May 7, 2007, https://www.washington examiner.com/weekly-standard/tooting-the-horn-of-pawlenty-14688.

154 **Much of that message** "The Huckabee Contradiction," *Wall Street Journal,* December 5, 2007, https://www.wsj.com/articles/SB119682363824414053.

157 **All told, then** Institute of Politics, John F. Kennedy School of Government, Harvard University, *Campaign for President: The Managers Look at 2008* (Lanham, Md.: Rowman and Littlefield, 2009), p. 67.

162 **But beyond the cheers** Tim Mak, "5 Best Couric-Palin 2008 Moments," *Politico,* April 2, 2012, https://www.politico.com/story/2012/04/5-best-couric-palin-2008-moments-074735.

163 **On the campaign trail** Gerald F. Seib, "Wall Street's Woes Challenge Both Candidates," *Wall Street Journal,* September 16, 2008, https://www.wsj.com/articles/SB122149887584837137.

164 **That simply set off** Henry M. Paulson Jr., *On the Brink: Inside the Race to Stop the Collapse of the Global Financial System* (New York: Grand Central Publishing, 2010), pp. 296–99.

Chapter 11: The Tea Party Erupts

168 **"This is America!"** Jeff Cox, "5 Years Later, Rick Santelli 'Tea Party' Rant Revisited," CNBC, February 24, 2014, https://www.cnbc.com/2014/02/24/5-years-later-rick-santelli-tea-party-rant-revisited.html.

176 **Republicans then proceeded** Jonathan Weisman, "GOP in Lead in Final Lap," *Wall Street Journal,* October 20, 2010, https://www.wsj.com/articles/SB10001424052702303550904575562493014465942.

180 **That was a compromise** Janet Hook, Corey Boles, and Siobhan Hughes, "Congress Passes Fiscal Cliff Deal," *Wall Street Journal,* January 2, 2013, https://www.wsj.com/articles/SB1000142412788732332040457821537335279 3876.

180 **The crusade went forward** Aaron Blake, "Tea Party Groups to Target Skeptical GOP Senators on Defunding Obamacare," *Washington Post,* August 19, 2013, https://www.washingtonpost.com/news/post-politics/wp/2013/08/19/tea-party-groups-to-target-skeptical-gop-senators-on-defunding-obamacare.

181 **The Tea Party Patriots distributed** Tea Party Patriots, "Defunding Obamacare Toolkit for Activists," http://cdn6.teapartypatriots.org/wp-content/uploads/2013/09/Tea-Party-Patriots-Defund-Obamacare-Toolkit-Final.pdf?x36556.

Chapter 12: Trump Storms In

188 **The other person** "Remarks by the President on Immigration," June 15, 2012, Barack Obama White House Archives, https://obamawhitehouse.archives.gov/the-press-office/2012/06/15/remarks-president-immigration.

188 **As Obama moved** "Romney's 'Self Deportation' Plan Draws Laughs, January 23, 2012, video, 1:34, CBS News, https://www.youtube.com/watch?v=ObVnA0nIx_s.

190 **Most important, though** "Growth & Opportunity Project," Republican National Committee, 2012, https://www.documentcloud.org/documents /624581-rnc-autopsy.html.

193 **The bill embodied** Jason Horowitz, "Marco Rubio Pushed for Immigration Reform with Conservative Media," *New York Times,* February 28, 2016, https://www.nytimes.com/2016/02/28/us/politics/marco-rubio-pushed-for -immigration-reform-with-conservative-media.html.

193 **Rubio also went on Rush** "Senator Rubio Discusses Immigration with Rush Limbaugh," press release, Office of Sen. Marco Rubio, January 29, 2013, https://www.rubio.senate.gov/public/index.cfm/2013/1/senator-rubio -discusses-immigration-with-rush-limbaugh.

193 **It didn't last** Ann Coulter, "If Rubio's Amnesty Is So Great, Why Is He Lying?" Ann Coulter (website), April 17, 2013, http://www.anncoulter.com /columns/2013-04-17.html.

194 **Donald Trump was watching** Beth Reinhard, "Some in N.Y. GOP Want Trump Banished from Party," *Wall Street Journal,* December 10, 2015, https:// www.wsj.com/articles/some-in-n-y-gop-want-trump-banished-from -party-1449769694.

196 **Throughout, the young Donald** Much of this recounting of Donald Trump's early business career can be found in Michael Kramish and Marc Fisher, *Trump Revealed: The Definitive Biography of the 45th President* (New York: Scribner, 2016).

196 **If Trump wasn't necessarily considered** Ralph Z. Hallow, "In CPAC Speech, Trump Hints at White House Bid," *Washington Times,* February 10, 2011, https://www.washingtontimes.com/news/2011/feb/10/in-cpac-speech -trump-hints-of-white-house-bid.

197 **After toying with** A history of the trademark filing can be found at https:// trademarks.justia.com/857/83/make-america-great-85783371.html.

197 **He appeared at CPAC** "Donald Trump Speech at CPAC, 2014," March 6, 2014, video, 18:20, *Politico,* https://www.politico.com/video/2014/03/donald -trump-speech-at-cpac-2014-003845.

198 **Trump had a prepared text** The original text of the speech can be found here: http://www.p2016.org/trump/trump061615sp.html. An account of the speech as actually delivered is here: "Here's Donald Trump's Presidential Announcement Speech," *Time,* June 16, 2015, https://time.com/3923128 /donald-trump-announcement-speech.

202 **Cruz hung on** This data comes from a June 2019 briefing prepared by the Public Opinion Strategies polling firm, entitled "What Republicans Need to Know as We Move Toward the 2020 Election."

203 **As Trump cruised** Peter Wehner, "Why I Will Never Vote for Donald Trump," *New York Times,* January 14, 2016, https://www.nytimes.com /2016/01/14/opinion/campaign-stops/why-i-will-never-vote-for-donald -trump.html.

203 **Senator Jeff Flake** Alexander Bolton, "Majority of GOP Senators to Attend

Trump Convention," *The Hill,* January 7, 2016, https://thehill.com/home news/senate/286753-majority-of-gop-senators-to-attend-trump-convention.

204 **But that was exactly** Gregory Krieg, "Trump Likens Carson's 'Pathology' to That of a Child Molester," CNN, November 12, 2015, https://www.cnn .com/2015/11/12/politics/donald-trump-ben-carson-child-molester/index .html.

205 **For other conservatives** Wehner, "Why I Will Never."

Chapter 13: Shock Waves

213 **This meant Trump simply didn't** Julie Creswell, "Trump and U.S. Chamber of Commerce Pull No Punches on Trade Policy," *New York Times,* July 11, 2016, https://www.nytimes.com/2016/07/12/business/us-chamber -of-commerce-donald-trump.html.

215 **Moreover, many business leaders** As was common in President Trump's Washington, Senator Schumer made his feelings known in a post on Twitter: Chuck Schumer (@SenSchumer), "Hang tough on China, President @realDonaldTrump," Twitter, May 5, 2019, 2:00 P.M., https://twitter.com /SenSchumer/status/1125143336837206016.

216 **But then he offered** Gerard Baker, Carol E. Lee, and Michael C. Bender, "Trump Says He Offered Better Trade Terms in Exchange for Help on North Korea," *Wall Street Journal,* April 12, 2017, https://www.wsj.com/articles /trump-says-he-offered-china-better-trade-terms-in-exchange-for-help-on -north-korea-1492027556.

217 **Oddly, this willingness** Donald J. Trump (@realDonaldTrump), "Because of my Administration, drug prices are down," Twitter, September 19, 2019, 2:42 P.M., https://twitter.com/realdonaldtrump/status/117480088705 6932864.

220 **A few days before** Steve Holland and David Shepardson, "Trump Meets with Airline CEOs over Qatar Subsidy Accusations," Reuters, July 18, 2019, https://de.reuters.com/article/usa-qatar-airlines-gulf/update-4-trump-meets -with-airline-ceos-over-qatar-subsidy-accusations-idUKL2N24J0Y9.

223 **Most advisers thought** "U.S. Active-Duty Military Presence Overseas Is at Its Smallest in Decades," Pew Research Center, August 22, 2017, https:// www.pewresearch.org/fact-tank/2017/08/22/u-s-active-duty-military -presence-overseas-is-at-its-smallest-in-decades.

225 **The reaction to Trump's** Again, in typical fashion, the communication be- tween the president and other players occurred on Twitter: Lindsey Graham (@LindseyGrahamSC), "American isolationism," Twitter, October 9, 2019, 8:00 A.M., https://twitter.com/LindseyGrahamSC/status/118194761605 0995200.

226 **Fellow Republican senator Rand Paul** Senator Rand Paul (@RandPaul), "I know this @realDonaldTrump," Twitter, October 9, 2019, 9:24 A.M., https://twitter.com/RandPaul/status/1181968653362835457.

Chapter 14: What Just Happened?

230 **Today, Democrats represent** A deep look into these changes in the two parties can be found in a detailed set of charts and graphs on *The Wall Street Journal*'s website, entitled "Democrats and Republicans Aren't Just Divided. They
Live in Different Worlds," https://www.wsj.com/graphics/red-economy
-blue-economy.

Chapter 15: What Now?

239 **That, in turn, prompted** Paul Rosenzweig, "I'm Proud to Be Called
Human Scum," *The Atlantic,* October 24, 2019, https://www.theatlantic.com
/ideas/archive/2019/10/trumps-tweet-makes-me-proud-be-human-scum
/600685.

241 **Above all, and odd as it seemed** Gerald F. Seib, "Trump's Impeachment Is
Virtually Over. What Did It Change?" *Wall Street Journal,* February 1, 2020,
https://www.wsj.com/articles/trumps-impeachment-is-virtually-done-what
-did-it-change-11580566870.

245 **"In the real world"** Oren Cass, "Resolved: That America Should Adopt an
Industrial Policy," *Law and Liberty,* July 23, 2019, https://www.lawliberty
.org/2019/07/23/resolved-that-america-should-adopt-an-industrial-policy.

Index

ABOUT THE AUTHOR

GERALD F. SEIB is the executive Washington editor of *The Wall Street Journal,* where he writes the weekly "Capital Journal" column. Over four decades in Washington, he has covered the White House, the State Department, the Pentagon, and national politics. He also reported from the Middle East for the *Journal* for three years. He has moderated three presidential debates and interviewed every president since Ronald Reagan. He has won the Merriman Smith Award for coverage of the presidency, the Aldo Beckman Award for coverage of the White House, the Edward Weintal Prize for Diplomatic Reporting, and the Gerald R. Ford Foundation Reporting Prize. He was part of a team of *Journal* reporters and editors who won the Pulitzer Prize in the breaking news category for their coverage of 9/11. In 2005 he won the William Allen White Foundation National Citation, and in 2009 the National Press Club's award for political analysis. He is a regular commentator on CNBC, Fox News, PBS's *Washington Week,* CBS's *Face the Nation,* and NBC's *Meet the Press.* With CNN's John Harwood, he previously wrote *Pennsylvania Avenue: Profiles in Backroom Power.* He lives in Chevy Chase, Maryland, with his wife, fellow journalist and editor Barbara Rosewicz.

Twitter: @GeraldFSeib

ABOUT THE TYPE

This book was set in Bembo, a typeface based on an old-style Roman face that was used for Cardinal Pietro Bembo's tract *De Aetna* in 1495. Bembo was cut by Francesco Griffo (1450–1518) in the early sixteenth century for Italian Renaissance printer and publisher Aldus Manutius (1449–1515). The Lanston Monotype Company of Philadelphia brought the well-proportioned letterforms of Bembo to the United States in the 1930s.

.